NEVADA POLITICS AND GOVERNMENT

*Politics and Governments
of the American States*

General Editor

John Kincaid
Robert B. & Helen S. Meyner Center
for the Study of State and Local
Government, Lafayette College

Founding Editor

Daniel J. Elazar
Temple University

Editorial Advisory Board

Thad L. Beyle
University of North Carolina
at Chapel Hill

Diane D. Blair
University of Arkansas

Ellis Katz
Temple University

Charles Press
Michigan State University

Stephen L. Schechter
Russell Sage College

Published by the University of
Nebraska Press in association
with the Center for the Study
of Federalism and the
Robert B. & Helen S. Meyner Center
for the Study of State and Local
Government, Lafayette College

DON W. DRIGGS AND LEONARD E. GOODALL

Nevada Politics & Government

CONSERVATISM IN AN OPEN SOCIETY

UNIVERSITY OF NEBRASKA PRESS
LINCOLN AND LONDON

⊛ The paper in this book
meets the minimum requirements of
American National Standard
for Information Sciences–Permanence of
Paper for Printed Library Materials,
ANSI Z39.48-1984.

Library of Congress
Cataloging-in-Publication Data
Driggs, Don W.
Nevada politics and government:
conservatism in an open society /
Don W. Driggs and Leonard E. Goodall.
p.   cm.–(Politics and governments
of the American states)
Includes bibliographical references and index.
ISBN 0-8032-1703-X (cl : alk. paper). –
ISBN 0-8032-6604-9 (pbk : alk. paper)
1. Nevada–Politics and government.
I. Goodall, Leonard E.
II. Title.   III. Series.
JN8516.D75   1996
306.2′09793–dc20
95-43756   CIP

CONTENTS

TABLES AND MAPS

JOHN KINCAID

Series Preface

The purpose of this series is to provide informative and interesting books on the politics and governments of the fifty American states, books that are of value not only to the student of government but also to the general citizens who want greater insight into the past and present civic life of their own states and of other states in the federal union. The role of the states in governing America is among the least well known of all the 85,006 governments in the United States. The national media focus attention on the federal government in Washington DC and local media focus attention on local government. Meanwhile, except when there is a scandal or a proposed tax increase, the workings of state government remain something of a mystery to many citizens—out of sight, out of mind.

In many respects, however, the states have been, and continue to be, the most important governments in the American political system. They are the main building blocks and chief organizing governments of the whole system. The states are the constituent governments of the federal union, and it is through the states that citizens gain representation in the national government. The national government is one of limited, delegated powers; all other powers are possessed by the states and their citizens. At the same time, the states are the empowering governments for the nation's 84,955 local governments—counties, municipalities, townships, school districts, and special districts. As such, states provide for one of the most essential and ancient elements of freedom and democracy, the right of local self-government.

Although, for many citizens, the most visible aspects of state government are state universities, some of which are the most prestigious in the world, and state highway patrol officers, with their radar guns and handy ticket books, state governments provide for nearly all domestic public services.

Whether elements of those services are enacted or partly funded by the federal government and actually carried out by local governments, it is state government that has the ultimate responsibility for ensuring that Americans are well served by all their governments. In so doing, all of the American states are more democratic, more prosperous, and better governed than most of the world's nation-states.

This is a particularly timely period in which to publish a series of books on the governments and politics of each of the fifty states. Once viewed as the "fallen arches" of the federal system, states today are increasingly seen as energetic, innovative, and fiscally responsible. Some states, of course, perform better than others, but that is to be expected in a federal system. Each state is unique in its own right. It is our hope that this series will shed light on the public life of each state and that, taken together, the books will contribute to a better, more informed understanding of the states themselves and of their often pivotal roles in the world's first and oldest continental-sized federal democracy.

DANIEL J. ELAZAR

Series Introduction

The more than continental stretch of the American domain is given form and character as a federal union of fifty different states whose institutions order the American landscape. The existence of these states made possible the emergence of a continental nation where liberty, not despotism, reigns and where self-government is the first principle of order. The great American republic was born in its states as its very name signifies. America's first founding was repeated on thirteen separate occasions over 125 years, from Virginia in 1607 to Georgia in 1732, each giving birth to a colony that became a self-governing commonwealth. Its revolution and second founding was made by those commonwealths, now states, acting in congress, and its constitution was written together and adopted separately. As the American tide rolled westward from the Atlantic coast, it absorbed new territories by organizing thirty-seven more states over the next 169 years.

Most of the American states are larger and better developed than most of the world's nations. Territorially, Nevada is one of the Union's larger states, but in terms of its population, it is still one of the smallest despite its rapid growth in recent decades.

The American states exist because each is a unique civil society within their common American culture. Nevada, though long considered an artificial entity established to secure Lincoln's majority in the 1864 presidential election and subsequently an economic and social appendage of California, nevertheless has come to have its own "personality" and a distinctive way of life within the American context. As in the case of every state, it was first given political form and then acquired these other characteristics. This personality development was especially pronounced for Nevada since it became a state when it was hardly more than a desert with a few silver mines and cattle ranches in the western pocket at the closest point to San Francisco. Since then the weight of the state has shifted southward from its original Reno–Carson City–Lake Tahoe area of settlement to the Las Vegas area, but those characteristics that make Nevada its own place have only intensified.

Each state has its own constitution, its own political culture, its own relationship to the federal union and to its section, all of which give each state its own law and history. For most, the longer that history, the more distinctive the state. Nevada's distinctiveness, however, owes more to its location in the heart of the Great Basin of the Pacific slope than to a long history.

It is in and through the states, no less than the nation, that the great themes of American life play themselves out. The advancing frontier and the continuing experience of Americans as a frontier people, the drama of American ethnic blending, the tragedy of slavery and racial discrimination, the political struggle for expanding the right to vote—all found, and find, their expression in the states.

The changing character of government, from an all-embracing concern with every aspect of civil and religious behavior to a limited concern with maintaining law and order to a concern with providing the social benefits of the contemporary welfare state, has been felt in the states even more than in the federal government. Some states began as commonwealths devoted to establishing model societies based on a religiously informed vision (Massachusetts—less so in its Maine district; Connecticut; Rhode Island). At the other end of the spectrum, Nevada is an expressly individualistic civil society, dedicated to allowing every person his or her pleasures. At least three states were independent for a significant period of time (Hawaii, Texas, and Vermont). Others, Nevada among them, were created from nothing by hardly more than a stroke of the pen. Several are permanently bilingual (California, Louisiana, and New Mexico). Each has its own landscape and geographic configuration that time and history transform into a specific geo-historical location. In short, the diversity of the American people is expressed in no small measure through their states.

Nevada Politics and Government is the fourteenth book in the State Politics and Governments of the American States series of the Center for the Study of Federalism and University of Nebraska Press. The aim of the series is to provide books on the politics and government of the individual states that will appeal to three audiences: political scientists, their students, and the wider public in each state. Each volume examines the specific character of one of the fifty states, looking at the state as a polity—its political culture, traditions and practices, constituencies and interest groups, constitutional and institutional frameworks.

Each book in the series reviews the political development of the state to demonstrate how that state's political institutions and characteristics have evolved from the first settlement to the present, presenting the state in the context of the nation and section of which it is a part, and reviewing the roles and relations of the state vis-à-vis its sister states and the federal government. The state's constitutional history, its traditions of constitution making and constitutional change, is examined and related to the workings of the state's political institutions and processes. State-local relations, local government, and community politics are studied. Finally, each volume reviews the state's policy concerns and their implementation from the budgetary process to particular substantive policies. Each book concludes by summarizing the principal themes and findings in order to draw conclusions about the current state of the state, its continuing traditions, and emerging issues. Each volume also contains a bibliographic survey of the existing literature on the state and a guide to the use of that literature and state government documents in learning more about the state and political system.

Although the books in the series are not expected to be uniform, they do focus on the common themes of federalism, constitutionalism, political culture, and the continuing American frontier in order to provide a framework within which to consider the institutions, routines, and processes of state government and politics.

FEDERALISM

Both the greatest conflicts of American history and the day-to-day operations of government are closely intertwined with American federalism—the form of American government (in the eighteenth-century sense of the term, which includes both structure and process). American federalism has been characterized by several basic tensions. One is between state sovereignty (the view that in a proper federal system, authority and power over most domestic affairs should be in the hands of the states) and national supremacy (the view that the federal government has a significant role to play in domestic matters affecting the national interest). The other tension is between dual federalism (the idea that a federal system functions best when the federal government and the states function as separately as possible, each in its own sphere) and cooperative federalism (the view that federalism works best when the federal government and the states, while preserving their own institutions, cooperate closely on the implementation of joint or shared programs).

Technically speaking, all of the public land states carved out of the American public domain west of the Appalachians were founded through the initial efforts of the federal government under the auspices of Congress and with its approval. Some of them actually were formed by fully following the procedures laid down by Congress. In others, local populations seized the initiative when they felt they were ready, if they thought Congress was reluctant to act, and essentially forced Congress to recognize them. Although the territorial legislature, in one of its first acts, called for a popular vote on convening a state constitutional convention and 82 percent of the voters approved the drive for statehood, Nevada achieved statehood during the Lincoln administration as a Civil War measure considerably before it had the requisite permanent population or motivation to achieve statehood. Lincoln needed the three electoral votes that a new state firmly in the Republican column would provide for the 1864 presidential election. Thus Nevada was born out of the nation's greatest crisis of federalism.

Whereas other states may complain of their loss of power vis-à-vis the federal government, Nevada today probably has more local control than ever before in its history simply because it now has the population and the resources to develop its own freestanding policies in many fields.

CONSTITUTIONALISM

American constitutionalism had its beginning in New England. Representatives of the Connecticut River valley towns of Hartford, Windsor, and Wethersfield met in January 1639 to draft a constitution. That document, the Fundamental Orders, established a federal union to be known as Connecticut and inaugurated the American practice of constitution making as a popular act and responsibility, ushering in the era of modern constitutionalism.

The American constitutional tradition grew out of the Whig understanding that civil societies are founded by political covenant, entered into by the first founders and reaffirmed by subsequent generations, through which the powers of government are delineated and limited and the rights of the constituting members are clearly proclaimed in such a way as to provide moral and practical restraints on governmental institutions. That constitutional tradition was modified by the federalists, who accepted its fundamental principals but strengthened the institutional framework designed to provide energy in government while maintaining the checks and balances they saw as needed to preserve liberty and republican government. At the same time, they turned nonbinding declarations of rights into enforceable constitutional articles.

American state constitutions reflect a melding of these two traditions. Under the U.S. Constitution, each state is free to adopt its own constitution, provided that it establishes a republican form of government. Some states have adopted highly succinct constitutions—the 6,600-word Vermont Constitution of 1793 is still in effect with only fifty-two amendments. Others are just the opposite; for example, Georgia's Ninth Constitution, adopted in 1976, has 583,000 words.

State constitutions are potentially far more comprehensive than the federal Constitution, which is one of limited, delegated powers. Because states are plenary governments, they automatically possess all powers not specifically denied them by the U.S. Constitution or their citizens. Consequently, a state constitution must be explicit about limiting and defining the scope of governmental powers, especially on behalf of individual liberty. So state constitutions normally include an explicit declaration of rights, almost invariably broader than the first ten amendments to the U.S. Constitution.

The detailed specificity of state constitutions affects the way they shape each state's governmental system and patterns of political behavior. Unlike the open-endedness and ambiguity of many portions of the U.S. Constitution, which allow for considerable interpretive development, state organs, including state supreme courts, generally hew closely to the letter of their constitutions because they must. This means that formal change of the constitutional document occurs more frequently through constitutional amendment, whether initiated by the legislature, special constitutional commissions, constitutional conventions, or direct action by the voters, and, in a number of states, the periodic writing of new constitutions. As a result, state constitutions have come to reflect quite explicitly the changing conceptions of government that have developed over the course of American history.

Overall, six different state constitutional patterns have developed. One is the commonwealth pattern, developed in New England, which emphasizes Whig ideas of the constitution as a philosophic document designed first and foremost to set a direction for civil society and to express and institutionalize a theory of republican government. A second is the constitutional pattern of the commercial republic. These constitutions reflect a series of compromises required by the conflict of many strong ethnic groups and commercial interests generated by the flow of heterogeneous streams of migrants into particular states and the early development of large commercial and industrial cities in those states.

The third pattern is that found in the South, which can be described as the southern contractual pattern. Southern state constitutions are used as instruments to set explicit terms governing the relationship between polity and society, such as those that protected slavery or racial segregation, or those that sought to diffuse the formal allocation of authority in order to accommodate the swings between oligarchy and factionalism characteristic of southern state politics. Of all the southern states, only Louisiana stands somewhat outside this pattern, since its legal system was founded on the French civil code. Its constitutions have been codes—long, highly explicit documents that form a fourth pattern in and of themselves.

A fifth constitutional pattern is that found frequently in the states of the Far West, where the state constitution is first and foremost a frame of government explicitly reflecting the republican and democratic principles dominant in the nation in the late nineteenth century, but emphasizing the structure of state government and the distribution of powers within that structure in a direct, businesslike manner. Finally, the two newest states, Alaska and Hawaii, have adopted constitutions following the managerial pattern developed and promoted by twentieth-century constitutional reform movements in the United States. Those constitutions are characterized by conciseness, broad grants of power to the executive branch, and relatively few structural restrictions on the legislature. They emphasize natural resource conservation and social legislation.

Nevada's constitution is of the fifth pattern. Based on California's, it was hastily written and adopted in Nevada's rush to statehood. Hence it is not much noted except by those professionally concerned with its implementation, and certainly is not celebrated, as this volume clearly indicates. It serves as a frame of government unique only in its protection (although not specifically) for certain human pleasures (gambling, brothel prostitution) long declared illegal in other states.

THE CONTINUING AMERICAN FRONTIER

For Americans, the very word *frontier* conjures up the images of the rural-land frontier of yesteryear—of explorers and mountain men, of cowboys and Indians, of brave pioneers pushing their way west in the face of natural obstacles. Later, Americans' picture of the frontier was expanded to include the inventors, the railroad builders, and the captains of industry who created the urban-industrial frontier. Recently television has begun to celebrate the entrepreneurial ventures of the automobile and oil industries, portraying the magnates of those industries and their families in the same larger-than-life frame as once was done for the heroes of that first frontier.

As is so often the case, the media responsible for determining and catering to popular taste tell us a great deal about ourselves. The United States was founded with a rural-land frontier that persisted more or less until World War I, spreading farms, ranches, mines, and towns across the land. Early in the nineteenth century, the rural-land frontier generated the urban frontier based on industrial development. The creation of new wealth through industrialization transformed cities from mere regional service centers into generators of wealth in their own right. That frontier persisted for more than one hundred years as a major force in American society as a whole and for perhaps another sixty years as a major force in various parts of the country. The population movements and attendant growth on the urban-industrial frontier brought about the effective settlement of the United States in freestanding cities from coast to coast.

Between the world wars, the urban-industrial frontier gave birth in turn to a third frontier stage, one based on the new technologies of electronic communication, the internal combustion engine, the airplane, synthetics, and petrochemicals. These new technologies transformed every aspect of life and turned urbanization into metropolitanization. This third frontier stage generated a third settlement of the United States, this time in metropolitan regions from coast to coast, involving a mass migration of tens of millions of Americans in search of opportunity on the suburban frontier.

In the 1970s, the first post–World War II generation came to a close. Many Americans were speaking of the "limits of growth." Yet despite that anti-frontier rhetoric, there was every sign that a fourth frontier stage was beginning in the form of the rurban, or citybelt-cybernetic, frontier generated by the metropolitan-technological frontier, just as the latter had been generated by its predecessor.

The rurban-cybernetic frontier first emerged in the Northeast, as did its predecessors, as the Atlantic Coast metropolitan regions merged into one another to form a six-hundred-mile-long megalopolis (the usage is Jean Gottman's)—a matrix of urban and suburban settlements in which the older central cities came to yield importance, if not prominence, to smaller ones. It was a sign of the times that the computer was conceived at MIT in Cambridge, first built at the University of Illinois in Urbana, and developed at IBM in White Plains, three medium-sized cities that have become special centers in their own right. This in itself is a reflection of the two primary characteristics of the new frontier. The new locus of settlement is in medium-sized and small cities and in the rural interstices of the megalopolis.

The spreading use of computer technology is the most direct manifestation of the cybernetic tools that make such citybelts possible. In 1979 the newspapers in the Northeast published frequent reports of the revival of the small cities of the first industrial revolution, particularly in New England, as the new frontier engulfed them. Countrywide, the media focused on the shifting of population growth into rural areas. Both phenomena are as much a product of direct dialing as they are of the older American longing for small-town or country living. Both reflect the urbanization of the American way of life no matter what lifestyle is practiced, or where.

Although the Northeast was first, the new rurban-cybernetic frontier, like its predecessors, is finding its true form in the South and West, where these citybelt matrices are not being built on the collapse of earlier forms, but are developing as an original form. The present sunbelt frontier—strung out along the Gulf Coast, the southwestern desert, and the fringes of the California mountains—is classically megalopolitan in citybelt form and cybernetic with its aerospace-related industries and sunbelt living made possible by air conditioning and the new telecommunications.

The continuing American frontier has all the characteristics of a chain reaction. In a land of great opportunity, each frontier has generated its successor and has been replaced by it. Each frontier has created a new America with new opportunities, new patterns of settlement, new occupations, new challenges, and new problems. As a result, the central political problem of growth is not simply how to handle the physical changes brought by each frontier, real as they are. It is how to accommodate newness, population turnover, and transience as a way of life. That is the American frontier situation.

Here, too, Nevada's situation is somewhat paradoxical. On one hand, its image is that of the last frontier state, where the land frontier actively dominated the state until World War I, with gold and other mineral rushes extending into the twentieth century in the old style, and where "wide open" frontier values of individualism have continued to exist long after other aspects of the land-frontier stage had spent themselves. Its landscape and general emptiness (its population almost entirely urban and concentrated at two points in the state) contribute to reenforcing this view, even for the traveler who passes through the state on the way elsewhere.

Yet in most respects this is a mythic view; Nevada, with two exceptions, has remained frozen in the modes of the land frontier while being bypassed by subsequent frontier phases. The two exceptions are the post–World War II history of Las Vegas and its boom based on gambling, and the supersonic flight program of the U.S. Air Force—which can be seen as manifestations of the metropolitan-technological frontier.

Now that Las Vegas is settling down to being a normal city and metropolitan concentration and that gambling has ceased to be a Nevada monopoly, there does not seem to be much evidence of the state finding a way onto the cutting edge of the rurban-cybernetic frontier. The Nevada desert is not made for rurban living and the state is likely to be a consumer of the products of cybernetics but not a pioneer of them.

THE PERSISTENCE OF SECTIONALISM

Sectionalism—the expression of social, economic, and especially political differences along geographic lines—is an integral part of American political life. The more or less permanent political ties that link groups of contiguous states together as sections reflect the ways in which local conditions and differences in political culture modify the impact of the frontier. This overall sectional pattern reflects the interaction of the three basic factors. The original sections were produced by the variations in the impact of the rural-land frontier on different geographic segments of the country. They, in turn, have been modified by the pressures generated by the first and subsequent frontier stages. As a result, sectionalism is not the same as regionalism, which is essentially a phenomenon—often transient—that brings adjacent state, substate, or interstate areas together because of immediate and specific common interests. The sections are not homogeneous socioeconomic units sharing a common character across state lines, but are complex entities combining highly diverse states and communities with common political interests that generally complement one another socially and economically.

Nevada's sectional position is fairly unambiguous. It is clearly part of the West. Indeed, it is usually thought of as at the very heart of the West, since it is located at the heart of the Great Basin and connected to the Rocky Mountain West to the east and California and the Pacific coast on the west.

Intrasectional conflicts often exist, but they do not detract from the long-term sectional community of interest. More important for our purposes, certain common sectional bonds give the states of each section a special relationship to national politics. This is particularly true in connection with those specific political issues that are of sectional importance, such as the race issue in the South, the problems of the megalopolis in the Northeast, and the problems of agriculture and agribusiness in the Northwest.

The nation's sectional alignments are rooted in the three great historical, cultural, and economic spheres into which the country is divided: the greater Northeast, the greater South, and the greater West. Following state lines, the greater Northeast includes all those states north of the Ohio and Potomac Rivers and east of Lake Michigan. The greater South includes the states below that line but east of the Mississippi plus Missouri, Arkansas, Louisiana, Oklahoma, and Texas. All the rest of the states compose the greater West. Within that framework, there are eight sections: New England, Middle Atlantic, Near West, Upper South, Lower South, Western South, Northwest, and Far West.

From the New Deal years through the 1960s, Americans' understanding of sectionalism was submerged by their concern with urban-oriented socioeconomic categories, such as the struggle between labor and management or between the haves and have-nots in the big cities. Even the racial issue, once the hallmark of the greater South, began to be perceived in nonsectional terms as a result of black migration northward. This is not to say that sectionalism ceased to exist as a vital force, only that it was little noted in those years.

Beginning in the 1970s, however, there was a resurgence of sectional feeling as socioeconomic cleavages increasingly came to follow sectional lines. The sunbelt-frostbelt rivalry is the prime example of this new sectionalism. *Sunbelt* is the new code word for the Lower South, Western South, and Far West; *frostbelt*, later replaced by *rust belt*, is the code word for the New England, Middle Atlantic, and Great Lakes (Near Western) states. Sectionalism promises to be a major force in national politics, closely linked to the rurban-cybernetic frontier.

A perennial problem of the states, hardly less important than that of direct federal-state relationships, is how to bend sectional and regional demands to fit their own needs for self-maintenance as political systems. One of the ways in which the states are able to overcome this problem is through the use of their formal political institutions, since no problems can be handled governmentally without making use of those formal institutions.

Some would argue that the use of formal political institutions to deflect sectional patterns on behalf of the states is "artificial" interference with the "natural" flow of the nation's socioeconomic system. Partisans of the states would respond not only by questioning the naturalness of a socioeconomic system that was created by people who migrated freely across the landscape as individuals in search of opportunity, but by arguing that the history of civilization is the record of human efforts to harness their environment by means of inventions, all artificial in the literal and real sense of the term, and with political institutions among the foremost of those inventions.

THE VITAL ROLE OF POLITICAL CULTURE

The United States as a whole shares a general political culture rooted in two contrasting conceptions of the American political order that can be traced back to the earliest settlement of the country. In the first, the polity is conceived as a marketplace in which the primary public relationships are products of bargaining among individuals and groups acting out of self-interest. In the second, the political order is conceived to be a commonwealth (a polity in which the whole people have an undivided interest) in which the citizens cooperate in an effort to create and maintain the best government in order to implement certain shared moral principles. These two conceptions have exercised an influence on government and politics throughout American history, sometimes in conflict and sometimes complementing each other.

The national political culture is a synthesis of three major political subcultures. All three are of nationwide proportions, having spread, in the course of time, from coast to coast. At the same time, each subculture is strongly tied to specific sections of the country, reflecting the streams and currents of migration that have carried people of different origins and backgrounds across the continent in more or less orderly patterns. Considering their central characteristics, the three may be called *individualistic*, *moralistic*, and *traditionalistic*. Each of the three reflects its own particular synthesis of the marketplace and the commonwealth.

The *individualistic political culture* emphasizes the democratic order as a marketplace in which government is instituted for strictly utilitarian reasons—to handle those functions demanded by the people it is created to serve. Beyond the commitment to an open market, a government need not have any direct concern with questions of the good society, except insofar as it may be used to advance some common view formulated outside the political arena. Since the individualistic political culture emphasizes the centrality of private concerns, it places a premium on limiting community intervention—whether governmental or nongovernmental—into private activities to the minimum necessary to keep the marketplace in proper working order.

The character of political participation in the individualistic political culture reflects this outlook. Politics is just another means by which individuals may improve themselves socially and economically. In this sense politics is a business like any other, competing for talent and offering rewards to those who take it up as a career. Those individuals who choose political careers may rise by providing the governmental services demanded of them and, in return, may expect to be adequately compensated for their efforts. There are varying interpretations of officeholders' obligations under this arrangement. Where the norms are high, such people are expected to provide high-quality public services in return for appropriate rewards. In other cases, the office-holders' primary responsibility is to serve themselves and those who have supported them directly, favoring supporters even at the expense of the public.

Political life within the individualistic political culture is based on a system of mutual obligations rooted in personal relationships. In the United States, political parties serve as the vehicles for maintaining the obligational network. Party regularity is indispensable in the individualistic political culture because it is the means for coordinating individual enterprise in the political arena and is the one way of preventing individualism in politics from running wild. Such a political culture encourages the maintenance of a party system that is competitive, but not overly so, in the pursuit of office.

Since the individualistic political culture eschews ideological concerns in its businesslike conception of politics, both politicians and citizens look upon political activity as specialized, being essentially the province of professionals and having no room for amateurs to play an active role. Furthermore, there is a strong tendency among the public to believe that politics is a dirty—if necessary—business, better left to those who are willing to soil themselves by engaging in it. In practice, then, where the individualistic political culture is dominant, there is likely to be an easy attitude toward the limits of the professionals' perquisites. Since a fair amount of corruption is expected in the normal course of things, there is relatively little popular excitement when any is found, unless it is of an extraordinary character. It is as if the public is willing to pay a surcharge for services rendered, rebelling only when it feels the surcharge has become too heavy. (Of course, the judgments as to what is normal and what is extraordinary are themselves subjective and culturally conditioned.)

Public officials, committed to giving the public what it wants, normally will initiate new programs only when they perceive an overwhelming public demand. The individualistic political culture is ambivalent about the place of bureaucracy in the political order. Bureaucratic methods of operation fly in the face of the favor system, yet organizational efficiency can be used by those seeking to master the market.

To the extent that the marketplace provides the model for public relationships in American civil society, all Americans share some of the attitudes that are of first importance in the individualistic political culture. At the same time, substantial segments of the American people operate politically within the framework of two political cultures.

The *moralistic political culture* emphasizes the commonwealth conception as the basis for democratic government. Politics is considered one of the great activities of humanity in its search for the good society—a struggle for power, it is true, but also an effort to exercise power for the betterment of the commonwealth. Consequently, both the general public and the politicians conceive of politics as a public activity centered on some notion of the public good and properly devoted to the advancement of the public interest.

In the moralistic political culture, there is a general commitment to utilizing communal—preferably nongovernmental, but governmental if necessary—power to intervene in the sphere of private activities when it is considered necessary to do so for the public good or the well-being of the community. Accordingly, issues have an important place in the moralistic style of politics, functioning to set the tone for political concern. Government is considered a positive instrument with a responsibility to promote the general welfare, though definitions of what its positive role should be may vary considerably from era to era.

Politics is ideally a matter of concern for every citizen. Government service is public service, placing moral obligations on those who serve in government more demanding than those of the marketplace. Politics is not considered a legitimate realm for private economic enrichment. A politician is not expected to profit from political activity and in fact is held suspect if he or she does.

The concept of serving the commonwealth is at the core of all political relationships, and politicians are expected to adhere to it even at the expense of individual loyalties and political friendships. Political parties are considered useful political devices but are not valued for their own sakes. Regular party ties can be abandoned with relative impunity for third parties, special local parties, nonpartisan systems, or the opposition party if such changes are believed helpful in gaining larger political goals.

In practice, where the moralistic political culture is dominant today, there is considerably more amateur participation in politics. There is also much less of what Americans consider corruption in government and less tolerance of those actions that are considered corrupt, so politics does not have the taint it so often bears in the individualistic environment.

By virtue of its fundamental outlook, the moralistic political culture creates a greater commitment to active government intervention in the economic and social life of the community. At the same time, its strong commitment to communitarianism tends to keep government intervention local wherever possible. Public officials will themselves initiate new government activities in an effort to come to grips with problems as yet unperceived by a majority of the citizenry.

The moralistic political culture's major difficulty with bureaucracy lies in the potential conflict between communitarian principles and large-scale organization. Otherwise, the notion of a politically neutral administrative system is attractive. Where merit systems are instituted, they tend to be rigidly maintained.

The *traditionalistic political culture* is rooted in an ambivalent attitude toward the marketplace, coupled with a paternalistic and elitist conception of the commonwealth. It reflects an older, precommercial attitude that accepts a substantially hierarchical society as part of the ordered nature of things, authorizing and expecting those at the top of the social structure to take a special and dominant role in government. Like its moralistic counterpart, the traditionalistic political culture accepts government as an actor with a positive role in the community, but it tries to limit that role to securing the continued maintenance of the existing social order. To do so, it functions to confine real political power to a relatively small and self-perpetuating group drawn from an established elite who often inherit their right to govern through family ties or social position. Social and family ties are even more important in a traditionalistic political culture than personal ties in the individualistic culture, where one's first responsibility is to oneself. At the same time, those who do not have a definite role to play in politics are not expected to be even minimally active as citizens. In many cases, they are not even expected to vote. As in the individualistic political culture, those active in politics are expected to benefit personally from their activity, although not necessarily by direct pecuniary gain.

Political parties are not important in traditionalistic political cultures because they encourage a degree of openness that goes against the grain of an elitist political order. Political competition is expressed through factions, an extension of the personal politics characteristic of the system. Hence political systems within the culture tend to have loose one-party systems if they have political parties at all. Political leaders play conservative and custodial, rather than initiatory, roles unless pressed strongly from the outside.

Traditionalistic political cultures tend to be anti-bureaucratic. Bureaucracy by its very nature interferes with the fine web of social relationships that lies at the root of the political system. Where bureaucracy is introduced, it is generally confined to ministerial functions under the aegis of the established powerholders.

Nevada is an individualistic state par excellence. Indeed, its statewide ethos cultivates individualism in both its general and political cultures and styles. Its constitution and laws and their administration all support these cultural characteristics, and its leaders cultivate both for economic as well as social reasons. Moreover, Nevada has an individualistic political culture in every part of the state and always has had except for that brief moment in its prehistory when Las Vegas was founded by the Mormons, who brought their moralistic political culture with them, as an outpost in Brigham Young's abortive march to the sea. (The more lasting and significant Mormon settlement in Carson Valley, where it was part of the Utah Territory, subsequently was submerged in the state's political culture.) All of that is long since gone, and there has been no other parallel attempt of any significance in the state's history.

NEVADA AS AN OUTPOST AND GROWTH NODE

In the last analysis, Nevada prides itself on continuing its nineteenth-century frontier tradition and adapting it to the twentieth century. But at the same time, it also has become a growth center in the last third of the twentieth century as advanced technological change has made possible the settlement of the desert in pursuit of those erstwhile frontier values. The invention of air conditioning is probably the most important single factor in Nevada's transformation from a place of uncomfortable temporary settlement in a severe environment to a place that could be inhabited comfortably, while the jet plane made Nevada accessible in a way that it had not been even when it had much better railroad service.

The opening of cyberspace enhances the possibilities for people to choose to live in Nevada while being closely connected with the rest of the world. Thus Nevada has a promising future as long as the water it needs is available and the energy it consumes holds out. None of this, however, enhances Nevada's political life. Its individualistic political culture has continued to direct people into their private pursuits, now enforced by the general privatism sweeping the United States. Government exists to do what it has to do and rarely arouses any serious concern or passion among the state's citizens.

As in any individualistic political culture, those who go into government choose their careers as others choose careers in business or law or medicine, and they are expected to pursue those careers in ways that will be profitable to themselves by providing expected governmental services to their constituents. One should not expect great new social or political visions from Nevada, but the state's economic prospects are good because it offers people what they seek in order to enjoy the new privatism.

Author's Preface

After thirty-nine years of observing, teaching, and participating in Nevada politics, I am pleased to coauthor the Nevada book in the Politics and Governments of the American States series of the University of Nebraska Press. Involvement in Nevada politics has been a fascinating experience, to say the least.

In a state where the population is six times what it was in 1956, I am amazed at how personal state politics still is. Nevada is a state where the individual can still make a difference, as I have observed over the years at the legislature and at county commission and city council meetings.

It was my good fortune to have Leonard E. Goodall, the former president of UNLV, agree to coauthor the book. He added the perspective of southern Nevada and expertise in public administration, government finance, and local government.

We wish to thank John Kincaid and Daniel J. Elazar for their excellent critiques of our manuscript. Their suggestions and encouragement were invaluable.

Although I am indebted to all the authors cited in the book, I wish to give special thanks to five history scholars at the University of Nevada, Reno— Russell R. Elliott, Jerome E. Edwards, James W. Hulse, Mary Ellen Glass, and Elizabeth Raymond—whose research, writing, and analyses of Nevada political history were most helpful in putting together the history chapters. In connection with the search for material and citations, I wish to acknowledge the excellent assistance rendered by Robert Erickson, Director of the Research Division of the Legislative Counsel Bureau; Chief Deputy Secretary of State Dale Erquiaga; Guy Rocha of the Nevada State Archives; Chris

Driggs of the Archives and the University of Nevada, Reno; Jill M. Winter of the Senator Alan Bible Center for Applied Research; Emeritus Professors James S. Roberts and Elmer Rusco of the University of Nevada, Reno; and Marty Sample, Deputy Superintendent of Public Instruction for the State of Nevada. I also wish to express my appreciation to Geraldine S. Graves and Gloria West for their assistance. However, the authors assume full responsibility for any errors of commission or omission.

NEVADA POLITICS AND GOVERNMENT

CHAPTER ONE

The Character and Political Culture of the State

In the 1970s, Eleanore Bushnell gave the title *Sagebrush and Neon* to a collection of articles on Nevada politics.[1] The title typifies the outsider's view of a state that is mostly desert and that has an economy heavily dependent on casino gambling. Yet the state contains some of the most spectacular scenery and man-made wonders in the world—from beautiful Lake Tahoe and the snow-capped Sierra Nevada and Ruby Mountains in the north to the brilliant red sandstone of the Valley of Fire, Hoover Dam, and Lake Mead in the south. Since the 1950s, the scenic attractions and gaming (the name Nevadans prefer when speaking of games of chance) have made tourism the dominant industry in the state.

Nevada became a state "before its time" because of the Civil War and Reconstruction, and it remained the smallest-population state from 1864 until the admission of Alaska in 1959. By 1990 Nevada had passed ten other states to rank thirty-ninth in population and was on track to pass four others by the 2000 census. The *growth* in population in the fifteen years from 1980 to 1995 exceeded the total population of the state in 1970.

INFLUENCE OF GEOGRAPHY

Thousands of forty-niners traversed the area that now constitutes Nevada on their way to California in quest of gold. Modern freeways have increased the number of tourists visiting the state, which continues to serve as a land bridge between the nation's most populated state and the rest of the country.

The politics and economy of Nevada have also been intertwined with its powerful neighbor to the west ever since the late 1850s when the discovery of silver in the fabulous Comstock Lode in the Virginia City area attracted large numbers of prospectors, bankers, and attorneys from northern California. Many of these Californians decided to settle in the new state. From an economic standpoint, money from California banks built most of the mining shafts, tunnels, and mills; in turn, the wealth extracted by the financiers helped build many of the first great mansions of San Francisco. The rush to Washoe, as the area was then called, was responsible for an increase in population sufficient to propel the western part of the Utah Territory toward separate territorial status in 1861 and statehood in 1864.

Geography and the mostly desert terrain of Nevada have also influenced its economic development or lack of same. Less than 1.5 percent of the almost 71 million acres of land in the state is under cultivation.[2] Hence, Nevadans have had to rely heavily on the agricultural production of other states. However, the state has been blessed with an abundance of mineral resources. In addition to the Comstock Lode, the state enjoyed other mining booms in the early decades of the twentieth century with the discovery of gold and silver in the Tonopah and Goldfield region and the uncovering of a large deposit of copper in White Pine County.[3] The large-scale mining of copper that began in 1900 led to a fifty-year period in which copper became the dominant metal in Nevada. The worldwide rise in the price of gold in the 1970s and the availability of new technology led to a substantial increase in gold mining in northern Nevada in the 1980s.

Geography played an important role in the development of sectional politics in Nevada after World War II, especially as the construction of large hotel-casinos in downtown Las Vegas and then along the famous "Strip" led to a population explosion in the southern part of the state. Las Vegas passed Reno as the largest city in the state during the 1950s, and Clark County's population, which includes the Las Vegas area, exceeded the total population of the rest of the state before the end of the 1960s. The legislative apportionment acts of 1971, 1981, and 1991 gave this one county 55, 57, and 62 percent, respectively, of the seats in each house of the state legislature.

AN INDIVIDUALISTIC POLITICAL CULTURE

In 1966 Daniel J. Elazar, a leading scholar of state politics and federalism, described three types of political cultures or subcultures that exist in the United States.[4] Of the three types—moralistic, individualistic, and traditionalistic—he termed Nevada's political culture as highly individualistic. Such a characterization is still true today. Almost all of the features that

Elazar notes as being typical of an individualistic state are part of the Nevada political culture.

Elazar notes that in an individualistic political culture, "government is instituted for strictly utilitarian reasons to handle those functions demanded by the people it is created to serve," that "government need not have any direct concern with questions of the 'good' society except insofar as it may be used to advance some common conception of the good society formulated outside the political arena," and that "public officials . . . are normally not willing to initiate new programs or open up new areas of government activity . . . [unless] they perceive an overwhelming public demand for them to act."[5] These statements accurately describe the attitudes of the average Nevadan, as indicated in public opinion polls in the 1980s and early 1990s.[6]

The mining booms of the nineteenth and early twentieth centuries attracted people to the territory and then the state who were motivated primarily by individualistic concerns. The western frontier, cattle ranching, the laissez-faire tradition, and the large amount of gambling activity, whether legal or not, further encouraged individualism. The concept of a limited role for government has been reinforced throughout Nevada's history by a belief in low resident taxation.

In November 1992 a University of Nevada opinion poll showed that most Nevadans were willing to support a modest tax increase to fund what they apparently believed to be elements of a "good society": more low-income housing and aid to the elderly, more spending for K–12 education, child care for low-income working mothers, mental health facilities, and law enforcement. However, when the respondents were asked about the type of taxation they preferred, they favored increases in gaming, cigarette, and liquor taxes and the imposition of a new tax on corporate profits. The respondents were thus interested in allowing the tourists and corporations to carry more of the tax load.

In 1990 the voters approved a constitutional amendment initiative prohibiting a state personal income tax by a 3-1 margin. In the poll taken two years later, Nevadans were strongly opposed to increases in the property and sales taxes, both of which would have hit state residents harder.[7] In the early 1990s, Clark County voters rejected ballot measures that would have provided for more schools, police officers, and parks—proposals that had been supported in the past. The recent large influx of retirees from southern California may have contributed to the defeat of the bond measures.

Elazar stated that because the emphasis in an individualistic political culture is on "the centrality of private concerns," the culture "places a premium on limiting community intervention—whether governmental or non-governmental—into private activities to the minimum necessary to keep the marketplace in proper working order."[8] This attitude is most visible nationally in the legalization of prostitution in much of Nevada. The "right of privacy" is important, too, to the average Nevadan, for 63 percent of the electorate voted in 1990 to restrict the legislature from making any changes in the 1973 abortion law. The statute basically concurs with the majority opinion in the *Roe v. Wade* (1973) decision of the U.S. Supreme Court.

Other features of the individualistic political culture include a "political life . . . based on a system of mutual obligations rooted in personal relationships" and opposition to big government, big business, and big labor.[9] The chapters on political history, the legislature, the governor, and interest groups illustrate the important role of personal relationships in Nevada, despite the phenomenal population growth in recent decades. Even conservative Republican Paul Laxalt was quick to attack big business while serving in the U.S. Senate.

Elazar's statements that, in an individualistic political culture, "politicians are interested in office as a means of controlling the distribution of favors or rewards of government rather than as a means of exercising governmental power for programmatic ends" and "since political corruption is not unexpected, there is relatively little popular excitement when any is found unless it is of an extraordinary character" describe the Nevada political scene.[10] The governor's most important impact on government is the apportionment of expenditures in the executive budget. Likewise, the preferred committee assignments in both houses of the legislature are seats on the money panels.

The old adage that "money is the mother's milk" of politics has been true in Nevada from the days of the "bag men" who bought elections to the present, when large campaign donations from the gaming industry guarantee generally favorable treatment in the legislature. A "sting" operation in the mid-1980s did result in one Nevada legislator serving time in federal prison, but other politicians who accepted campaign donations from reputed mobsters in the gaming industry have been able to survive. In Nevada's U.S. Senate races, the contributions of national political action committees (PACs) and party organizations have led to campaign spending of several million dollars in a single campaign.

Because of more reliance on television advertising, the population growth of recent decades has reinforced rather than decreased the importance of the individual as compared to party in "high-profile" elections. Republicans elected governors in 1966 and 1978, despite a huge Democratic registration edge, and the GOP carried the state in six straight presidential elections prior to 1992. Throughout Nevada's history, powerful individuals and interest groups have been more important than parties in determining the outcomes of the political process.

THE SINGLE-INDUSTRY ECONOMY

Through most of its history, Nevada's economic well-being has been tied to a single industry. In the first ninety years of statehood, mining was the major industry, and the accompanying "boom-and-bust" periods resulted in large swings in both the economy and the population of the state. Thus, the "playing out" of the Comstock Lode in the Virginia City area led to economic recession and large losses of population in the last two decades of the nineteenth century; likewise, the discoveries of gold and silver in the first decade of the twentieth century led to boom times and larger populations, followed by later recessions in the 1920s after the closing of most of the mines.

The decline of mining activity was an important consideration in the Nevada legislature's legalization of casino gambling in 1931. With enactment of a state tax on gross gambling revenues in 1945 and the building of large hotel-casinos in the Las Vegas area after World War II, Nevada's economic well-being—both private and public—became tied to a new dominant industry. Although mining revived in the 1970s and 1980s and economic diversification efforts by Governors Richard Bryan and Bob Miller in the 1980s and 1990s had some limited success, gambling and the accompanying tourism continue to dominate Nevada's economy.

CONSERVATISM IN AN OPEN SOCIETY

In a University of Nevada poll in late 1992, Nevadans were asked to identify themselves as liberal, moderate, or conservative on economic and social issues (see table 1). The telephone poll involved 1,252 randomly selected interviews, with approximately 400 in each of three regions in the state: Clark County (South); Washoe County, Carson City, and Douglas County (North); and the remaining thirteen rural counties (Rural).[11] Proportional weighting in accord with the population of each region was used to determine the statewide figures.

The poll shows that in all three regions, the respondents were more conservative on economic issues than on social issues. In Clark County, the con-

Table 1: Orientation of Nevadans on Economic and Social Issues

| | *Orientation in Economic Issues (in Percent)* | | | |
	South	*North*	*Rural*	*State*
Liberal	19	19	16	19
Moderate	44	37	38	42
Conservative	35	41	42	37
	Orientation on Social Issues (in Percent)			
	South	*North*	*Rural*	*State*
Liberal	27	23	17	25
Moderate	42	41	43	42
Conservative	28	33	37	31

Source: Jill M. Winter, Judy Calder, and Donald E. Carns, from "Public Opinion on Selected Legislative Issues: November 1992," in Jill M. Winter and Glen Atkinson, eds., *Nevada Public Affairs Review* 1993, p.4. Reprinted with permission.

servatives outnumbered the liberals almost 2-1 on economic issues, as compared to an almost even split on social issues. There are many conservative Democrats in the rural areas; thus, the region's more conservative position on social issues is not surprising. A 42 percent plurality of respondents statewide identified themselves as moderates on both economic and social issues.

Periods of Liberal Reform

Given the moderate conservatism of the majority of Nevadans in the last half of the twentieth century, the periods of liberal reform in the state's early history are often overlooked. The free-coinage-of-silver question led most Nevadans to support the populists and William Jennings Bryan in the decades around the turn of the twentieth century. The individualistic ethic caused them to give especially enthusiastic support to the plank in Bryan's campaign platform that called for adoption of the progressive reforms of initiative, referendum, and recall.

The influx of miners, some of whom were associated with the Wobblies labor union in the early 1900s, also led to the election of four members of the Socialist party to the Nevada legislature in the 1912–14 period. William Howard Taft, the incumbent Republican president, not only finished behind Democrat Woodrow Wilson and Progressive candidate Theodore Roosevelt but also Socialist candidate Eugene Debs in the 1912 election in Nevada. Even as late as 1924, Progressive party candidate Robert LaFollette finished second in the presidential election—ahead of the Democratic party's candidate, who was a Wall Street lawyer. There have been other examples of political liberalism in the state's electoral behavior in the last seventy years, including support for Franklin D. Roosevelt, Harry S. Truman, John F. Kennedy, and Lyndon B. Johnson in presidential elections.

An Open Society

The western frontier and mining activities in the nineteenth century, as noted above, produced a strong individualistic tradition and a large amount of open gambling even when it was illegal. In the early years of organized government, gambling was prohibited by the first Nevada territorial legislature in 1861, yet there was little, if any, attempt to enforce the law. The same was true from 1909 to 1931.

The existence of brothel prostitution in the state from the early mining days to the present has generally been tolerated by most Nevadans.[12] Prior to 1971, as noted by Ellen Pillard, courts in Nevada had stated that even though brothels were not mentioned in state law, "the common law definition of brothel prostitution as a nuisance allowed counties to eliminate brothels because they (the counties) could abate nuisances."[13] In 1971 the legislature enacted a statute that prohibited the licensing of a "house of ill fame or repute for the purpose of prostitution" in a county with a population of 250,000 or more.[14] In 1978 the state supreme court ruled that this 1971 law implicitly allowed the sixteen counties not covered by this prohibition—Clark being the only county with that large a population—to license brothel prostitution.[15] Five rural counties and six towns have not only legalized brothel prostitution but regulate and tax it as well.

Although brothel prostitution was not mentioned in state law until 1971, street prostitution was outlawed by the legislature in 1911 in the midst of the progressive period of social reform.[16] As Pillard has pointed out, "the number of women working in legal brothels is fairly small in comparison to the total numbers of prostitutes statewide."[17] The reason for the predominance of illegal prostitution in Nevada is that in the two metropolitan areas of the state—Las Vegas and Reno—street prostitution and call-girl services are widespread. Pillard notes that the legalization of prostitution in some areas of Nevada is more in line with the international view of prostitution, for most developed nations have decriminalized it and the United Nations has endorsed decriminalization.[18] A University of Nevada poll of in 1988 showed that only 34 percent of Nevadans believed that the existence of legalized prostitution in many of the rural counties had a negative effect on the way non-Nevadans view the state.[19]

The attitudes of Nevadans toward divorce and gun control also fit the concept of an open society. The shortening of the residency requirement for divorce was an example of economic benefits to the state being placed ahead of any moral or religious strictures against making divorce easier to obtain. In 1931, in the midst of the Great Depression, the legislature lowered the residency requirement to six weeks in order to attract divorce seekers from states having more restrictive laws.

Given the state's frontier background and wide-open spaces, gun control has been very unpopular in Nevada. Politicians realize that any leaning in the direction of gun control can be a "kiss of death" in an election campaign. In 1966 Walter Baring, then Nevada's lone congressman, was challenged in the Democratic primary by Ralph Denton, a Boulder City attorney. In the closing stages of the campaign, Denton indicated in a radio interview in Ely that he would favor some regulation of handguns in certain circumstances. Charlie Bell, Baring's campaign chief, saw the opportunity to turn the tide against Denton and sent a mailing to all Democrats in the state in which Denton was quoted out of context, implying that the congressman's challenger favored gun control in general. Political observers believed that this issue saved Baring from defeat; the fate of Denton in losing a close election that he seemed to be winning was a warning to other politicians who might favor minimal gun control laws.

Racial Prejudice

In contrast to the individualistic, open attitude toward social activities noted above, Nevadans have been generally conservative on many other matters. For example, racial prejudice raised its ugly head very early in the state's history. Although the majority of Nevadans had supported the Union party and President Abraham Lincoln during the Civil War, many Nevada legislators were reluctant to ratify the Fifteenth Amendment to the U.S. Constitution because of prejudice against the Chinese, who had come into the state to work on the railroad and who made up by far the state's largest ethnic minority.[20] Nevada's William Stewart, who served as the amendment's floor manager in the U.S. Senate, sent a telegram "explaining that the word 'nativity' had been struck from an early version of the Negro suffrage resolution specifically in order to exclude the Chinese."[21] However, some Nevada legislators were still not convinced; the resolution of ratification passed the assembly with only three votes to spare.[22]

The Chinese workers made a great contribution to the construction of the Central Pacific Railroad in the late 1860s. Those who remained in Nevada afterward turned to jobs such as cooking and laundry and had to put up with discriminatory laws and practices.[23] The Chinese population in Nevada, which had reached a peak of 8.7 percent of the state's total population in the 1880 census, declined rapidly until it was less than 1 percent by 1920.

In 1880, when there were 5,416 Chinese in Nevada, there were only 396 blacks in the state. The black population did not reach 1 percent of the state's population until World War II. Many blacks migrated from the South during the war to work for the Basic Magnesium Corporation in Henderson (located halfway between Hoover Dam and Las Vegas), which was the largest magnesium plant in the world. The only places where these blacks could obtain housing of any kind were in the company-owned Carver Park and the McWilliams Townsite, which became known as Westside.[24] After the war, as Joseph Crowley has noted, blacks in the Las Vegas area were hard-pressed to find housing or lodging anywhere outside Westside.[25] Those who had spent most of their lives in the South were used to segregated housing, but well-known entertainers, such as Sammy Davis Jr., who were featured at the new hotel-casinos in the 1950s, were outraged that they were relegated to inferior housing in Westside.[26] Discrimination against blacks in Nevada in the 1950s went beyond housing. Blacks were not welcome in most eating establishments and gaming facilities. Some civil rights supporters referred to Nevada as the "Mississippi of the West" because of its slowness in responding to discrimination.[27]

The election of Grant Sawyer, a liberal on civil rights, as governor in 1958 marked a turning point in discrimination against minorities in the state. Elmer Rusco has noted that Sawyer "was courageous in advocating and working for civil rights legislation throughout his eight years as governor."[28] However, the young governor was thwarted in his efforts to move strongly against discrimination by the opposition of the large hotel-casinos and a conservative state senate. The legislature did pass laws to outlaw discrimination in public employment in 1959 and to set up the Nevada Equal Rights Commission in 1961, although the commission was given an annual budget of only $2,500.[29]

Following the enactment of the federal Civil Rights Act of 1964, the 1965 legislature passed a more comprehensive law that outlawed discrimination in employment and public accommodations and gave the Equal Rights Commission both the power and increased funding to enforce the law. Because of opposition of the real estate lobby, an open-housing law was not enacted until 1971.[30]

The phenomenal growth in the total population of the state in the last two decades has been accompanied by an even larger growth in the minority population. By 1990 minorities made up 26.2 percent of the total state population, with Hispanics being 10.4 percent, blacks 6.6 percent, those of Asian extraction 3.2 percent, and Native Americans 1.6 percent. Ninety percent of the blacks and two-thirds of the Hispanics in the state resided in Clark County. As Thomas Wright and Dina Titus have noted, "it is now indisputable that Las Vegas has become a city of ethnics."[31] Still, prior to the 1994 election there was little minority representation in the legislature, except for the three seats that were set up in the Westside–North Las Vegas area to assure the election of blacks.

Native Americans constituted the largest minority in the 1900 census, when they were 11.3 percent of the state's population. However, the percentage of American Indians dropped to a low of 1.6 percent in the 1970 census and has remained below 2 percent. In the 1970s and 1980s, the Reno-Sparks Indian Colony engaged in economic development that produced jobs for many of its members.[32] An agreement between the State of Nevada and the Southern Nevada Mojave Tribe to permit gaming on its reservation was used as a model for a portion of the federal Indian Gaming Regulatory Act (IGRA) enacted in 1988.[33] In 1994 the state Gaming Commission approved the plans for a large hotel-casino to be built on the Mojave reservation on the banks of the Colorado River.

Women's Rights

Another political battle over rights in Nevada that found the state taking a more conservative position than other northern states involved the ratification of the proposed Equal Rights Amendment (ERA) to the United States Constitution. In 1975 Nevada became a key battleground as the national ERA movement attempted to gain the approval of the last few state legislatures needed to satisfy the constitutional requirement of ratification by three-fourths of the states. To the surprise of many observers, the Nevada Assembly voted to support ratification by a 27-13 margin, with the Washoe County delegation voting 9-1 in favor.[34]

The more conservative senate proved to be a more serious problem for the pro-ERA forces. In Clark County, Mormon women's groups who opposed the Equal Rights Amendment concentrated their efforts on the upper house; they held letter-writing meetings and deluged the senators with their epistles.

Although Democrats controlled the Nevada Senate by a 17-3 margin and national polls showed Democrats overwhelmingly in favor of the ERA in 1975, eleven of those Democrats voted against the ratification resolution, which lost by a vote of 12-8.[35]

Despite their success in stopping ratification in 1975, opponents of the ERA were concerned that thirty-five of the sixty legislators had voted for ratification. Therefore, the anti-ERA forces intensified their efforts in the 1976 legislative election campaigns. In the meantime, the hierarchy of the Mormon church made an official pronouncement against the proposed amendment, citing its belief that the ERA would be detrimental to the family; subsequently, legislative candidates in Clark County were questioned by a committee of Mormon leaders about their positions on the amendment. It was obvious in the course of the campaign that some legislators were modifying their positions. However, the defeat of two anti-ERA state senators in the Democratic primaries by two strong supporters of the amendment heartened ERA advocates; both ERA supporters won in the general election.

Because of the better than 2-1 margin by which the assembly had approved the Equal Rights Amendment in 1975 and the pickup of two seats in the senate, the pro-ERA forces were optimistic that the legislature would ratify in 1977. The key battleground was expected to be the upper house, where there was a possibility of a tie vote. The ERA forces felt that they had an "ace-in-the-hole" in the strong support of Lieutenant Governor Bob Rose, who had pledged that he would vote to break a tie in favor of the amendment, even though the state constitution was ambiguous on the question of whether the lieutenant governor could vote on the final passage of a bill or resolution. Rose did use a controversial maneuver to exercise the power to break a tie and thus declare that the proposed amendment had been approved by the upper house, but the assembly did a remarkable about-face from its 1975 position by rejecting the ratification resolution by a vote of 25-14.

After all the heat they had taken from both sides on the ERA issue, the legislators decided to place the question on the ballot in the 1978 general election in a nonbinding advisory referendum. (The U.S. Constitution gives the power of ratification of amendments to the state legislatures or to popularly elected conventions in the states. Even the governors have no official role in the ratification process.) The voters buried the amendment by a 2-1 margin. The difference in the legislative votes in 1975 and the vote of the people in 1978 indicates that Nevadans were much more conservative on this issue of women's rights than were the majority of legislators.

Abortion has been another volatile question, dividing the people similarly in Nevada as in the nation as a whole. The individualistic ethic, as noted above, is still strong in the state and has led many people to support the right-of-privacy position. However, the Roman Catholic and Mormon hierarchies, representing the two dominant churches in the state, have strongly opposed legislation making abortions easier to obtain.

A study of legislative voting on bills attempting to liberalize the state's abortion laws in 1967 and 1969 showed a strong correlation between religious affiliation and the way an individual legislator voted. Moreover, many Mormon legislators who served in both legislatures displayed a dramatic shift in voting behavior after the official church position against the reform legislation was published just prior to the vote in 1969.[36] Both of the liberalization efforts failed; however, the 1973 legislature did amend Nevada's abortion laws to conform with *Roe v. Wade*.[37]

Perhaps because of fear of single-issue voting by constituents with strong religious views, Nevada legislators in 1975 passed a resolution asking the Congress to propose a "human life" constitutional amendment that would restrict abortion and, following the lack of action on the first request, to call a constitutional convention to propose such an amendment.[38] With this legislative history in mind, pro-choice groups in the abortion controversy moved to block action of the legislature following the U.S. Supreme Court's 1989 *Webster* decision, which seemed to invite the legislatures to decide the abortion issue in their respective states.[39] Petitions were circulated for a referendum vote of the people on the 1973 pro-choice law. (The Nevada Constitution provides that if a law is upheld by the people in a referendum vote, that law "shall not be amended, annulled, repealed, set aside, suspended or in any way made inoperative except by the direct vote of the people."[40]) In the subsequent election in 1990, as noted above, the voters supported the pro-choice law by almost a 2-1 margin. Thus, the Nevada electorate appeared to be just as liberal on abortion in 1990 as it was conservative on the Equal Rights Amendment twelve years before.

Social Welfare

On social welfare issues, individualism has once again been an important factor in the generally conservative attitude of most Nevadans. Mining and gambling emphasize individualism and thus do not enhance a feeling of social responsibility for the poor and the less fortunate. Also, the extensive welfare programs of the Mormon church have instilled in its membership a feeling that government welfare should be only a last resort. Rusco has pointed out that between the years 1915 and 1935, "Nevada was among the states most willing to support welfare." Since that period, the state's support of the Aid to Families with Dependent Children (AFDC) program has declined compared to other states.[41] Rusco offers the ethnic and religious mix of the population as a hypothesis for partially explaining the difference in Nevada's support of welfare programs, citing the "high proportion of Catholics of southern or eastern European origin" in the earlier period and the influx of Protestants of northwestern European origins since the 1930s.[42]

The legalization of gambling in 1931 may have had some effect on the changing attitudes toward the government's responsibility for welfare. In another hypothesis, Rusco states that the pervading influence of gambling in Nevada since the 1930s may have encouraged "greater cynicism about the motives of other persons; hence, Nevadans are more likely to oppose welfare on the grounds that it mainly aids 'cheaters.'"[43]

In line with the national trend, welfare reform became a "hot button" issue at the 1995 legislative session. First-term senator Maurice Washington, a black Republican, made an impassioned appeal for passage of a strong reform bill that would have placed a two-year limit on welfare payments and would have denied benefits to children conceived after the mother had started receiving welfare. After passage in the upper house, the bill died on a 21-21 party-line vote in the assembly, as the Democrats complained that the proposal was too punitive to poor mothers and children. The 1995–97 budget includes, as per Governor Miller's proposal, money for the employment and training of six thousand additional welfare mothers.

The attitude of Nevadans toward social welfare can also be partially explained by their generally conservative preference for low taxes and low government expenditures. With legalization and taxation of gambling in the 1930s, some leading politicians sponsored a constitutional amendment to prohibit estate and inheritance taxes in the hope of encouraging wealthy individuals in other states to retire in the "One Sound State." The voters ratified the amendment in 1942, and it probably was an important factor in the decisions of some multimillionaires, such as Max Fleischmann and E. L. Cord, to move to Nevada.

Over the years Nevada lost countless millions of dollars because of the amendment; one notable example was that the state was not a "player" in the court fights over the disposition of billionaire Howard Hughes's fortune, even though Nevada was arguably Hughes's state of residence at the time of his death.[44] The amendment also meant that Nevada was the only state not to take advantage of the estate tax "pickup" permitted by federal legislation prior to 1986, when the voters finally approved an amendment allowing the "pickup," which otherwise would have continued to go into the federal treasury.

In keeping with its attitude toward taxation, Nevada has never had personal or corporate income taxes. With gambling taxes providing the largest amount of revenue for the state's general fund, the state and local taxes paid by Nevadans themselves when measured against tax capacity have been among the lowest in the nation in the last three decades.[45]

Thus, the national image of Nevada as an open society because of casino gambling, legalized prostitution, and easy divorce laws masks generally conservative attitudes on many social, political, and economic issues. This conservatism has not prevented the election of many candidates who are more liberal than the electorate because of the tendency of the voters to place the emphasis on the individual in high-profile election campaigns. However, from the mid-1960s on, most political candidates in Nevada have avoided the "liberal" label and have referred to themselves as "conservatives" or "moderates."

CONCENTRATION OF THE STATE'S POPULATION

Some people are startled to find out that in a state that is the seventh largest in area, but with most of that area being desert, 86 percent of the population resides in urban areas. The 1990 census disclosed that 62 percent of the state's population lived in the Las Vegas metropolitan area, with almost 24 percent residing in the Reno–Carson City metropolitan district.

Although most of the post–World War II population explosion has taken place in Clark County (see table 2), the Virginia City area completely dominated the population figures at the time Nevada became a state in 1864, with one estimate stating that Storey County had about three-fourths of the new state's population. After the Comstock Lode ran its course, the population of the state became more scattered. In the census figures from 1900 through 1950, Washoe County was the largest county in population; however, the highest percentage of the total state population that Washoe had during that period was 31.4 percent in 1950. The 1950 census disclosed that over half of the state's population resided in the urban areas of Reno and Las Vegas; the percentage of urban dwellers increased in each of the next four censuses to approximately 74 (1960), 81 (1970), 83 (1980), and 86 (1990) percent.

Despite the increasing urbanization and concentration of the state's population, the small rural counties have fared well in the legislature since the

Table 2: Population Increases in the State of Nevada and Clark County, 1940–1990

Year	Nevada		Clark County	
	Population	% Increase	Population	% Increase
1940	110,247	21.1	16,414	92.4
1950	160,083	45.2	48,289	194.2
1960	285,278	78.2	127,016	163.0
1970	488,738	71.3	273,288	115.2
1980	800,508	63.8	463,087	69.5
1990	1,201,833	50.1	741,459	60.1

Source: U.S. Department of the Census, Bureau of the Census, 1980, 1990.

court-ordered reapportionment in 1965 gave the urban counties control of both houses. Political observers have been hard-pressed to find instances in which the two dominant counties discriminated against the rural areas. However, given the increasing majorities of both houses from Clark County, the interests of the Las Vegas area will undoubtedly receive top priority in the future.

CONCLUSION

The moderately conservative positions of most Nevadans on economic issues and their more liberal positions on some social issues are consistent with a generally libertarian view of society. This belief in individualism and a smaller role for government can also explain why a majority of Nevadans have supported a liberal position on abortion and a conservative stance on the Equal Rights Amendment.

The end of the century may see the Las Vegas metropolitan area's population top the million mark and the Reno–Carson City area's population reach 340,000. The state will have to concentrate on the problems that have been plaguing large urban areas in the nation for some time. However, there are no signs that the political culture of Nevada will depart from Daniel Elazar's "individualistic" category.

CHAPTER TWO

Nevada in the Federal System

The average Nevadan's belief in an individualistic political culture is extended to belief in the rights of an individual state in its relationship with the federal government. This tenet has been strongly asserted recently in the nuclear waste depository controversy. Armed with polls showing that Nevadans were strongly opposed to a high-level nuclear waste site in the state, two governors and Nevada's entire congressional delegation have battled both the executive and legislative branches of the federal government for over a decade on the issue.

Nevada's history illustrates the important role that the federal government has played in the state and the types of questions that arise in a federal system, as can be noted by the following examples:

• Nevada's admission to statehood was facilitated by President Lincoln's desire for more support in Congress for his views on issues related to the Civil War. Lincoln believed, correctly, that Nevada's representatives would support his views when they took their seats in Congress.

• The use and control of federally owned land, which constitutes 87 percent of all acreage in Nevada, has been a major political issue throughout the state's history.

• Water issues have often involved conflicts with other states as well as with the federal government.

• The construction of Hoover Dam, the interstate highway system, and defense installations such as the Nevada Test Site and Nellis Air Force Base illustrate the importance of federal government expenditures to the economy of the state.

THE MEANING OF FEDERALISM

The idea of federalism implies a legal relationship between the nation and the states,[1] but it is also a political relationship. States sometimes compete with the federal government or each other, but most of their relationships are cooperative. Federal, state, and local governments all have roles in providing services such as law enforcement, public education, and highways. Dramatic conflicts between federal and state governments—such as in the historic battles over school desegregation—make good headlines, but most federal-state relations are routine and are more the product of careful negotiation than of public confrontation.

There is no definitive answer to the question of how authority is divided between the federal and state governments. Times change, new problems arise, and the allocation of powers between the governments must be adjusted accordingly. The resolution of this question is not just a matter for the courts. Congress and the executive branch also are often involved in helping determine whether specific functions should be undertaken by the federal or state governments. The process also involves negotiation between, for example, state and federal health officials or state and federal highway administrators. As a result, many public services are provided through the cooperative efforts of state and federal officials rather than as a result of conflict or competition between them.

Deil Wright refers to this trend toward cooperative action as "cooperative federalism."[2] Wright and others have advocated more use of the term "intergovernmental relations" as an alternative to federalism. They believe the term more accurately emphasizes the cooperative nature of the relationship rather than the state-federal competition that some associate with federalism.

The U.S. Constitution states that "This Constitution . . . shall be the supreme law of the land; and the judges in every state shall be bound thereby, anything in the constitution or laws of any state to the contrary notwithstanding."[3] Nevada is unique among the states in that its constitution contains what is known as the "paramount allegiance clause," which states, "The paramount allegiance of every citizen is due to the federal government, in the exercise of all its constitutional powers, as the same have been, or may be, defined by the Supreme Court of the United States, and no power exists in the people of this or any other state of the federal union to dissolve their connection therewith, or perform any act tending to impair, subvert, or resist the supreme authority of the government of the United States."[4]

This firm stand in favor of national supremacy is best understood in the context of the historical period in which it was written. Nevada's fundamental law was drawn up in the midst of the Civil War, and the framers were solidly on the side of the North and Lincoln. With feelings running high in the Nevada Territory against the South, it was not surprising that the constitution contained strong support for the concept of the supremacy of the federal government.

FEDERALISM IN PRACTICE

Relations in a federal system are dynamic and ever changing. The following five issues illustrate the evolving relationship between Nevada and the federal government and the importance of federal projects in the development of the state: the Newlands Reclamation Project, the construction of Hoover Dam, northern Nevada water rights, the "Sagebrush Rebellion," and the debate over nuclear and military projects in the state.

The Newlands Reclamation Project

Nevada has had to face the reality that most of its land is desert and inhospitable to the growth of agricultural products. Politicians have long attempted to alleviate the problem by securing irrigation water through federal assistance.

In 1902 the Congress enacted a law introduced by Nevada Congressman Francis G. Newlands to allow the federal government to construct irrigation systems with money obtained from the sale of public lands. The first such project was started on the Truckee and Carson Rivers and included the construction of the Truckee Canal, the Lahontan Dam, and the Lahontan Reservoir. As a result of the project, the community of Fallon became the center of a prosperous agricultural area.

The Newlands Project also generated controversy. There were years when the water supply was not adequate to meet agricultural needs; in 1934 the federal government eased drought conditions in the Truckee Meadows and Fernley areas by releasing water from Lake Tahoe into the Truckee.[5] The residents around Lake Tahoe protested the "raid" and the use of their treasured lake as a reservoir of water for farmers and ranchers. Eventually the federal government stepped in as a referee and established maximum and minimum levels for the lake.

This federal action did not settle the entire controversy. Native Americans in the Pyramid Lake area objected to the amount of water used by farmers and ranchers under the terms of the Newlands Project; the Paiutes called on the federal government to help prevent infringement upon their Pyramid Lake water rights.

Northern Nevada Water Rights

The Pyramid Lake Indian Reservation, located northeast of Reno and home of the Paiute Lake Indians, occupies about 475,000 acres, 115,000 of which are the lake itself. The lake is the reservation's most important economic resource, and its water level began dropping as much as a foot a year after construction of the Newlands Project. Little was done about the problem until the 1980s, when the tribe sued to require the U.S. Department of the Interior to enforce water conservation measures. In response to court direction, Interior Secretary Rogers Morton began enforcing regulations aimed at the Truckee-Carson Irrigation District. The resulting water conservation measures did lead to a greater availability of water, and the tribe's next task was to establish its rights to a portion of the water.

After his election to the U.S. Senate in 1986, Harry Reid began an effort to settle this complex set of water disputes, which stretched back to 1913. Issues involved the allocation of water between California and Nevada, environmental matters such as protection of wetlands and rare species of fish, and the water rights of northern Nevada cities, certain agricultural areas, and the Indian reservation. Budget questions were also involved, as a settlement that appeared to require excessive federal spending faced the possibility of a veto by President George Bush.

In the last hours of the 1990 congressional session, Senator Reid, with the help of the three other members of the Nevada delegation and some key members of the California delegation, managed to get a bill passed that guaranteed the water rights of the Paiutes and provided a total of $108 million for tribal development programs. The legislation also allocated 90 percent of the Truckee River water, 80 percent of the Carson River water, and 33 percent of Lake Tahoe water to Nevada. The Interior Department was authorized to protect wetlands and wildlife refuge areas and to establish protection programs for two species of rare fish. Finally, the act attempted to build some stability into the agreement by forbidding either the irrigation district or the Pyramid Lake Paiutes from going to court to challenge the water allocation plan prior to 1997. Senator Reid and his supporters in Congress breathed a sigh of relief when President Bush signed the bill, thus ending seventy-three years of dispute among the states of Nevada and California and the federal government, representing the Pyramid Lake Indian Reservation.[6]

Hoover Dam

Perhaps no federal project has had a greater impact on the economy of Nevada, especially southern Nevada, than Hoover Dam. The idea of harnessing the Colorado River to control flooding, produce electricity, and provide recreation had been debated for years. Finally, in December 1928, President Calvin Coolidge approved the Boulder Canyon Project Act, which provided for construction of Boulder Dam. Begun in 1931, the project was a mammoth one, including construction of 22 miles of railroad track from the Union Pacific line in Las Vegas to the dam site. Paved roads were built from Las Vegas, and an electric transmission line was brought over 220 miles from San Bernardino, California.

The construction project gave an important boost to the Great Depression–era economy of southern Nevada. The construction employed between three thousand and five thousand workers. When the project began, workers had to commute from Las Vegas or live in temporary tents or buildings near the dam. The U.S. Bureau of Reclamation then spent over $2 million to construct an entire new city—Boulder City—in order to provide living accommodations and commercial facilities for those working on the project. The city was well designed by professional city planners and became one of Nevada's most beautiful and desirable living areas. For years the federal government owned the entire city. When Congress eventually approved the sale of the property to the residents, the state legislature approved a charter giving the Boulder City government authority similar to that of other Nevada municipalities.

The completed dam brought significant permanent changes to the economy and lifestyle not only of southern Nevada but also of areas throughout the southwest. Low-cost electricity flowed to Arizona and the Los Angeles area as well as to Nevada, where it facilitated the economic development of Las Vegas. Availability of a dependable and inexpensive supply of electricity created a dramatic expansion of the defense industry in the area, especially the production of magnesium during World War II.[7]

The creation of Lake Mead spurred recreational activity and gave impetus to tourism in the Las Vegas area. Many of those who visited the casinos went to the lake for fishing, boating, and water skiing. In addition, the construction of dams farther down the Colorado River added recreational facilities to that area.

Flood control was another economic benefit of the dam. Farmers in Arizona and California had suffered for years from unpredictable flooding. The dam provided for the storing of flood waters for use during drought, bringing much needed economic stability to the agriculture of the region.

The dam also helped provide a rational allocation of water among various users. It made possible the direction of Colorado River water to those in Nevada, Arizona, and California to whom the water had been allocated. The building of a dam, of course, does not create new water. Water is a limited resource, and its availability will continue to be a major factor in the politics and economic development of southern Nevada for years to come.

The "Sagebrush Rebellion"

If the construction of Hoover Dam was an example of federalism working to the advantage of Nevada, the "Sagebrush Rebellion" a half-century later illustrated the state's concern about too much intrusion and dominance by the federal government. The controversy focused on the question of whether the national government or state governments should own and control the vast amounts of public land in the western states. The federal government owns one-third or more of the land in almost every state west of the Rocky Mountains, with the figures being highest in Alaska (96 percent), Nevada (87 percent), Utah (66 percent), and Idaho (64 percent).

In the late 1970s, rural Nevada officials began a movement to have much of the federal land turned over to the state. Other states joined the effort, working through organizations such as the Western Conference of State Governments and the Western Interstate Region of the National Association of Counties.

Several western states also took legislative and judicial action to attempt to claim ownership of federal lands within their boundaries. The 1979 Nevada legislature, for example, passed the "Sagebrush Rebellion Bill," which asserted state ownership over all federal lands in Nevada that were being administered by the Bureau of Land Management (BLM). Although few Nevada legislators were willing to defend the BLM, state Senator Clifton Young of Reno, an ardent conservationist, stated that the measure was futile and a "combination of demagoguery, avarice, and animosity and a handy way of venting spleen against the hated feds."[8] Other western states enacted similar legislation, but to no avail; BLM ignored the claims.

Some western states also took action in the courts, arguing that the states were entitled to receive the federal lands on the basis of the "equal footing doctrine." Under the doctrine, federal courts have held that new states entering the Union are entitled to do so on an "equal footing" with states already in the Union. The U.S. District Court rejected the argument, pointing out that the doctrine had historically been applied to political equality but not to issues concerning economic development or land. Nevada originally appealed to the U.S. Court of Appeals but then dropped the case before it was heard.

Opposition to the "Sagebrush Rebellion" developed rapidly. Environmentalists feared that public lands would not be protected as vigorously if they were administered by the states. Likewise, outdoor recreation activists believed their interests would be advanced more effectively if the lands remained under federal control. Others were concerned that transfer to the states would be a step toward transfer to private ownership and potential exploitation by real estate, ranching, and other interests.[9]

Senator Orrin Hatch of Utah introduced a bill to transfer federal lands to the states. However, no action was taken on the bill. Thus, despite much legislative activity in various states and Washington, no federal land was transferred to the states. Although the "Sagebrush Rebellion" did not accomplish its goal of shifting the ownership of land to the states, it provided an outlet for the increasing frustration of many people who worried that the federal government had become too large, too intrusive, and too unresponsive to concerns of its citizens. This frustration came to the fore again in 1993 when the Nye County Commission claimed that the state controlled all land within its county, including all roads.

Military and Nuclear Issues

Since World War II, Nevadans have faced a series of questions concerning military and nuclear policy issues. Nellis Air Force Base, the largest military presence in the state, opened in 1941 north of Las Vegas. The base was deactivated briefly at the end of World War II; however, it was reopened during the Korean War and has been an important military installation ever since. It is the site of one of the air force's most advanced technical training centers, where American as well as foreign pilots receive sophisticated flight training under simulated combat conditions.

To the northwest of Nellis is the Tonopah Test Range, administered by the U.S. Department of Energy. Its isolated location makes it ideal for projects demanding high security. In the 1950s and 1960s, missiles, helicopters, and other weapons and aircraft were tested there. In the 1980s, the air force developed the top-secret Stealth fighter aircraft at Tonopah.

The Nevada Test Site, located about seventy-five miles northwest of Las

Vegas, is one of the state's best known and most controversial federal installations. The federal government has conducted hundreds of nuclear explosions at the site since its opening in 1951. Activities at the test site provide a major source of employment and other economic benefits for Clark and Nye Counties. A long series of above-ground nuclear tests were undertaken there prior to 1963, when a partial test-ban treaty was negotiated with the Soviet Union. Since 1963 underground nuclear weapons tests have continued at the site. With the thawing of the Cold War in the late 1980s, many Russian scientists and military personnel have visited the test site.[10]

In recent years three major controversies have emerged concerning the test site. First, the public has become increasingly aware of the potential long-term health hazards of nuclear testing. There is concern that both military and civilian personnel who worked at the site during the years of above-ground testing may have been exposed to conditions causing serious health problems, including cancer, which sometimes did not become apparent until years or even decades later.

A second issue at the test site has been raised by activists in the anti-war movement. Some protesters philosophically oppose all war; others oppose the use of nuclear weapons in war. Many of them have chosen to participate in periodic demonstrations at the Nevada Test Site. The protesters have normally achieved their goal of publicizing their belief that all testing of nuclear weapons should be discontinued.

The third, and recently most controversial, issue is the proposed establishment of a nuclear waste repository at Yucca Mountain. There is currently no designated permanent site for the storage of radioactive waste material created by nuclear-powered generating plants.

The Nuclear Waste Policy Act passed by Congress in 1982 and signed by President Ronald Reagan in 1983 established an elaborate procedure for choosing nuclear waste repository locations. The original plan called for two locations, one in the eastern part of the country and one in the West. The bill allowed the affected states to exercise a veto over the site selection, but the measure also gave Congress the power to override a state veto by a simple majority vote. It was obvious that under such procedures, states with small populations and correspondingly small congressional delegations would be at a political disadvantage in the site selection process.

Three locations were initially identified: Hanford, Washington; Deaf County, Texas; and Yucca Mountain, Nevada. Political leaders and interest groups in all three areas soon expressed vigorous opposition to opening a repository in each location. In Nevada, substantial numbers of people spoke out both for and against the location of the repository in the state. Advocates saw the repository as a source of jobs, construction contracts, and a continuing flow of federal dollars into the state. Opponents emphasized the potentially harmful health effects of the repository and the deleterious impact it would have on the state's gaming and tourist industries. Critics also feared that location of the repository in Nevada would make it harder to convince other businesses to locate in the state.

It soon became apparent that opponents of the waste repository, led by Governor Richard Bryan, were winning the political battle. While a few legislators from Clark County originally advocated further study of the matter, most officials took a strong and unequivocal stand against its location in the state.[11] Public opinion polls consistently showed that a large majority of residents were opposed to having the repository at Yucca Mountain.[12] By the late 1980s, virtually every candidate for public office took a strong stand in opposition to the site; to do otherwise was almost a sure recipe for political suicide.

Although three possible sites for the nuclear waste repository had been identified, it soon became apparent that the U.S. Department of Energy was focusing on Yucca Mountain. In 1987 Senator Bennett Johnston introduced a bill to study only one site rather than three; the bill soon became known as the "Screw Nevada" bill.[13] Nevadans have succeeded in slowing down the selection process, but it is far from clear that in the long run they will keep the site out of the state. The reality of being a small state with few allies in Congress on the issue may ultimately prove to be more important than any objective study of the relative merits of the three sites.[14]

The Yucca Mountain controversy raises the question of whether the state should continue to oppose the project or whether it should compromise with the federal government in hopes of getting the maximum possible amount of federal funds as "compensation" for hosting the site. In a survey conducted by the two state universities in the fall of 1988, 89 percent of the respondents agreed with the following statement: "If the high level nuclear waste site ends up in Nevada, the state should begin planning now to get the best possible economic deal in return."[15]

Routine Federal Activity

Although federalism is sometimes characterized by controversies over water or land or construction of a dam, it usually operates through routine activities that gain little attention. Over twelve thousand federal government employees work in Nevada and have an impact on the economy. Much of the state's in-migration consists of retirees whose pensions and Social Security payments also boost the local economy. Federal funds provide a major portion of spending for the state's Medicaid and highway construction programs, and the university system annually brings millions of federal research dollars into Nevada. In 1991 direct federal expenditures in Nevada amounted to more than $4.8 billion, including $2.5 billion in direct payments to individuals, such as federal employment retirement payments and Social Security.

These activities make the news only when there is a major controversy or scandal. Most of the time these functions proceed without notice. Federalism, or intergovernmental relations, usually proceeds as a set of important, but mostly routine, relationships among federal, state, and local governments.

FEDERAL MONEY AND FEDERAL MANDATES

A federal system constantly experiences strains between the national government and the regional governments. In recent years these strains have been exacerbated in the United States as the federal government has mandated more state expenditures. At the same time, federal funding declined from a high of 26 percent of the total fifty-state and local outlays in 1978 to 22 percent by 1993. While most Nevadans possess an individualistic spirit, they face a paradox in their relationship with the federal government. Although they welcome federal money and programs, such as Hoover Dam and the Nevada Test Site, they resent the power and control exercised by the federal government, as reflected in the "Sagebrush Rebellion" and Yucca Mountain controversies.

These concerns about federal control have increased in recent years as the state budget has had to absorb the increasing costs of federally aided and mandated programs. Two programs illustrate this trend: Aid to Families with Dependent Children (AFDC) and Medicaid. Table 3 shows the increased impact on the state budget of these two programs in the 1980s.

These programs are federally aided rather than mandated. Legally, states have the right not to participate in them, but from both political and fiscal standpoints, no state would dare to withdraw from participation. Federal requirements that states assume the costs of environmental protection programs are examples of federal mandates that have impacted state budgets.

Sharp budget increases in AFDC and Medicaid programs are also found in the budgets of other states. Although the federal government sets the gen-

Table 3: State General Fund Budgets for Federally Mandated Aid to Families with Dependent Children and Medicaid, 1981 and 1990

	1981 (Millions)	% of General Fund	1990 (Millions)	% of General Fund	% Increase, 1981–90
AFDC	$ 7.6	.82	$ 26.5	1.2	248.7
Medicaid	48.6	5.24	146.7	6.5	202.2

Source: State of Nevada, Executive Budget, 1981–83 and 1991–93.

eral guidelines for the programs, it gives the states some discretion in determining eligibility for benefits. States that are conservative on welfare issues, such as Nevada, are more restrictive in defining eligibility; yet program costs continue to grow rapidly in those states as well.[16]

About half of the cost of these programs is offset by federal aid. In 1991 Nevada joined other states in taking advantage of what some would call a loophole in federal law. The legislature imposed a tax on hospitals, with the revenue to be used to increase the state's Medicaid expenditures. This increase generated more federal matching money. Each hospital was then reimbursed for the amount of the tax paid. The use of this ploy meant that the federal government paid for the entire increase in the state's Medicaid expenditures. The loophole was terminated by Congress, effective in 1995. Therefore, the state will have to look for other sources of revenue, cut Medicaid, or hope that health-care reform will produce savings.

Federal requirements for state spending, especially in the health-care area, are likely to remain a major issue for the foreseeable future. The election of a Republican Congress in 1994, as well as the growing opposition of both Republican and Democratic governors to unfunded mandates, increases the likelihood that future mandates will be reduced or restricted.

INTERSTATE FEDERALISM

Political questions concerning intergovernmental relations also involve relations among the states. Sometimes relationships are formalized through compacts between states. Nevada's most important interstate compacts have involved the environment in the Lake Tahoe area and the distribution of water.

Lake Tahoe

The Lake Tahoe region, on the Nevada-California border, is a beautiful area of water, mountains, and forest. It is also the scene of a long debate over the extent to which it should be developed for residential and commercial purposes or preserved as nearly as possible in its pristine state. Numerous interest groups, both state governments, and the federal government have all been involved in the controversy.

As early as 1931, California and Nevada created the Lake Tahoe Interstate Water Conference Committee to study development issues of the region; later, in 1955, the Congress established the California-Nevada Interstate Compact Commission. These and other agencies made some progress in resolving the issues facing the Tahoe region. Throughout the 1960s, both states discussed the creation of a regional governing body—with only limited enforcement powers—for the area. Finally, in 1969 both states agreed to the creation of the Tahoe Regional Planning Agency (TRPA), which received the approval of the federal government.

Since 1969, then, TRPA has been the primary regional planning body for the Tahoe area. While some progress has been made in solving the environment-versus-growth problem, the agency remains a battleground on which a variety of interests contend with one another. Local governments in the area are fearful of TRPA as a "supergovernment" impinging on their authority. Private property owners believe that they should be able to use and build on their land just like property owners elsewhere. The interests of those who favor growth and commercial expansion conflict directly with those who favor preservation and more restricted development.[17]

The Lake Tahoe region is a good example of how policy differences result from conflicts among governments as well as among political and economic interest groups that have very different goals. The fundamental differences about the future of the region will not likely be resolved soon. When solutions to the problems are ultimately found, they will probably be the result of cooperation among several governmental units rather than the action of any single government acting alone.

Water Issues

All of Nevada has had to face the problems of a limited water supply. The previous discussion of the Newlands Reclamation Project illustrates the importance of water in northern Nevada. In the southern part of the state, the allocation of Colorado River water has long been a crucial matter for the area's development. The river, which flows along Nevada's southeastern border and then divides the states of California and Arizona as it flows toward Mexico, is a vital water source for the Las Vegas region.

Congress long ago recognized the importance of the river to the growth of the southwestern states; in 1921 it authorized the states adjoining the river to negotiate an agreement for allocating water among them. The states were almost immediately skeptical and fearful of one another. Arizona and Nevada were especially fearful that California would claim nearly all the water and leave them without adequate amounts. Eventually an agreement was reached in 1928 whereby each basin, the Upper Colorado River Basin and the Lower Colorado Basin, would receive 7,500,000 acre feet of water. The lower basin water was to be allocated as follows: California, 4,400,000 acre feet; Arizona, 2,800,000 acre feet; and Nevada, 300,000 acre feet.

As time passed, new issues arose. California—the Los Angeles area in particular—was growing even more rapidly than Arizona and Nevada, which feared that California would demand ever more water. There was disagreement over whether the water in the tributaries should count against a state's allocation. There was also concern that the political power in Congress of the more populous California would be used to the disadvantage of Arizona and Nevada.

In 1952 Arizona sued California to assure a guarantee of its water rights; a year later Nevada entered the suit as an ally of Arizona. Under the U.S. Constitution, suits between states are to be adjudicated by the U.S. Supreme Court. The case took over ten years to be resolved, as a court master attempted to settle the dispute.[18] In 1963 the Supreme Court handed down a decision that was mainly favorable to Arizona and Nevada. The decision stated that the original negotiated allocation of water among the states was not a binding agreement; however, the Court went on to allocate the water in exactly the same amounts as in the original agreement. The decision also supported Arizona's contention that water in the Gila River should not be counted against the state's allocation of Colorado River water.[19]

The dispute among the three states illustrates the difficulty of states resolving such conflicts when a scarce resource such as water is involved and when the economic stakes are so high. It became necessary for the Supreme Court to serve as a referee to resolve the issue. As the three states continue to make demands on a limited amount of water, the controversy will continue.

CONCLUSION

Based on the above illustrations of federalism in action, it is possible to make four generalizations about how our federal system works. First, public policy in a federal system results from interaction of private interest groups as well as units of government. States and the federal government may contend with one another, but property owners, conservationists, tourism officials, agricultural interests, and others contend as well.

Second, the economic and political stakes are often so high that affected groups cannot voluntarily arrive at solutions. Thus, state and local officials and private interests—who may well be skeptical of federal power—may have to look to the federal government to serve as the final decision maker.

Third, all three branches of the federal government often get involved in working out solutions to problems with states. In addition to the Supreme Court, Congress and the executive branch agencies—such as the Department of Defense, Bureau of Land Management, and the Bureau of Indian Affairs—are important players in settling disputes with the states.

Fourth, the federal government is integrally involved in virtually every aspect of state and local policymaking in Nevada. These intergovernmental relations are usually routine and cooperative, although occasionally there will be conflicts and policy disagreements. There are no final resolutions of these intergovernmental issues because federalism is not a static concept; one of its virtues is its ability to respond to changing times and conditions.

CHAPTER THREE

Political History: The Early Years

Before its power declined in the Western Hemisphere during the Napoleonic Wars of 1805–15, Spain established two provinces—New Mexico and California—with the land that now constitutes the state of Nevada being in one or the other. Mexico staged a successful revolt against Spain in 1821 and laid claim to the two provinces. The Republic of Mexico in turn ceded the provinces to the United States in the Treaty of Guadalupe Hidalgo that ended the Mexican War on 2 February 1848.

THE UTAH AND NEW MEXICO TERRITORIAL GOVERNMENTS

The Compromise of 1850 divided the two provinces into the state of California and the territories of Utah and New Mexico. Seven counties of the Utah Territory extended across present-day Nevada to the boundaries of the state of California. The same extension of the three counties of Rio Arriba, Santa Ana, and Bernalillo of the New Mexico Territory was also made across the southern triangle that now makes up the most populous area of Nevada.

After ignoring the people who had settled in the Carson Valley for three years, the Utah territorial legislature in January 1854 created Carson County out of the extreme western sections of four preexisting counties. The new county included all or parts of ten present-day counties in northern Nevada. Brigham Young, who had been appointed governor of the Utah Territory by President Millard Fillmore, then appointed Orson Hyde, one of the apostles of the Mormon church, as the probate judge for Carson County.[1]

Sending Orson Hyde to Carson County was in line with a decision of Mormon church leaders to send colonizing groups to various locations in the West. Another mission was established at a stopping place along the Old

Spanish Trail that went from Santa Fe to Monterey; this mission was called Las Vegas Spring and was in the New Mexico Territory. A group of Mormons led by William Bringhurst arrived in the area that is now the city of Las Vegas on 14 June 1855 and proceeded to establish the first white settlement in what is now Clark County.[2] This community or mission did not last long. A series of financial setbacks and repeated attacks by Indians caused Brigham Young to recall the members to Salt Lake City in early 1857. O. D. Gass developed the abandoned site and renamed it the Las Vegas Ranch.[3]

The Mormons and the Federal Government

Meanwhile, in late 1856 deterioration of relationships between the federal government and the Utah Territory threatened Mormon control of the Carson County government. The Mormons had been pleased and relieved when President Fillmore appointed Brigham Young as governor of the Utah Territory. However, Franklin Pierce and James Buchanan, Fillmore's successors, did not share his generally positive feeling toward the Mormons. Pierce appointed federal judges who clashed with the Mormon leader. In his resignation letter to President Buchanan in March 1857, Chief Justice W. W. Drummond wrote a scathing denunciation of the Mormons and the Utah territorial government.[4] This letter may have been the main factor in President Buchanan's decisions to relieve Brigham Young as governor and to send troops to put down the "rebellion" in the Utah Territory.[5]

In June 1857 Buchanan found a suitable candidate for governor in Alfred E. Cumming of Georgia. Influenced by the Drummond letter, Buchanan felt that he needed to send federal troops to accompany Governor Cumming and restore law and order to the Utah Territory. Not knowing the objective of the troops but fearing the worst, Young prepared his own military strategy. Most of the plans dealt with delaying the march of the army in the hope that winter would prevent its entrance into the Salt Lake Valley and that negotiations could then take place with the federal officials on the existing problems.[6]

With the Mormons mobilizing to resist a possible attack in the Salt Lake Valley, Young decided to recall the missionaries from Europe and the members of the colonies in the Carson Valley and San Bernardino, California. Most Mormons living in the Carson Valley, including almost all of the elected officials of the county government, unhesitantly responded to the call to return to the Salt Lake Valley.[7] When they arrived back in the Salt Lake Valley in November 1857, they found that things were working out as Brigham Young had hoped. While the federal troops were camped for the winter in

Fort Bridger, in what is now Wyoming, President Buchanan decided to send a commission to the Utah Territory to bring an end to the so-called Mormon War that had proved to be an embarrassment to his administration.

The Period of Anarchy and Confusion

While the Buchanan administration and the Mormon leaders were working out their settlement, the residents of the Carson Valley were without a local government. A mass meeting in August 1857 approved a memorial to Congress requesting that a separate government be established for the western part of the Utah Territory. The petition charged that the only law that existed in the Utah Territory was the rule of the Mormon church.[8] The people at the meeting elected James Crane, a Whig politician in Virginia, as their delegate to present the memorial to Congress and to represent the new territory when it came into being.

In June 1859 the discovery of major deposits of gold and silver thirty miles from Genoa led to a decline of interest in politics.[9] Mining activity increased even more with the discovery of the nearby Comstock Lode the next year.

Delegate Crane died in September 1859. John J. Musser, who was elected to replace him, engendered some support for the creation of a separate territory. However, in May 1860 the House of Representatives tabled the territorial bill.[10]

The silver and gold discoveries in the Virginia City area and the subsequent "rush to Washoe" brought swarms of people into Carson County. The large increase in population and the impending break between the North and the South following the election of Abraham Lincoln as president were opening the door for congressional passage of a separate territorial bill. With the help of California's U.S. senators, William Gwin and Milton Latham, Musser was able to push the bill through Congress during its short lame-duck session from December 1860 to 3 March 1861.[11] Two days after President Buchanan signed the Nevada bill into law, Lincoln was inaugurated.

THE NEVADA TERRITORY AND STATEHOOD

Eighteen days after taking office, President Lincoln named James W. Nye as governor and Orion Clemens of Missouri as secretary of the Nevada Territory. Both were patronage appointments.

A native of New York, Nye had served as police commissioner of New York City, where he became a close friend of William Seward, the powerful U.S. senator from New York.[12] Although Nye had supported Seward for the Republican nomination in 1860, he campaigned hard for Lincoln during the presidential campaign. When Lincoln asked Seward to be his secretary of state, Seward put in a good word for an appointment for Nye; the president rewarded the latter with the territorial governorship.[13]

Orion Clemens had worked in the St. Louis law office of Edward Bates, Lincoln's attorney general. Clemens had also stumped for Lincoln during the presidential campaign. Thus, he had the credentials for a patronage appointment when Bates dropped the name of his former employee to Lincoln. Clemens was accompanied to his new position in the Nevada Territory by his brother Samuel, who became better known by his pen name, Mark Twain.[14]

Nye arrived in Carson City in July 1861 and immediately commissioned a census of the new territory. The population was determined to be 16,374, exclusive of Indians and transients. Nye also called for an election for members of the territorial legislature and the delegate to Congress. Former federal judge John Cradlebaugh was elected the delegate to Congress, where he became known for his strong anti-Mormon speeches.[15]

The First Territorial Legislature

Governor Nye convened the first territorial legislature on 1 October 1861 in Carson City in the upper story of Curry's Warm Springs Hotel, the present site of the first Nevada State Prison. The member of the first territorial legislature who went on to the greatest fame was William M. Stewart, a Carson City lawyer at the time, who later served as a powerful U.S. senator from Nevada for twenty-eight years. A New York native, Stewart attended Yale University for a year and a half before joining the gold rush to California in early 1850. He served for six months as acting attorney general of California and for a short time became a member of the Know-Nothing party before returning to the Democratic party. In March 1860 he moved to Virginia City and set up a law partnership, specializing in mining cases.[16]

Stewart and his friend Abraham Curry, the founder of Carson City, worked at the first legislative session to make Carson City the territorial capital. Stewart framed the bill so that several of the towns within a comparatively short distance of Carson City were made county seats, thus assuring the support of legislators from those towns for Carson City as the capital, even though it meant the establishment of some geographically small counties.[17] Thus, despite the much larger population of Virginia City, Carson City was designated as the capital.

The Statehood Question

On 20 December 1862 the territorial legislature passed a bill "to frame a Constitution and State Government for the State of Washoe." The act set up an election for September 1863 to vote on statehood and to choose delegates to a state constitutional convention in case the vote was in favor of statehood.[18]

On the last day of the 1862–63 lame-duck session of Congress, the U.S. Senate passed an enabling bill to authorize the Nevada Territory to draft a state constitution.[19] However, a motion to suspend the rules in the House so that it might take up the bill did not muster the necessary two-thirds majority. Despite the lack of authorization from Congress, officials in the Nevada Territory proceeded with the September election. The voters overwhelmingly (better than 4-1) approved of statehood, so that the delegates elected to the constitutional convention prepared to meet in Carson City in November.

All but four of the thirty-nine delegates to the 1863 convention had come to the territory after residing in California, and all but two had lived in Nevada less than five years.[20] Given this background and the fact that the delegates included a former governor (J. Neely Johnson) and attorney general (William M. Stewart) of California, the convention decided to use that state's constitution as the starting point for deliberations.

The taxation of unproductive mining property and the holding of elections for state officials at the same time as the ratification vote on the constitution turned out to be the most critical decisions at the convention.[21] Stewart lost on both issues; however, he pledged that he would support the constitution in the ensuing election.[22]

As Elliott has written, "The forces favoring adoption of the constitution appeared invincible when the ratification fight began."[23] Most newspapers and the San Francisco interests that dominated the Comstock Lode were in favor of ratification and statehood. However, the anti-ratification forces used the mining tax article and the election process to defeat the constitution and the Stewart forces in the election.

David A. Johnson, who exhaustively researched the contemporary newspapers in both Nevada and California, came to the conclusion that "Nevada rejected statehood because . . . [the people] believed that William Stewart would capture the state government and use it to serve the purpose of San Francisco financiers in control of Nevada's largest mining corporations."[24] The *Virginia Daily Union,* previously favoring ratification, changed its position after Stewart completely controlled the Union party convention and the nomination of the party's candidates for the election. The paper's editorial stated that Stewart and "California speculators would run the state government" if the constitution were ratified and that the paper "would prefer 'Uncle Abe' to Bill Stewart as an appointing power."[25]

At the election on the proposed constitution on 19 January 1864, only 2,157 votes were cast in favor of ratification, with 8,851 voting against.[26] Thus, the people voted better than 4-1 against a proposed state constitution only four months after voting by approximately the same margin in favor of statehood.

The Nevada Enabling Act

Meanwhile, the Radical Republicans in Congress were anxious to admit new states likely to elect representatives who would support their plans for Reconstruction after the Civil War. Therefore, just three weeks after the vote of Nevadans against the unauthorized state constitution, Senator James R. Doolittle of Wisconsin introduced another Nevada statehood bill.[27] Congress passed the bill through both houses in less than three weeks; Lincoln signed the enabling act on 21 March 1864.

In the enabling act, Congress specified certain matters to be included in the state constitution.[28] The Republicans, who held the majority of the seats in both houses, wished to have the new state vote in the presidential election. Thus, the enabling act provided that the president rather than Congress would determine whether the document had complied with the directives of the act.

The Second Constitutional Convention

On 6 June 1864 voters selected delegates to a convention that had been officially authorized by Congress. Only ten delegates had also served at the 1863 convention.

The delegates immediately passed a resolution stating "that the constitution adopted by the late convention be taken as the basis of the constitution to be adopted by this convention."[29] The most important change made in the 1863 constitution concerned the mining clause that had caused such a stir both during and after the first convention. David A. Johnson's research convinced him that the mining depression of 1864 was a major factor in the decision of the delegates to change the mining clause.[30] The convention also decided to separate ratification of the constitution from the election of the new state officials.

The changes made at the second constitutional convention appeared to clear the way for approval of the constitution. The economic depression and the popular belief that statehood would get rid of the allegedly corrupt territorial judiciary also probably contributed to the popular support for statehood.[31]

In the election on ratification on 7 September 1864, the voters overwhelmingly approved the document and statehood, 10,375 to 1,284. Given the nearness to the presidential election, the complete text of the constitution was telegraphed to President Lincoln at a cost in excess of $3,400.[32] Having been empowered to act in the Nevada enabling act, Lincoln proclaimed Nevada a state on 31 October 1864, just eight days prior to the election.

Thus, Nevada became a state of the Union only fourteen years after the first white settlements in the area and thirty-two years prior to the admission of the more populous Utah Territory. The discovery of the Comstock Lode, the Civil War, and the issue of Reconstruction were primarily responsible for Nevada's early admission, whereas problems between the Mormon church and the federal government—especially concerning polygamy—delayed the admission of Utah.

EARLY STATEHOOD, 1864–1892

Most of the voters in the 1864 election voted a straight Union (Republican) party ticket. The final tally showed that about 60 percent voted for the Republican presidential electors, the GOP candidate for the U.S. House of Representatives, and the Union candidates for all the statewide offices. The voters elected only one Democrat to each house of the legislature.

The first state legislature met in December 1864. The election of the first two U.S. senators was one of the first orders of business and attracted considerable public interest. William Stewart showed that he was the most powerful politician in the new state by easily winning one of the seats on the first ballot. However, James W. Nye, the territorial governor, won an unexpectedly tough fight for the second seat.

In contrast to travel by airplane today, the first Nevada delegation to the nation's capital in January 1865 had an arduous journey. Stewart, Nye, and Congressman H. G. Worthington went by stagecoach to Sacramento and then by riverboat to San Francisco; they then took an ocean steamer to the

Isthmus of Panama. After riding horses to the Atlantic side of the Isthmus, the group boarded a ship to New York City. A train trip completed the journey to the nation's capital.[33] A welcoming party met Worthington and whisked him to the House to vote on the Thirteenth Amendment (prohibition of slavery). The amendment was approved by a vote of 119-56, just two votes more than the two-thirds requirement.

The first session of the state legislature passed a resolution that would have tremendous consequences for the future history of the state. The joint resolution asked Congress to add an additional degree of territory, at the expense of the Utah Territory, on its eastern border. On 5 May 1866, over the strong opposition of the Utah and Arizona territorial delegates, Congress not only extended the Nevada border to the east but added the triangle below the 37th parallel to its southern border (see map 1). The latter addition was subject to the approval of Nevada's legislature, which was granted on 18 January 1867. The main argument used in the congressional debate on the two additions was that the territory "was valuable for its mining . . . and Nevada was a mining state."[34] Nevada was able to add this territory because it had voting membership in Congress—something the Utah and Arizona territories did not have.

U.S. Senators

The most powerful political figures in this early period and throughout most of the state's first century were the two U.S. senators. The prestige of the office, which had equal voting power with senators from the populous states, attracted experienced politicians as well as wealthy tycoons. Prior to the Seventeenth Amendment, the legislature elected the senators. More often than not, the selection of the U.S. senator was the dominant issue in the November legislative elections.

As shown in table 4, the Republican party, the party of Lincoln, dominated the politics of Nevada during the first twenty-eight years of statehood. John P. Jones and William Stewart, who served for twenty and sixteen years, respectively, during this first period, still hold the record for the most years served by Nevadans in the upper house of Congress (see table 5). Stewart had the backing of the mining interests, the Bank of California crowd that dominated the financing of the Comstock mines, and the Central Pacific Railroad.[35] Jones had made a fortune while superintendent of the Crown Point mine. He was the first Nevadan who, in effect, bought the office. The millionaire, who was a popular campaigner, reportedly spent as much as

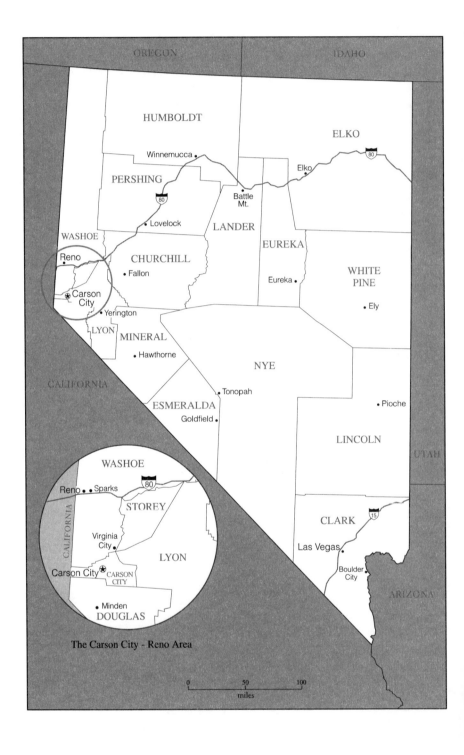

The Carson City - Reno Area

Table 4: Years of Party Control of Major Statewide Elective Offices and Legislative Houses, 1864–1892

Office	Republican Control	Democratic Control
U.S. Senate	50	6
U.S. House	20	8
Governor	16	12
Lieutenant Governor	16	12
Attorney General	20	8
Secretary of State	28	0
Treasurer	20	8
Controller	28	0
State Senate	24	4
State Assembly	24	4

Source: Frankie Sue Del Papa (secretary of state), *Political History of Nevada*, 9th ed. (Carson City: State Printing Office, 1990).

$800,000 contributing to the campaigns of legislative candidates who in turn promised to support him in the vote for the U.S. Senate.[36]

After serving ten years in Washington, Stewart announced in 1874 that he would not be a candidate for reelection. Although he implied that financial difficulties dictated that he return to the practice of law, Russell Elliott, his biographer, believes that the declaration of candidacy for the Senate seat by Comstock millionaire William Sharon was probably the main reason for Stewart's retirement.[37] Sharon's attendance record during his six-year term was probably the worst case of absenteeism in the history of the U.S. Senate, as he "was recorded on less than 1 percent of all roll calls."[38] He was replaced by Democrat James G. Fair, another Comstock millionaire, whose attendance record was almost as bad as his predecessor's.[39]

In 1885 Stewart moved back to Nevada and launched a campaign to regain his seat. He chose Charles C. "Black" Wallace, the paid agent and lobbyist for the Central Pacific Railroad in Nevada, to run his campaign—a clear indication that the railroad was backing Stewart.[40] With the support of mining magnate John Mackay, the Bank Crowd, and popular Senator Jones, Stewart easily won election at the January 1887 legislative session.

Stewart and Jones proved to be effective senators. They accumulated enough seniority to gain committee assignments that were important to the state. However, the nine individuals who served in Nevada's lone seat in the lower house were generally ineffective in exercising influence on Capitol Hill. None of them served more than two consecutive two-year terms.

Table 5: Nevadans with the Most Years in the U.S. Senate

Senator	Party	Years of Service	Total Years
1. John P. Jones	Republican, Silver	1873–1903	30
2. William M. Stewart	Republican, Silver	1865–75, 1887–1905	28
3. Key Pittman	Democrat	1913–40	27+
4. Howard W. Cannon	Democrat	1959–82	24
5. Patrick A. McCarran	Democrat	1933–54	21+
6. Alan Bible	Democrat	1954–74	20
7. Francis G. Newlands	Democrat	1903–17	14+
8. Tasker L. Oddie	Republican	1921–33	12
George W. Malone	Republican	1947–59	12
Paul Laxalt	Republican	1974–86	12

Source: Frankie Sue Del Papa, *Political History of Nevada*, 9th ed. (Carson City: State Printing Office, 1990).

Governors

Despite the overall dominance of the Republican party during this early period, Democrats won three of the seven gubernatorial elections. The first Democratic breakthrough occurred in 1870 when the integrity and personality of Lewis R. "Broadhorns" Bradley, a cattleman from the northeastern part of the state, overcame the general Republican proclivities of the electorate. Bradley was reelected in 1874; however, he failed in his bid for a third term when the mining interests opposed him because of his veto of a bill decreasing mining taxes.[41]

Republican John Kinkead, the candidate of the mine owners, defeated Bradley in 1878. Kinkead's appeal to the legislature for more stringent regulation of the railroads went unheeded.[42] This reaction typified the general legislative response during this period when a governor's position was contrary to that of the dominant interest groups. The governors were no match for the power exercised by the mine owners and the railroads.

Power of the Mining and Railroad Interests

From 1864 to 1878, the economy of the state was tied to the Comstock Lode, which experienced a number of booms and busts. When the Comstock did not revive after 1878, the state fell into a depression that lasted until the discoveries of silver and gold at Tonopah in 1900. The depression itself did not end Republican political dominance, but the silver question became so important in the politics of Nevada during the last decade of the century—partially as a result of the depression—that officeholders and political hopefuls were forced to jump to the new Silver party as a matter of political survival.

Although mining was the dominant interest in nineteenth-century legislative sessions, the railroads had the most effective lobbyists. During the 1870s and the early 1880s, the premier lobbyist was Henry M. Yerington, the general manager of the Virginia and Truckee Railroad. The main goal of the Central Pacific Railroad was to control the U.S. senators from Nevada, but it also relied on Yerington indirectly in the early years of statehood to protect railroad interests in general.[43] Elliott has outlined how Yerington and the railroads achieved their ends. First, they distributed money to legislators "who promised to work for the railroad interest." Second, Yerington "attempted to control the delegates" to the Republican county and state conventions in order to obtain platform planks favorable to the railroads. Finally, the railroads controlled the legislature when in session "by means of lobbying and additional money if necessary and by liberal uses of railroad passes."[44]

In the mid-1880s, Black Wallace, who had been the protégé of Central Pacific Railroad president Collis P. Huntington prior to his assignment as the company's Nevada agent, joined Yerington in lobbying for railroad interests. Wallace quickly mastered the politics of the state. He was described by a contemporary journalist as being "smooth and diplomatic when the occasion called for such tactics, and a rough and ready fighter when cornered, and he was seldom cornered. His chief personal asset was unwavering fidelity to his word, which once passed, was as good as any United States Government Bond anywhere in Nevada."[45] A newspaper editorial decried the power that Wallace exercised in the legislature and sarcastically suggested that "the taxpayers should by all means engage his services and have him exercise his genius in their interests, instead of going through the farce of electing men every two years."[46] Wallace was prescient enough to know that the Central Pacific and the other railroads could only remain an important political force in Nevada if they joined the silver bandwagon in the early 1890s. Thus, he became an important figure in the formation of the Silver party in 1892.

DOMINANCE OF THE SILVER QUESTION, 1892–1908

By 1892 remonetization of silver had become the number one issue in western mining states. Senator Henry M. Teller of Colorado, a leading "silverite" in Congress, called for the organization of "nonpartisan political associations" to promote the cause of the free coinage of silver.[47]

George Nixon, a Winnemucca banker and editor of the influential newspaper *Silver State,* organized Nevada's first silver club in April 1892. A silver state convention that met in Reno on 24 June 1892 created, in effect, a Silver party.

Less than five months after its formation, the Silver party scored an amazing victory. The party convention in September had instructed its three presidential electors to cast their votes for General James B. Weaver, the candidate of the national People's or Populist party whose platform supported the free coinage of silver. The voters gave the Silver electors 67 percent of the vote for president, the GOP electors 26 percent, and the Democratic electors 6 percent. Democrat Grover Cleveland, who favored the gold standard, won the national election.

The election for Nevada's lone seat in the U.S. House of Representatives was even more one-sided than the presidential race. Francis G. Newlands, the son-in-law of former U.S. senator William Sharon, won 73 percent of the vote as the Silver party candidate compared to 23 percent for the Republican candidate and 3 percent for the Democrat. There was a great upheaval in the party composition of the legislature, where the Republicans had held a 36-4 margin over the Democrats in the 1891 assembly. In 1892 the voters elected only one Republican and two Democrats; when the assembly convened in January, all thirty members declared themselves to be "silver men"[48] (see table 6).

The 1896 Democratic National Convention nominated William Jennings Bryan for president and adopted a platform that was very similar to the People's party platform of 1892, including a free-coinage-of-silver plank. These actions encouraged cooperation between the remnants of the Democratic party in Nevada and the Silver party. The Silver-Democratic fusion ticket swept all the statewide elections in 1896, winning 76 percent of the vote for Bryan and 67 percent of the vote for Congressman Newlands. The Silver-Democratic coalition carried almost all the statewide offices in the next five elections. However, the 1906 election proved to be the last hurrah for the remnants of the Silver party movement, as silver was no longer the all-important issue.

U.S. Senators

Both Stewart and Jones "saw the handwriting on the wall" and joined the Silver party prior to their first race for reelection during this period. Afraid of antagonizing the Bank Crowd and the railroad leaders, who were strong Republicans, Stewart delayed making a commitment to the new party until 8

Table 6: Years of Party Control of Major Statewide Elective Offices and Legislative Houses, 1892–1908

Office	Republican	Democrat	Silver	Silver-Democrat	Democrat-Silver
U.S. Senate	8	6	18	0	0
U.S. House	0	0	4	12	0
Governor	2	0	8	4	2
Lieutenant Governor	2	0	8	4	2
Attorney General	2	0	8	4	2
Secretary of State	8	0	8	0	0
Treasurer	2	0	8	4	2
Controller	4	0	8	4	0
State Senate	2	0	10	0	4
State Assembly	2	0	10	0	4

Source: Frankie Sue Del Papa, Political History of Nevada, 9th ed. (Carson City: State Printing Office, 1990).

August 1892.[49] After the Silver landslide in November, Stewart's was the only name placed in nomination when the legislature met in January.

Although a strong supporter of silver, Senator Jones was reluctant to leave the Republican party and did not join the Silver party until 1894. Jones easily defeated the last-minute candidacy of George Nixon in the 1897 legislature.[50]

The Silverites at the 1899 legislature were split on Stewart's candidacy for a fifth term in Washington. Congressman Newlands, who had been encouraged to move to Nevada by Stewart in 1888, had long been ambitious for a seat in the U.S. Senate.[51] Black Wallace was able to use his considerable skills to "outmaneuver and outcorrupt" Newlands's forces and secure a narrow victory in the legislature for the longtime senator.[52]

In 1902 the decision of Senator Jones not to seek reelection enabled Congressman Newlands to achieve his longtime goal. Newlands had served five distinguished terms in the lower house, topped by the passage of the Newlands Reclamation Act—a major piece of legislation providing for the reclamation of arid lands. Newlands differed from most contemporary politicians in Nevada in that he believed, in the words of Russell Elliott, "that the federal government should be a positive force in the economic and social welfare of the people."[53]

Senator Stewart worked hard to try to defeat Newlands's Senate bid, but Stewart's return to the Republican party in 1900 after having been elected by the Silverite legislature a year earlier had antagonized the silver forces. The death of Black Wallace, Stewart's ally, also helped the congressman win the support of silver legislators. Newlands's independent fortune was an important factor in the election, just as it had been in his previous campaigns.[54] Newlands easily won the Senate seat, as the GOP elected only a total of eight members to the legislature.

While Senator Stewart, now seventy-eight years old, was still considering whether to run for reelection in 1904, George Nixon announced that he was returning to the Republican party. The railroad interests, which had supported Stewart in the past, promised their support to Nixon for the Senate seat.[55] With his base of support gone, Stewart withdrew from the race, and Nixon became the sole Republican candidate. In the November election, the popularity of Theodore Roosevelt helped the Republicans gain a majority of the seats in the legislature and ensured the election of Nixon to the U.S. Senate.

Thus, the end of the dominance of silver in Nevada politics coincided with the retirement from the U.S. Senate of William Stewart and John Jones, whose time in the upper house reached from 1864 to 1905. The election of Nixon in 1904 initiated a period of almost fifty years in which at least one of the U.S. senators had a connection with the discovery of gold and silver in Tonopah and Goldfield in the first decade of the twentieth century.

The Railroads and Silver

Prior to his death in 1901, Black Wallace was a dominant force in state politics and the legislature during this period. His activities as a paid agent of the Central Pacific Railroad and as a leader of the Silver party would appear to be incongruous. However, when Newlands announced his opposition to a plank in the 1894 Silver party platform calling for government ownership of the railroads, Wallace told the congressman "that a pro-railroad stand would interfere with the railroad's plans."[56] The "plans" included the election of legislative candidates who would support Wallace and his candidate for the U.S. Senate; a pro-railroad stand would threaten the election of such individuals, given the public's strong anti-railroad sentiments.

The people were critical of the railroads because of the fare structure that forced ranchers and farmers to pay high rates to transport goods and because of the huge land grants given the transcontinental railroad. However, the railroads were not concerned about platform planks and campaign stands of the legislators; they were confident that campaign donations and the lobbying of Black Wallace would ensure that the legislators would vote the "right" way.

Why were the lobbyists able to exercise so much control over the legislators and, in effect, "buy" them? One of the reasons was the transiency of the population. With the mining depression, the state lost one third of its population in the last two decades of the century. Very few legislators served more than one term during the period—an average of less than 10 percent of the members of the lower house returned for a second term each election during the sixteen-year period. The legislatures lacked experience and leadership; thus, there was not a power base to oppose the powerful lobbyists.

CONCLUSION

During the first twenty-eight years of statehood, the Republican (Union) party was the overwhelming party of choice because of its ties to President Lincoln and the North in the Civil War. However, party loyalty gave way to political expediency when the free coinage of silver became the overriding issue in the state in the 1890s. This early statehood period set the precedent for powerful interest groups and individuals—and the money they dispersed—to be more important than party in elections and legislative actions. The most powerful interest groups were the mining and railroad interests, and the most powerful individuals during this time were U.S. senators Stewart and Jones, Congressman and later Senator Newlands, and railroad lobbyists Wallace and Yerington.

CHAPTER FOUR

Political History:
The Twentieth Century

The turn of the century marked a watershed in Nevada's history. Part-time prospector Jim Butler's discovery of silver and gold in 1900 near Tonopah set off a mining boom that ended the state's twenty-year economic depression.[1] Two years later, gold was discovered in Goldfield, about thirty miles south of Tonopah.

Tasker L. Oddie, a young attorney from Austin, became a partner of Jim Butler. Oddie's chance involvement in the Tonopah mines ultimately led to his entry into politics and his election as governor and U.S. senator.[2] The two most important figures in financing the Goldfield mines were George Wingfield, who had used poker winnings to start his investment in mining, and George Nixon, the prosperous Winnemucca banker, editor of *Silver State*, and cofounder of the Silver party.[3] After Tonopah, Wingfield became a wealthy banker and powerful behind-the-scenes political boss in Nevada.[4] Other individuals who moved to Tonopah and Goldfield during the mining boom and later became important political figures in the state included Key Pittman and Pat McCarran, two of the state's most powerful U.S. senators; Vail Pittman, Key's brother, who later became governor; George Bartlett, a two-term congressman; and George Thatcher, who became a leader of the state Democratic party as well as a business partner of Wingfield.[5] The friendships formed in the Tonopah area among these individuals had a great impact on the state's politics during the first half of the twentieth century.

CLOSE PARTY COMPETITION, 1908–1932

Nevada returned to two-party politics after the 1906 election, and the parties came close to splitting the number of victories during the next twenty-four

Table 7: Years of Party Control of Major Statewide Elective Offices and Legislative
Houses, 1908–1932

Office	Republican	Democrat	Democrat-Silver
U.S. Senate	16	32	0
U.S. House	18	6	0
Governor	10	12	2
Lieutenant Governor	10	12	2
Attorney General	0	22	2
Secretary of State	2	22	0
Treasurer	6	16	2
Controller	12	12	0
State Senate	18	6	0
State Assembly	16	8	0

Source: Frankie Sue Del Papa, *Political History of Nevada*, 9th ed. (Carson City: State Printing Office, 1990).

years, as shown in table 7. William Jennings Bryan carried the state for a third time in 1908, but he again lost the national election. In 1912 the state started a run of sixteen straight presidential elections in which it cast its electoral votes for the winner in the presidential race.

George Wingfield, whose only elective office was university regent, was the foremost economic and political leader in the state during this period. In 1896, at the age of nineteen, he left his family in Oregon and migrated to Nevada. In the words of Elizabeth Raymond, his biographer, "through an incredible combination of ability, luck, and gambling prowess, including the fortuitous acquisition of a phenomenal gold mine," he had become a multimillionaire and the business partner of a U.S. senator by the time he was thirty.[6] In an era of close party competition, Wingfield had close connections with leaders of both political parties.

U.S. Senators

The big Democratic edge in the U.S. Senate seats in the period was due to the popularity of two men: Francis Newlands and Key Pittman. Newlands was elected to a second term by the legislature after winning an advisory election in 1908 and to a third term in 1914 in the first direct election of U.S. senators.[7]

In the 1910 election, incumbent senator George Nixon and Democrat Key Pittman, who were both part of the Tonopah crowd, agreed prior to the election to abide by the results of the nonbinding popular vote. This agreement turned out to be crucial. Nixon won the popular vote; however, the voters elected Democrats to a majority of the seats in the legislature. After some hesitation, Pittman asked his fellow Democrats in the legislature to vote for Nixon. Pittman did not have to wait long to claim the seat, as Senator Nixon died on 5 June 1912. The Democrat won a four-person race to serve out the last four and a half years of Nixon's term. In 1916 Pittman won reelection in a three-person race with a plurality of 39 percent of the vote. That proved to be the last close call for Pittman—he received at least 59 percent of the vote in each of his next four reelection races.

In 1920 former governor Tasker Oddie challenged Charles Henderson, who had been elected to the last two years of Newlands's term after the latter's death in 1917. Oddie defeated the incumbent Democrat by 4 percent of the vote. The presence of independent candidate Anne Martin, the leader of the women's suffrage movement in Nevada, probably cost Henderson the election. She carried 18 percent of the vote, most of which was probably taken from Henderson inasmuch as her political views were closer to his than to Oddie's.[8] Oddie easily won reelection in 1926.

Governors

The death of Governor John Sparks in May 1908 marked the end of an era in which the first nine elected governors were rarely strong legislative leaders; lobbyists such as Yerington and Wallace exercised the real power. Starting with acting governor Denver Dickerson in 1908, the next four Nevada governors had progressive agendas and exercised stronger leadership.

Republican Tasker Oddie defeated Dickerson in the 1910 election and worked well with the Democrats—who controlled the state senate in 1911 and both houses of the legislature in 1913—to enact much progressive legislation. He was opposed in his bid for reelection in 1914 by Emmet D. Boyle, a thirty-five-year-old civil engineer who had served in the Oddie administration as state engineer and as a member of the State Tax Commission. Personal factors favored Boyle. He not only had a reputation for integrity but would also be the first native-born governor as well as the first to have graduated from the state university.[9] Boyle won by 5 percentage points in 1914 and was reelected in a rerun against Oddie in 1918.

Midway through his second term, Boyle decided not to run for a third term.[10] The governor supported State Engineer James G. Scrugham, former dean of Engineering at the University of Nevada, to be his successor. Running on the Boyle record and benefiting from Key Pittman's name being at the head of the Democratic ticket, Scrugham won the governor's race in 1922.

Scrugham had an admirable record of accomplishments—including the creation of state parks and the improvement of the state road system to promote tourism—in his four years as governor. He also served as a member of the federal Colorado River Commission that proposed the construction of what came to be called Hoover Dam. Republican secretary of commerce Herbert Hoover, who chaired the commission, stated that Scrugham was the "outstanding executive in the Western states."[11] However, Scrugham lost his reelection bid in 1926.

Republican state chairman Fred Balzar, who has been described by Elliott as "one of the most popular campaigners in Nevada history," received 53 percent of the vote to defeat Scrugham.[12] The election showed the power and influence of Wingfield and his associates. Wingfield coordinated a network of local campaign workers from the Republican party headquarters in Reno and also made a trip around the state to ensure that the party machinery was working properly.[13] Wingfield also gave personal financial help to both Balzar and Senator Oddie.

Balzar had an engaging personality, but he was over his head in the governor's chair. After his election in 1926, Wingfield told a friend that "Fred will absolutely play the game."[14] Wingfield expected personal allegiance, and Balzar did not disappoint. The contrast between the gubernatorial performances of Scrugham and Balzar could not have been much greater.[15] Balzar delegated much of his decision making to Jay White, his personal secretary. In 1930 Balzar was reelected in a close race with Democratic congressman C. L. Richards.[16]

Wingfield was especially successful in exercising influence over both Balzar and the legislature in 1931. At the end of the session, Wingfield told banker friends in San Francisco that "we got everything we wanted and killed everything we did not want."[17] The two laws that pleased Wingfield the most were the reduction of the residency period for divorce from three months to six weeks and the legalization of casino gambling.[18] He believed that these actions would be a boon for tourism in the Reno area.

A Bipartisan Political Machine?

In the early 1920s, Wingfield became associated with the law firm of Thatcher and Woodburn in Reno. George Thatcher was especially close to Wingfield, who shared a large office complex and phone number with the law firm. Both Thatcher and William Woodburn were longtime Democratic party leaders in the state. This association led to charges by some political observers, including the editor of the influential *Reno Evening Gazette,* Graham Sanford, that Wingfield was actually the head of a bipartisan machine that controlled both political parties in the state.[19]

The proponents of the bipartisan-machine theory pointed to the fact that from 1921 to 1933 the two U.S. senators—Democrat Key Pittman and Republican Tasker Oddie—had both been associates of Wingfield in Tonopah and had continued to be close friends. Elizabeth Raymond, who examined Wingfield's papers, believes that the preponderance of evidence indicates that any Wingfield "machine" was connected with the Republican party.[20] Wingfield obviously enjoyed the access he had to Pittman and was not disappointed when the senator was reelected in 1922. However, in 1928 Wingfield vigorously supported Republican Sam Platt in his losing effort to unseat Pittman.[21]

In 1926 Wingfield hired John Mueller, an assistant state engineer in the Scrugham administration, to be his lobbyist at the legislature. Mueller was responsible for much of Wingfield's success at the 1927, 1929, and 1931 legislative sessions.[22] Norman Biltz, who made a fortune in real estate in the Lake Tahoe area in the late 1920s, also worked with Wingfield to increase tourism and attract wealthy individuals to the state. Mueller and Biltz were to become principal players in a real bipartisan machine in Pat McCarran's heyday.

DEMOCRATIC DOMINANCE, 1932–1996

Democrats have generally been predominant in Nevada's elections during the sixty-four years that constitute the fourth period in the political history of the state (see table 8). The dominance has not been across the board, for Republican candidates carried the electoral votes in eight of the sixteen presidential races during the period, including six straight from 1968 through 1988. However, Democrats have won 79 percent of the elections for U.S. senator, 68.4 percent of the races for the House, 75 percent of the gubernatorial elections, and 67.5 percent of the elections for the other five elected state offices. Democratic party splits and the personal appeal of some Republican candidates led to several breakthroughs for the GOP in high-profile elections.

U.S. Senators

During this period, several Nevada senators became key players in the upper house of Congress. After serving as the second-ranking Democrat on the

Table 8: Years of Party Control of Major Statewide Elective Offices and Legislative
Houses, 1932–1996

Office	Republican	Democrat
U.S. Senate	30	98
U.S. House (two from 1982 to 1996)	24	54
Governor	18	46
Lieutenant Governor	26	38
Attorney General	16	48
Secretary of State	6	58
Treasurer	16	48
Controller	40	24
State Senate (one divided session)	36	26
State Assembly (one divided session)	6	56

Source: Frankie Sue Del Papa, Political History of Nevada, 9th ed. (Carson City: State Printing Office, 1990).

Foreign Relations Committee for ten years, Key Pittman served as chairman from 1933 until his death in 1940. After several ill-timed attempts to defeat incumbent Democrats, Pat McCarran's fortunes changed in 1932 due to a number of fortuitous circumstances.[23] The strongest candidates for the U.S. Senate from the Pittman wing of the Democratic party were Thatcher and Scrugham, but both refused to run because of their friendship for Republican senator Oddie. McCarran then took advantage of the situation by cutting deals with Pittman Democrats at the two conventions in Las Vegas and Carson City to obtain endorsements as the party's candidate for the Senate seat.[24] McCarran ran well behind Franklin Roosevelt and Democratic congressional candidate Scrugham; however, he won Clark County by 1,961 votes, which was enough to overcome Oddie's margin of 269 votes in the rest of the state. As Jerome Edwards has noted, "The crucial element of McCarran's margin of victory was the inflow of the Democratic-oriented workers [to help in the construction of Hoover Dam] into southern Nevada."[25]

McCarran went back to Washington during the last regular lame-duck congressional session and lobbied influential senators for key committee assignments. Senator Key Pittman may have played a role in McCarran's assignment to two of the most powerful Senate committees—Appropriations and Judiciary.[26] McCarran easily won reelection in 1938 and was catapulted into the chairmanship of the Judiciary Committee when Senator Frederick Van Nuys suddenly died in January 1944. He needed the new prestige to turn back a strong challenge from Lieutenant Governor Vail Pittman in the Democratic primary later that year. Pittman was supported by many Democrats who were upset with McCarran's prewar isolationism and friendship with Spanish dictator Francisco Franco, an ally of Adolph Hitler. However, McCarran easily won the general election over perennial candidate George Malone. The 1944 election was significant in that twelve years after the demise of Wingfield's power, two of his closest associates—Biltz and Mueller—played a major role in the McCarran victory. The two Republicans were especially valuable as fund-raisers.[27]

McCarran lost his powerful chairmanship for two years when the Republicans captured control of the Senate in the 1946 election. However, by the time he came up for reelection in 1950, he was once again chairman and was mainly responsible for the enactment of the McCarran Internal Security Act. He was more powerful than ever in his home state and was not challenged seriously in either the primary or general election. In 1952 McCarran attracted national attention as the principal author of the McCarran-Walter Immigration Act and as chairman of the Senate Internal Security Subcommittee. The subcommittee investigated communist influences in certain labor unions but did not turn up anything new. McCarran was an ally of Senator Joseph McCarthy of Wisconsin in the latter's charges that the State Department was riddled with communists. When McCarthy visited Las Vegas in October 1952, he leveled a vicious attack on McCarran foe Hank Greenspun, owner of the *Las Vegas Sun*, and referred to the newspaper as the "Local Daily Worker."[28] McCarran died in September 1954; if he had lived three months longer, he probably would have been one of the few senators to vote against McCarthy's censure by the Senate.[29]

The deaths of Key Pittman in 1940 and Pat McCarran fourteen years later removed from the Nevada political scene the two most powerful figures of the twentieth century. After Pittman had served for over twenty-seven years, three different individuals ended up serving out the remainder of his sixth term.[30]

The 1954 and 1958 elections sent to Washington two individuals, Alan Bible and Howard Cannon, who were each reelected three times and thus gained seniority and considerable influence in the Senate. Bible, a McCarran protégé and two-term attorney general, was a very different person than his mentor. He was well liked by almost everyone and became an excellent campaigner after being upset by the door-to-door campaign of Tom Mechling, a young newcomer to the state, in the Democratic primary in 1952. Bible was a moderate Democrat who strongly supported Presidents Kennedy and Johnson in contrast to McCarran's opposition to many of the key programs of Roosevelt and Truman.

Because of his closeness to Lyndon Johnson, the majority leader, Bible gained a seat on the powerful Appropriations Committee in 1959.[31] Bible became known as "Mr. National Parks" because of his subcommittee chairmanships on the Appropriations and Interior Committees that had jurisdiction over national parks and recreational areas. The National Park Service enjoyed its greatest period of growth during Bible's tenure in those key positions.[32] He retired from the Senate in 1974 because of a back problem, thus becoming the first popularly elected Nevada senator to give up the position voluntarily.

In 1958 Las Vegas City Attorney Howard W. Cannon won a close Democratic primary over Reno physician and university regent Fred Anderson and went on to unseat George Malone, a two-term senator who had been helped by Democratic party splits in 1946 and 1952. Cannon, a much-decorated bomber pilot during World War II, was a member of the Armed Services Committee for all his twenty-four years in the Senate but never rose higher than the panel's number three Democrat in seniority. However, he did serve for almost two decades as the chair of the committee's Aviation Subcommittee and became known as "Mr. Aviation" on Capitol Hill. In 1973 he became chair of the Committee on Rules and Administration, just as the Watergate scandal placed the minor committee in the national spotlight.[33] He took over chairmanship of the Committee on Commerce, Science, and Transportation in January 1978 and played a major role in the deregulation of the airlines.

Cannon almost lost his first reelection try in 1964, when he was challenged by popular Lieutenant Governor Paul Laxalt. While President Lyndon Johnson carried the state with 58.6 percent of the vote, Cannon bested Laxalt by only eighty-four votes. However, Cannon won reelection easily in 1970 and 1976.

Bible first disclosed his 1974 retirement plans to Governor Mike O'Callaghan and former governor and Democratic national committeeman Grant Sawyer. Either man would have been a big favorite to retain the seat for the Democrats, but both declined to run. With the elimination of the two political heavyweights, thirty-four-year-old lieutenant governor Harry Reid, a former student and protégé of O'Callaghan, easily won the Democratic nomination in the September primary.[34] Reid then faced the popular Paul Laxalt, whom Republicans had lured out of retirement. Early polls showed that Reid, because of his popularity and residency in vote-rich Clark County, had a large lead over the former governor.

With the election apparently being his to lose, Reid made a strategic error in October. In order to cut into Laxalt's base in northern Nevada, Reid's campaign chairman talked him into attacking Laxalt and his family concerning the financing of the Ormsby House hotel-casino in Carson City. A Reno newspaper blasted Reid in headlines and editorials for the attacks, and Reid's lead began to dwindle.[35] Reid carried Clark County by over 15,000 votes, but Laxalt carried the rest of the state by even more and won by 611 votes after a recount.

In his 1980 bid for reelection, Laxalt had the advantage of running on the same ticket with Ronald Reagan, a close friend from the time the two had been neighboring governors, from 1967 through 1970. Laxalt easily defeated Mary Gojack, a former state senator from Reno. In his second term, Laxalt, a man of great personal charm, had the closest relationship with an American president that any Nevada U.S. senator had ever had. As a result of the relationship, more Nevadans served in important positions in Washington than ever before, including Laxalt's close friend Frank Fahrenkopf as national chairman of the Republican party and Sig Rogich as a presidential adviser. In 1986 Laxalt surprisingly announced that he would not run for reelection and joined a prestigious law firm in Washington.

In 1982 Cannon decided to seek a fifth term, even though former colleague Bible advised him to retire. Four-term congressman James D. Santini, who had long desired a Senate seat, decided to take on the seventy-year-old incumbent in the Democratic primary. Given Nevada's closed primary, Cannon had an advantage over Santini because a strong nucleus of Democratic party activists—especially those who were liberals—were upset with Santini's conservative voting record and support for President Reagan's program. Cannon won the primary by taking 57.6 percent of the vote in Clark County, which was enough to offset Santini's margin in the rest of the state.

The primary win and the general feeling that Republican nominee Chic Hecht, a former state senator from Las Vegas, would not be a strong opponent apparently lulled Cannon into a false sense of complacency.[36] The Cannon staff's optimism was further boosted when an independent poll commissioned by two of the state's major newspapers showed Cannon leading Hecht by thirteen percentage points in mid-October.[37] Not until a poll taken a few days before the election disclosed a possible dead heat did Cannon's strategists realize that Hecht had closed the large gap. An attempt to purchase additional television time in the state's two major urban areas was unsuccessful because Hecht's staff had tied up the available advertising slots.[38]

The key to Hecht's remarkable turnaround in the 1982 campaign was the strategy crafted by Ed Allison, a top aide on Laxalt's staff in Washington, and Lyn Nofziger, the longtime key campaign aide to Ronald Reagan. The two advisers decided that Hecht should rely heavily on the "transfer" and "testimonial" techniques in television and radio ads instead of making speeches himself.[39] President Reagan and Senator Laxalt then proceeded to make ads in which they extolled Hecht's virtues and exhorted Nevada voters to send him to Washington, where he would give much-needed support to the president. Thus, the popularity of the two Republican leaders in Nevada was used effectively to aid a candidate who lacked their charisma and charm. Hecht won with 51.2 percent of the major party vote. The election meant that from 1983 to 1987, Nevada was represented in the U.S. Senate by two *elected* Republicans for the first time since the Seventeenth Amendment was adopted in 1913. During his six-year term, Hecht compiled a stronger presidential-support rating than Laxalt.

In 1986 two-term congressman Harry Reid won the Democratic primary and the opportunity to recapture the seat that had been held by Democrats McCarran and Bible for forty-two years prior to Reid's loss to Laxalt in 1974. His opponent in the general election was former congressman James Santini, who had been encouraged to defect to the Republican party by Laxalt and Republican National Committee chairman Frank Fahrenkopf, a fraternity brother at the University of Nevada. Although the two candidates campaigned personally across the state, the public's focus was on the ads that saturated the state's media markets. With the polls showing Reid with a comfortable lead statewide, President Reagan heeded the pleas of Laxalt and Fahrenkopf and made two visits to Nevada in the closing days of the campaign. However, Reid had blunted the impact of the Reagan visits earlier by running "David and Goliath" television ads in which Washington politicians were pictured as trying to gang up on Reid.[40]

Just as in 1982, Clark County proved to be Santini's Achilles heel. Although Santini carried fifteen of the state's seventeen counties, Reid finished 24 percentage points ahead in Clark County to best his opponent by 5.5 percent statewide. Reid, a Mormon, was probably helped by the return to active participation in the Democratic party in Clark County of many Mormon church leaders who had defected to work for Laxalt and Reagan in previous elections.[41]

Reid obtained a seat on the Appropriations Committee during his first term and gained a reputation among his colleagues for being able to forge compromise solutions to problems. In Nevada he was mainly responsible for achieving a breakthrough agreement on the distribution of water rights between Fallon farmers and the Pyramid Lake Indians. In 1992 Reid's 61,883-vote margin in Clark and Washoe Counties over Republican Demar Dahl, an Elko rancher, easily overcame Dahl's 8,146 edge in the rural counties.

After the GOP captured control of the Senate in 1994, Reid became chair of the Democratic Policy Committee, thus becoming the first Nevadan to hold a Senate party leadership post since Key Pittman served as president pro tem in the 1930s.

The 1988 senatorial campaign started early when Senator Chic Hecht announced in April 1987 that he would run for a second term. The early announcement might have been prompted by a public opinion poll taken a month before that showed Governor Richard Bryan with a 61-20 percent lead over the incumbent senator.[42] The race turned out to be a reinforcement of the conclusion drawn by analysts after Hecht's surprise win in 1982 that a heavily financed, astute television ad campaign can dramatically change public attitudes toward candidates. A Peter Hart poll in December 1987 showed Bryan with better than a 2-1 lead over Hecht;[43] however, after five months of negative Hecht television ads, Bryan admitted that his own poll showed his lead having dropped to only 10 percent.[44] Hecht's ads attacked Bryan for filing for another office in the middle of his second term as governor and questioned the suitability of Lieutenant Governor Bob Miller to succeed him in the governor's office.

The presence on the Democratic ticket of Michael Dukakis, an avowed liberal who was very unpopular in Nevada, also helped to reduce Bryan's vote margin. Dukakis ran 21 percentage points behind George Bush in Nevada, while Bryan defeated Hecht by about four percentage points. Hecht carried the small counties by about 12,000 votes, but Bryan took the two large counties, Clark and Washoe, by over 26,000 votes. He became the first sitting Nevada governor ever elected to the U.S. Senate.

In his first term, Bryan achieved national attention as chairman of the Senate Ethics Committee during the investigation of sexual harassment charges against Senator Robert Packwood (R-OR). As a member of the Commerce Committee, he received high marks from environmental groups for leading the fight for higher fuel efficiency standards for automobiles. In his reelection campaign in 1994, Bryan stated that he was "an independent voice for Nevada," stressing the times that he had opposed President Clinton on key issues. Appearing on the statewide ballot for the sixth time since 1974, Bryan's 57 percent of the two-party vote in Clark and Washoe Counties easily overcame Republican Hal Furman's slight edge in the fifteen smaller counties.

Thus, during this period the Republicans elected only three U.S. senators who served a total of thirty years, compared to a total of ninety-eight years served by Democrats. Five Democrats achieved enough seniority to be influential on Capitol Hill, while Paul Laxalt was the only Republican to gain such a distinction.

Governors

In the gubernatorial elections, the Democrats—helped by the popularity of Franklin D. Roosevelt and the New Deal—easily won the first four races in the period 1932–96. With the collapse of his banking empire, George Wingfield had lost his power to control the political affairs of the state.

The election of 1950 marked the start of a thirty-eight-year period in which no governor turned over the mansion to a person of the same party. Charles H. Russell, former longtime state legislator and congressman, won a surprisingly large percentage (57.6) of the vote against Democratic incumbent Vail Pittman. Russell's election was due in part to the split between the Pittman and McCarran wings of the Democratic party. McCarran allowed much of his campaign organization, led by financier Norman Biltz and Reno postmaster Pete Petersen, to work quietly for Russell.[45]

McCarran sent one of his top aides in Washington, Chet Smith, to Carson City to be Russell's budget director. Russell also appointed other friends of McCarran to important positions in his administration. However, when he found that one such appointee was reporting on confidential meetings to Norman Biltz, the aide was dismissed.[46] Biltz soon became disenchanted with Russell for other reasons and withdrew his support from the governor when he ran for a second term in 1954.[47] McCarran decided to mend his fences with the Democratic party by endorsing Vail Pittman in the rerun election, although the senator informed Russell that he "would make only a few desultory speeches for the [Democratic] nominee and then leave the state."[48] Russell won reelection by a smaller margin than he had garnered four years before.

Russell's attempt to be reelected for an unprecedented third term in 1958 was thwarted by Democrat Grant Sawyer, the thirty-nine-year-old district attorney for Elko County. Sawyer had been one of the "McCarran boys" for whom the senator had arranged patronage jobs on the Hill to help them through law school.[49] Although Sawyer capitalized on the McCarran connection in getting a start as an attorney in Elko, he was much more liberal in his politics than the senator. A group of professors at the University of Nevada in Reno, where Sawyer had been a student, helped to convince him that he should run for governor against Attorney General Harvey Dickerson, the candidate endorsed by conservative Democrat E. L. Cord.[50] The wealthy Cord had strong ties with Biltz and John Mueller, and the media often referred to their bipartisan machine. After defeating Dickerson by using a grass-roots, anti-machine campaign in the primary, Sawyer easily unseated Governor Russell by garnering 60 percent of the vote.[51]

Sawyer was a more activist governor than his recent predecessors and was reelected in 1962 with a record 66.9 percent of the vote. However, popular Lieutenant Governor Paul Laxalt used his charisma and the anti-third-term tradition to defeat Sawyer in the 1966 election with 52 percent of the vote.

Laxalt worked well with a Republican assembly and a Democratic senate, and probably could have been reelected. However, he announced that he would not run for reelection, citing personal considerations, including a pending divorce.

In the 1970 election, Democrat candidate Mike O'Callaghan, a former teacher who had been a member of the Sawyer administration and had more recently served in a federal position during Lyndon Johnson's presidency, bested Republican lieutenant governor Ed Fike by four percentage points in a four-candidate election. O'Callaghan turned out to be a strong popular governor. He won reelection in 1974 with a record percentage (67.4) of the votes cast in a three-candidate race.

O'Callaghan announced early in 1978 that he would not be a candidate for reelection. Republican attorney general Bob List faced off against Lieutenant Governor Bob Rose in the general election. List pinned the "eastern liberal" label on Rose and carried 58.6 percent of the two-party vote.

The national recession of 1981–82 forced Governor List to make midyear budget cuts and to lay off state workers. Thus, he was the underdog when he faced Attorney General Richard Bryan in the 1982 election. Bryan, a proven vote-getter in his home county of Clark, had served ten years in the assembly and senate and had barely lost his first try at the attorney general's office in 1974, when List won reelection to that office by only 701 votes. Bryan won 56 percent of the two-party vote in the 1982 rematch.

Governor Bryan showed strong leadership at the 1983 and 1985 legislative sessions. In 1986, the state's booming economy helped him win reelection with 72 percent of the vote—a record high for a gubernatorial election in Nevada.

When Bryan was elected to the U.S. Senate in 1988, Lieutenant Governor Bob Miller assumed the governor's chair. His veto of a bill that would have substantially raised legislators' pensions increased his popularity, and the voters resoundingly removed the *acting* from his title in the 1990 election. Receiving 65 percent of the vote, Miller became the sixth consecutive Democratic governor to serve more than four years as the state's chief executive; Charles Russell was the only Republican to so serve during the sixty-four-year period.

The national recession hit Nevada in 1991. Overly optimistic revenue projections in the 1991–93 state budget forced Governor Miller to freeze hiring, withhold some funds from state agencies and higher education, and lay off 266 state workers. In the wake of these conditions, popular Las Vegas mayor Jan Laverty Jones decided to challenge the incumbent in the 1994 primary.

By the time Miller filed for a second elective term in early 1994, the state's economy, sparked by several new family-oriented large hotel-casinos in the Las Vegas area, was booming. Jones's campaign concentrated on attacking the governor's position on abortion. As a Catholic, Miller was personally opposed to abortion, but he countered that he had favored a popular referendum on the abortion question in 1990. Already behind in the polls, Jones did not make up ground against the governor in televised debates. Miller easily won the primary with 63 percent of the vote to Jones's 28 percent. The governor won 62 percent of the two-party vote in his home county of Clark and 56 percent statewide to defeat Reno assemblyman Jim Gibbons in the general election. At the completion of his term, Miller will have served ten years—two years longer than any governor in Nevada history.

Members of the U.S. House of Representatives

As shown in table 9, five of the nine members who served the longest in the House of Representatives were elected during the period 1932–96. Democrats held the lone congressional seat for forty-four of the first fifty years of the period.

James Scrugham, the only Nevadan to be elected to the governor's office and both houses of Congress, was a strong supporter of Franklin Roosevelt and the New Deal in his ten years in the House. He stood up to McCarran in some battles over patronage appointments and claimed that the senior senator was "almost unbearable in his arrogance."[52] Scrugham gave up the chairmanship of the Naval Subcommittee of the House Appropriations Committee to run for the U.S. Senate in 1942.

Walter Baring was born in Goldfield and was a strong supporter of mining

Table 9: Nevadans with the Most Years in the U.S. House of Representatives

Representative	Party	Years of Service	Total Years
1. Walter S. Baring	Democrat	1949–53, 1957–73	20
2. Barbara Vucanovich	Republican	1983–97	14
3. Francis G. Newlands	Silver-Democrat	1893–1903	10
Samuel S. Arentz	Republican	1921–23, 1925–33	10
James G. Scrugham	Democrat	1933–43	10
6. E. E. Roberts	Republican	1911–19	8
James Santini	Democrat	1975–83	8
James Bilbray	Democrat	1987–95	8
9. William Woodburn	Republican	1875–77, 1885–89	6

Source: Frankie Sue Del Papa, Political History of Nevada, 9th ed. (Carson City: State Printing Office, 1990).

throughout his twenty years in Congress. He was first elected as a "Fair Deal" Democrat in 1948 with the support of organized labor. After two terms, he lost two congressional elections to attorney Clifton Young, a moderate Republican who was aided in 1952 by Eisenhower's coattails. Baring regained the seat in 1956 when Young made a try for the U.S. Senate.

In the late 1950s Baring changed ideologically. Perhaps influenced by Raymond I. Smith, the principal owner of Harold's Club in Reno, he became very conservative in his congressional voting behavior. Baring was personally attacked in the 1964 and 1966 Democratic state party platforms for his failure to support many of the programs of Presidents Kennedy and Johnson. He barely survived strong primary challenges in both years from Ralph Denton, a Boulder City attorney who was close to Governor Sawyer. Baring was a lackluster campaigner who stayed away from television; a common comment about his electoral success was "No one loves Walter but the voters." In the 1970 election, Mike O'Callaghan was furious when he heard that Baring was supporting his Republican opponent in the governor's race. Two years later, Baring was upset in the primary by James Bilbray, whose support in his home county of Clark overcame the ten-term congressman's voting margin in the rest of the state.

James Santini, grandson of a longtime president of the University of Nevada and nephew of writer Walter Van Tilburg Clark, was an influential member in the eight years he served in Congress. He was elected to the lower house the same year that Senator Alan Bible retired, and thus was able to obtain the services of Jack Carpenter, Bible's administrative assistant. Carpenter used his connections with Speaker Carl Albert to obtain choice committee positions for the freshman congressman. Santini was the key player, which was unusual for a first termer, in the passage of the "in lieu of taxes" measure that resulted in payments of millions of dollars over the years to Nevada counties with substantial federal land. In his last two terms, Santini chaired the Interior Subcommittee on Mines and Mining.

Barbara Vucanovich, who had run Senator Laxalt's office in Reno, has represented the state's Congressional District 1, covering a portion of Clark County and the other sixteen counties, since its creation in 1983. The first woman to represent Nevada in the U.S. Congress, she was a strong supporter of Presidents Reagan and Bush, and her influence in Congress was heightened because of Laxalt's close ties with the White House. By 1993 her seniority allowed her to claim membership on the Appropriations and Natural Resources Committees. After serving in the minority party for twelve years, Vucanovich became secretary of the Republican Conference when the GOP took control of the House in 1995. She is the first Nevadan to hold a House party leadership position.

Harry Reid represented Congressional District 2 for the first four years of its existence before he moved to the U.S. Senate in 1987. James Bilbray, a state senator who had lost a bid for Congress fourteen years before, won the seat representing most of Clark County in 1986 and was reelected easily for three more terms. Bilbray was a moderate Democrat, but his general support of President Clinton's legislative program hurt him in his bid for a fifth term in 1994. He lost to veterinarian John Ensign by less than one percent of the vote. Ensign was rewarded by the Republican leadership with a seat on the powerful Ways and Means Committee, a rare assignment for a freshman.

From Political Machine to the Mass Media

This last political period began with McCarran's election to the U.S. Senate in 1932. The junior senator immediately proceeded to fight for patronage appointments in the state. As a member of the Senate Appropriations Committee, McCarran had an important say in the amount of highway funds to be allocated to Nevada. He used that influence to pressure Governor Richard Kirman to appoint some of his friends to important positions in the state highway department. As a member of the Senate Judiciary Committee, McCarran influenced the appointment of deputy U.S. marshals in the state. Kirman was reported to have told a friend of senior senator Key Pittman that "Pat wants every job in the state."[53] Thus, McCarran began assembling the nucleus of the machine that would make him the most powerful politician in the state.

As Jerome Edwards has noted, "McCarran's most important patronage appointment was that of the Reno postmaster."[54] The senator nominated labor leader Pete Petersen for the position in 1936; Petersen then became the glue that held the McCarran machine together in the state. The passage of the Hatch Act of 1939, which made political activity by federal employees illegal, did not deter Petersen's activities. Newspaper columnist Denver Dickerson wrote that "Senator Hatch would have had a nervous breakdown within two weeks if he had ever visited the state."[55] The McCarran machine did not survive the senator's death in 1954. It was too much of a personal organization, which had as its main goal the political advancement of its founder.[56]

The 1950s marked the end of the political machine as an important force in Nevada politics and its replacement by the mass media. The key to Tom Mechling's upset victory over Alan Bible in the Democratic primary for the U.S. Senate in 1952 was the strong endorsement of Hank Greenspun, the editor of the *Las Vegas Sun* and outspoken McCarran opponent. Greenspun charged that Bible's endorsement by the McCarran machine "makes Mechling's independence shine like a beacon."[57] Mechling's 62.6 percent of the vote in Clark County gave him a narrow 475-vote margin over Bible in the state. McCarran was very upset by the outcome.

In 1960 a reform movement led by Reno attorney Charles Springer challenged the remnants of the McCarran machine that still controlled Washoe County Democratic politics. Two sets of precinct meetings and county conventions were held, and two separate delegations were elected to represent the county at the state convention in Ely. At the state convention, Governor Sawyer and Senator Bible threw their support behind the Springer delegation, which was then seated by vote of the entire convention. The old McCarran crowd, including some who had used threats of physical force to have their way at earlier county conventions, were furious, but the times had changed.

Television became the dominant media in Nevada politics in the 1960s, just as it did nationally. The charisma of Paul Laxalt, a small-county district attorney, came through on the television screen when he made strong races against three formidable Democratic opponents. With the Democrats having a 2-1 edge in the major party registration, Laxalt defeated former U.S. senator and congressman Berkeley Bunker for lieutenant governor in 1962, came within 84 votes of unseating U.S. senator Howard Cannon in 1964, and took half the Clark County vote (with 73 percent Democratic registration) to defeat two-term governor Grant Sawyer in 1966. Television helped Laxalt defeat Harry Reid in 1974 and was a major factor in all U.S. Senate races in Nevada in the 1980s and early 1990s.

Thus, in the last forty years of this period, the old-style political machine was no longer a factor in the major statewide elections in Nevada. It had been superseded by personal campaign staffs and fund-raising and by the use of the mass media, with television being the most powerful medium by far.

CONCLUSION

The Wingfield and McCarran political machines were the most important influences in Nevada politics in the first half of the twentieth century. The members of both machines were more loyal to the individual leader than to a particular ideology or party. The gambling industry, education, and certain governors, legislators, lobbyists, and U.S. senators have been the key players in the last half of the twentieth century. Political power has been much more diffuse than in earlier periods. Whereas U.S. senators were generally the dominant politicians in the state during its first century, they have had to share the limelight with strong governors during the last forty years. Although television has come to dominate the high-profile statewide elections, informality still prevails in other aspects of politics in the state.

CHAPTER FIVE

The Nevada Constitution
and Popular Control

The seventeenth-century colonists brought with them the English common law tradition, which became the primary basis of the American legal system. When the colonists declared their independence from Britain in 1776, they adopted written state constitutions. In so doing, the states departed from the English tradition of an unwritten constitution based loosely on historical documents, such as the Magna Carta and the Petition of Rights and certain important acts of Parliament.

The framers of the early state constitutions were used to having a written document that served as the basic law for each of the colonies. The British monarchy granted charters to individuals and groups with the understanding that actions of the colonial governments, including the laws passed by popularly elected legislatures, had to be in accordance with the basic law set forth in the charters. Prior to landing at Plymouth in 1620, the Pilgrims signed the Mayflower Compact, which spelled out the basic rules that would govern their new settlement.

Although the early state constitutions were drafted prior to the U.S. Constitution, Article 6 stipulates that the federal Constitution and the laws and treaties made thereunder have supremacy over the constitutions and laws of the various states. However, the Tenth Amendment reserves to the states or to the people all ''powers not delegated to the United States by the Constitution nor prohibited by it to the states.''

California's constitution of 1849 served as the model for the framers of the Nevada Constitution; California's basic law in turn relied heavily on the 1846 constitution of Iowa. As a reaction to the power exercised by colonial governors, many of the early state constitutions had given the legislature almost plenary authority. By the middle of the nineteenth century, there was widespread disillusionment with the performance of state legislatures. Therefore, framers of the Iowa and California constitutions expressly limited the powers of the legislature. The Nevada Constitution, following the example of the California document, enumerates a long list of cases in which the legislature may not pass special legislation for private benefit, such as divorce (Article 4, Sec. 20), and is forbidden to deal with certain subjects, such as establishment of a lottery (Article 4, Sec. 24) or granting a charter to a specific corporation (Article 8, Sec. 1).

Overall, Nevada's fundamental law fits Daniel Elazar's "frame of government pattern" of classification of state constitutions. In this pattern, the "constitutions are frames of government first and foremost. They explicitly reflect the republican and democratic principles dominant in the nation in the late nineteenth century."[1]

Nevada's constitution is more than twice as long as the federal Constitution, but it is shorter than the fundamental law of twenty-six states.[2] As of 1995, the Nevada Constitution had been amended 116 times; 75 other proposed amendments had been rejected by the voters at the polls. From 1976 to 1994, inclusive, the Nevada electorate approved 60 percent of the 77 amendments that were proposed, excluding the four amendments proposed by initiative that were approved for the first time in 1994 and will be voted on again in 1996. During the previous 112 years of the state's history, only 114 amendments had been proposed by the legislature or the initiative process. While recent legislatures have been much more active in proposing amendments, the electorate has not been any more inclined to approve the changes in the state's basic law. From 1878 through 1974, the voters approved approximately the same percentage (61.5) of proposed amendments as in the most recent eighteen-year period.

CONTENT OF THE CONSTITUTION

The Declaration of Rights

Article 1 of the Nevada Constitution, entitled "Declaration of Rights," and the Bill of Rights in the California Constitution are similar; both include most of the rights enumerated in the first nine amendments to the U.S. Constitution. Some of the state constitutions that predated the U.S. Constitution contained these same rights, and most nineteenth-century constitutions repeated them because the pre–Civil War judiciary interpreted the federal Bill of Rights as restrictions on the federal government alone. The drafters of these state constitutions wanted to make sure that state officials, including state legislatures, could not infringe on the same basic rights. In 1925 the

U.S. Supreme Court decided that the freedom of speech and press rights of the First Amendment were protected against infringement by state governments through the Fourteenth Amendment.[3] Since then, the Supreme Court has ruled that most, but not all, of the rights of the federal Bill of Rights are applicable to state and local governments, whether or not a particular state constitution protects such rights.

The first section of Article 1 of the Nevada Constitution was copied word for word from California's basic law. In language reminiscent of the philosophy expressed by Thomas Jefferson in the Declaration of Independence, the section states: "All men are, by nature, free and equal, and have certain inalienable rights, among which are those of enjoying and defending life and liberty; acquiring, possessing and protecting property, and pursuing and obtaining safety and happiness." This wording is almost identical to that of the first section of the Virginia Declaration of Rights, which was written by George Mason in 1776.[4] Section 2 of Article 1 of the Nevada Constitution contains language that was in keeping with the strong pro-Union sympathies of its drafters in the midst of the Civil War. The section states that "the paramount allegiance of every citizen is due to the federal government" and that this government "may employ armed force in compelling obedience to its authority." This provision is similar in spirit to the supremacy statements in Article 6 of the federal Constitution.

The original Nevada Constitution guaranteed against state infringement the rights contained in the Bill of Rights of the U.S. Constitution, with the exception of the right to bear arms. Once more, the Nevada framers were influenced by the action of the California constitutional convention, which rejected placing the right in the constitution on the grounds that the legislature should not regulate "matters of this kind."[5]

In accordance with the strong support for gun ownership in Nevada, the voters in 1982 approved a constitutional amendment adding a subsection to Section 11 of the Declaration of Rights providing for the right of a citizen "to keep arms for security and defense, for lawful hunting and recreational use and for other lawful purposes." An important difference between this right and the Second Amendment to the federal Constitution is that the latter is prefaced by the phrase "a well regulated militia being necessary to the security of a free state." Many constitutional scholars believe that the intent of the framers of the Second Amendment was to protect the right of those who belonged to a state militia to bear arms. If the U.S. Supreme Court were to so rule sometime in the future, the above guarantee in the Nevada Constitution would still apply to citizens in the state.

Section 9 of Article 1 expands on the terse provisions of the First Amendment to the U.S. Constitution regarding freedom of speech and the press by stating: "Every citizen may freely speak, write and publish his sentiments on all subjects, being responsible for the abuse of that right; and no law shall be passed to restrain or abridge the liberty of speech or of the press." The framers of the Nevada Constitution were explicitly stating that the freedom-of-speech guarantee is not absolute. The U.S. Supreme Court has also consistently ruled that there are limits on the freedoms of speech and the press. Justice Oliver Wendell Holmes stated in a famous 1919 case: "No person has the right to shout 'fire' in a crowded theatre when there is no fire."[6] The Nevada framers were also aware of libel laws, as they added: "In all criminal prosecutions and civil actions for libels the truth may be given in evidence to the jury, and if it shall appear to the jury that the matter charged as libelous is true, and was published with good motives, and for justifiable ends, the party shall be acquitted or exonerated."

Since the mid-1970s, some state supreme courts—perhaps motivated by conservative interpretations of individual rights by the U.S. Supreme Court under Chief Justices Warren Burger and William Rehnquist—have relied more on the rights guaranteed by their state constitutions. John Kincaid has described this "new judicial federalism" as "the willingness of state courts to exercise their long dormant authority to base the protection of individual rights on independent interpretations of state constitutional rights rather than U.S. constitutional rights."[7] Kincaid explains that the new judicial activism rests on the supposition that the U.S. Supreme Court, in its interpretation of the U.S. Constitution, "establishes a floor, namely, a minimum level of rights protection for all persons across the nation." State courts may interpret rights found in state constitutions more broadly than similar rights in the U.S. Constitution have been defined by the U.S. Supreme Court. State constitutions may also include rights not present in the federal document. For example, the constitutions of eighteen states now contain an equal rights amendment forbidding discrimination on the basis of gender.[8] The Nevada Supreme Court has not been in the vanguard of state courts that have expanded individual rights through the assertion of this "new federalism" doctrine.

Suffrage and Popular Control

The Nevada Constitution generally incorporates populist views of voting rights. The electorate has amended Article 2, entitled "Right of Suffrage," several times in keeping with national voting-rights trends. A few of the amendments are considered "housekeeping" because the changes had previously been placed in effect by federal constitutional amendments, laws, or decisions by the U.S. Supreme Court. In 1880 the voters eliminated the provision in the original Nevada Constitution restricting the suffrage to white males ten years after the ratification of the Fifteenth Amendment to the federal Constitution prohibiting the denial by the United States or by any state of the right to vote on the basis of "race, color, or previous condition of servitude." The original state constitution gave the legislature the power to make payment of a poll tax a requirement for voting; in 1910 voters approved an amendment eliminating this power. Then, after the ratification of the Twenty-Fourth Amendment to the U.S. Constitution in 1964 prohibiting payment of a poll tax as a prerequisite for voting in a federal election, Nevada voters in 1966 approved an amendment deleting the entire section of the poll tax from the state's basic law.

The voters have not always gone along with the so-called housekeeping amendments. For example, in 1976 the Nevada electorate rejected an amendment to change the residency requirement for voting from six months to thirty days, even though the U.S. Supreme Court had previously ruled that individuals could register after thirty days of residency in a state. Undoubtedly, some voters were expressing their dissatisfaction with the court's decision and their opposition to dictation by the federal government on the question, but the six-month residency requirement of the constitution is null and void.

Nevada was ahead of most states on one important suffrage issue. After a campaign led by women's suffragette Anne Martin, voters approved an amendment extending to women the right to vote six years prior to the ratification of the Nineteenth Amendment to the U.S. Constitution in 1920.[9] However, the 1914 amendment did not specifically remove the aforementioned Article 18 that stated: "The rights of suffrage and office-holding shall not be withheld from any male citizen by reason of his color or previous condition of servitude." The obsolete article remained in the Nevada Constitution until the legislature proposed and the electorate approved its removal in 1992.

The progressive movement that swept over much of the nation around the turn of the twentieth century was especially strong in the West. In addition to casting its electoral votes for James B. Weaver, the populist third-party candidate, in the 1892 presidential election, Nevada adopted the progressive reforms of referendum (1904), initiative (1912), and recall (1912) through constitutional amendment.

Nevada voters have used the referendum process, by which a petition may be filed to challenge an existing law at the polls, very sparingly. The voters upheld a police bill passed by the legislature in a close vote in 1908, repealed creation of a state rabies commission by a razor-thin margin in 1930, upheld a fish and game law in 1934, upheld the 2 percent sales tax enacted by the 1955 legislature in 1956, and upheld an abortion law in 1990.

Subsection 2 of the referendum section of Article 19 states that if the people uphold a law that is placed on the ballot by petition, the law cannot "be amended, annulled, repealed, set aside, suspended or in any way made inoperative except by direct vote of the people." Thus, any change in the original 2 percent sales tax has to be approved by the voters. Pro-choice forces took advantage of this provision by engineering a petition drive to place the abortion law, which was similar to the *Roe v. Wade* (1973) decision of the U.S. Supreme Court, on the ballot. Approval by the voters—by a sizable margin—makes it difficult for anti-abortion groups to change the law because any changes will have to be approved by the electorate.

In 1912, when 84 percent of presidential votes were cast for candidates of the Democratic, Progressive, and Socialist parties—all of which favored the populist reform agenda—Nevadans resoundingly added the initiative to Article 19 and recall to Article 2 with an approval vote of 90 percent. The people first used the initiative process to propose a law in 1918, when voters approved prohibition of the sale of alcoholic beverages.

The electorate first voted in favor of a constitutional amendment that was placed on the ballot by initiative petition in 1958; ironically, the amendment made the initiative process more difficult. After the legislature had refused to pass a "right-to-work" bill opposed by organized labor, supporters of the bill were able to obtain enough signatures to place it on the ballot in 1952. The electorate approved the measure, and labor reacted by using the initiative process to try to repeal it in 1954 and 1956; both repeal efforts were turned down by the voters. After enduring a debate over "right-to-work" in three consecutive general elections, business interests spearheaded a drive to place the 1958 amendment proposal on the ballot. The amendment stiffened the signature requirements for initiative petitions by making an addition to the requirement that a petition must include signatures of "registered voters equal to 10 percent or more of the number of voters at the last preceding election." Now the signatures must include 10 percent or more of the number of voters in "not less than 75 percent of the counties in the state." Thus, since 1958, signature gatherers in the initiative process cannot concentrate on only the most populated counties.

Recall makes public officials continuously responsible to the people. The first state to adopt the procedure was Oregon in 1908. Nevada is one of only eleven other states that have added recall since then.

In Nevada, recall applies to all elected state and local officials. Citizens can initiate the process against any elected official who has served a minimum of six months (ten days of a legislative session for legislators) by filing a petition signed by "a number of registered voters not less than 25 percent of the number who actually voted in the state, county, district, or municipality electing such an officer, at the preceding general election." Critics are opposed to the recall of judges, claiming that a judge might be recalled because of unpopular decisions and not because he or she has been incompetent.

Other Articles of the Constitution

Articles 3 through 7 provide for a separation of powers among the three branches of government and describe the qualifications, powers, and duties of the elected officials. The branches will be examined in the following four chapters.

Article 8 spells out the powers of the legislature concerning both private and municipal corporations. The almost total legislative control over municipal corporations (cities) in the original constitution was modified by a 1924 amendment that authorizes "the electors of any city or town to frame, adopt and amend a charter for its own government."

Articles 9, 10, and 11 cover state debt, taxes, and education and will be discussed in later chapters. Articles 12, 13, 14, and 15 deal with miscellaneous matters, such as the militia, benevolent institutions, the state prison, the state's boundary, the limit on the size of the legislature, and the establishment of a merit system for government employment.

The framers included Article 17, entitled "Schedule," to provide guidelines for the transition from territorial status to statehood. In a 1968 decision, the Nevada Supreme Court ruled that the article should remain a part of the constitution "to the extent that its provisions are still applicable."[10]

PROCEDURES FOR CHANGING THE CONSTITUTION

Article 16 provides for two ways to change the fundamental law: amendment and revision. Amendment is used to change a section of the constitution or to add a new section. Revision involves a rewriting of the document at a constitutional convention.

The Amendment Process

Until 1912 only the legislature could initiate an amendment. This process requires approval of a proposed amendment by both houses in *two successive legislatures* (separated by a biennial legislative election), with a *majority* of those *elected* to each house approving. With the present membership of twenty-one senators and forty-two members of the assembly, the constitution requires the affirmative vote of eleven senators and twenty-two members of the assembly, regardless of how many actually vote on the proposal. This procedure differs from the amendment process for the U.S. Constitution, which requires—once a quorum is established—the approval of *two-thirds* of the members *present and voting* in each house of *one* Congress. In Nevada, as for the federal government, the executive has no official role in the amendment process.

Once a proposed amendment has been approved by two successive legislatures, it must be approved by a vote of the people at a general, primary, or special election set by the legislature. All of the states, except Delaware, provide for legislative proposal of amendments and ratification by the people.

The original initiative section of Article 19 made no distinction between the proposal of a law and the proposal of a constitutional amendment. In contrast, there are substantial differences in the procedures for the enactment of a law and the proposal of a constitutional amendment by the legislature. Therefore, the voters in 1962 approved an amendment proposed by the legislature to make amendment by initiative more difficult. The amendment eliminated the requirement that an initiative petition proposal go to the legislature and added a requirement that such proposed amendments must be approved by the voters at *two successive* general elections before going into effect.

The Revision Process

Revision, the second way of changing the constitution, has never been used successfully in Nevada. The Constitutional Convention of 1787 was called to revise the Articles of Confederation. However, the delegates who met in Philadelphia decided to rewrite the entire document and thus set a precedent that has been followed in over three-fifths of the states that have had constitutional conventions to rewrite their fundamental laws.

Article 16 of the Nevada Constitution states that two-thirds of the members *elected* to each house of the legislature may vote to recommend to the electorate that a convention be called for the purpose of rewriting or revising the constitution. In Nevada's early history, four different legislatures voted to place the revision question on the ballot. The people voted by a 2-1 margin in 1876 and by close to a 3-2 margin in both 1884 and 1888 to reject the calling of a constitutional convention. Only 35 percent of the voters who went to the polls in 1888 bothered to vote on the convention issue, indicating how little public interest there was in constitutional revision at that time.

The 1889 legislature persevered and placed the question on the ballot again in 1890. This time a majority of those voting on the question appeared to have voted for a convention; however, Article 16 requires that the question must be approved by a "majority of the electors voting at such election." The article defines the number of electors voting at the election as "the highest number of votes cast at such election for the candidates for any office or on any question." On this basis, the revision question needed 6,205 "yes" votes, since 12,408 people voted for superintendent of public instruction, but the measure fell short of the required votes. Someone who does not vote on a ballot question involving revision of the constitution is, for all practical purposes, voting "no."

If a constitutional majority of the electorate does approve a constitutional convention, Article 16 stipulates that the next legislative session must set up a convention to meet within six months of the election. The article does not mention an election by the people to select delegates to the constitutional convention, although that has been the procedure followed by other states when revising their constitutions. The article also omits any mention of a requirement that a new constitution drafted by a convention be ratified by a vote of the people. Given the political precedents of court decisions in other states, however, it is likely that the electorate would have to approve such a document before it could become effective.

CONCLUSION

As Daniel Elazar has noted, the development of state constitutions is "affected by the political cultures of each state."[11] Nevadans showed their support of the individualistic ethic with their overwhelming approval of populist constitutional amendments in the early years of the twentieth century. Another example occurred when the legislature refused to propose a constitutional amendment to prohibit a state personal income tax. The people responded by signing petitions to place such an amendment on the ballot and subsequently approved it by large margins at the 1988 and 1990 general elections.

CHAPTER SIX

The Legislature

Individualism and personal politics have continued to thrive in the workings of Nevada's legislative branch, even with the great population growth in recent decades. A dedicated citizen legislator or lobbyist who is willing to "play the game" by the informal norms of the legislature can still make a difference.

Informality has marked the relationships between the legislators and governors throughout Nevada's history as well. This personal relationship is critical to the functioning of the state government, given the separation of powers spelled out in the constitution and the tendency of most Nevada voters to vote for individuals rather than a straight party ballot. The same party has controlled both houses of the legislature and the governor's office during only twenty-two of the sixty-seven regular sessions of the legislature through 1995. From 1905 through the 1995 session, the governor's party controlled both legislative houses during less than a fifth of the regular sessions, with this party unity prevailing during only two sessions from 1911 to 1965. Nevada politicians have thus learned to work within the framework of divided party government between the executive and legislative branches. Indeed, the control of both houses of the legislature by the governor's party does not guarantee a smooth working relationship during a session, especially when there is a slim majority in both houses, as was the case in 1991.

STRUCTURE

Like all states except Nebraska, Nevada has a bicameral legislature. The terms of office are four years for the senate and two years for the assembly. If a proposed constitutional amendment is approved a second time in 1996, legislators will be limited to twelve years in each house. The total membership of the two houses cannot exceed seventy-five, and the assembly must be between twice and three times the size of the senate.

Apportionment of Seats

Section 13 of Article 1 of the Nevada Constitution provides that "representation shall be apportioned according to population," and Section 13 of Article 15 states that the federal decennial census "shall serve as the basis of representation in both houses of the legislature." The 1915 legislature apportioned the Senate on the basis of one senator for each county, even though state senator John J. Kenney warned that the law was unconstitutional.[1] This action was not protested in the courts, and in 1946 the U.S. Supreme Court ruled in *Colegrove v. Green* that the apportionment of legislative seats was a "political question" to be decided by the political branches.[2] As was the case with many states, the Nevada practice of having one senator per county continued until the *Reynolds v. Sims* decision in 1964 when the Warren Court stated that both state legislative houses had to be apportioned on the basis of population.[3]

The *Baker v. Carr* decision of the U.S. Supreme Court in 1962 ruled that federal courts could act in cases in which action or inaction by state legislatures had led to malapportionment.[4] After the 1965 regular legislative session failed to reapportion, the federal district court, in *Dungan v. Sawyer,* ordered Governor Sawyer to call a special session to reapportion the legislature on the basis of the aforementioned decisions.[5]

Sawyer called the legislature into special session in the fall of 1965. The legislature, faced with the certainty of judicial reapportionment if it did not act, reluctantly apportioned the twenty seats in the senate and the forty in the assembly on the basis of population. Both houses decided to allow multi-member districts.[6]

The 1971, 1981, and 1991 legislatures followed the decennial census figures precisely in apportioning the seats in both houses. In 1971 Clark County was allocated a majority of the seats in both houses, and the assembly decided to change to all single-member districts. The 1981 legislature increased the size of the senate to twenty-one and the assembly to forty-two so that Washoe and the rural counties would not lose seats. During the 1970s and 1980s, Clark County's population increased by 171 percent while the rest of the state showed a 113.6 percent increase. Thus, in 1994 Clark County elected thirteen senators and twenty-six members of the assembly.

The 1981 legislature was the first in the state's history to have the opportunity to draw district lines for congressional seats, because Nevada was granted a second seat in the U.S. House of Representatives. The legislators from Clark County used their majorities in both houses to pass a districting measure that would have divided the state so that half of the population of each of the three political subdivisions—Clark, Washoe, and the rural counties—would have been included in each of the two districts. Clark County, which had 58.5 percent of the state's population then, would thus have had a majority in each district and an opportunity to elect Clark County residents to the two seats. However, Governor Bob List vetoed the plan. The final act divided the state so that one seat was made up of 85 percent of the Clark County population, with the remainder of the county's population being placed in the second district with the rest of the state. After the 1991 redistricting, District 1 contained 75 percent of the population of Clark County and had a Democratic edge in registration. District 2 contained about 200,000 residents of Clark County, including Boulder City and the conservative suburbs of Las Vegas, along with Washoe and the rural counties, and had a solidly Republican registration edge.

LEGISLATIVE ELECTIONS

All members of the assembly run in every general election, along with approximately half of the twenty-one senators. The actual number of legislators who run for reelection has varied greatly in the state's history. In the thirty-one legislative elections from 1866 through 1940, the voters reelected only an average of about four members of the assembly and two senators at each general election. American entry into World War II marked a change in the number of legislators seeking to return for another term. From 1942 through 1994, the voters reelected an average of twenty-four members of the assembly and over five senators to their respective houses in each general election.

In ten legislative elections from 1974 through 1994, most legislators who sought reelection were successful. Of the 79 senators who sought reelection during that period, 65 (82.3 percent) were returned to office. In the assembly, 288 or (83 percent) of the 346 incumbents who ran for reelection were victorious. The percentages for the assembly would have been higher except for the unusual number of incumbents—thirteen—who were defeated in 1990. Most of the incumbent losses were due to a strong reaction against legislators who had supported a fourfold increase in legislative pensions at the

1989 session. The reaction of the public, the media, and a petition by Common Cause led Governor Bob Miller to call a special session on 21 November 1989. The legislature, in the shortest special session in Nevada's history—two hours—overwhelmingly rescinded the pension increase that had been passed over Miller's veto.

THE LEGISLATORS

Although most states have annual legislative sessions, Nevadans seem to prefer a "citizen" legislature that meets in regular session for about six months during odd-numbered years. Thus, members must have occupations that allow them the flexibility to be away for the length of the legislative session. After the 1994 election, two newly elected legislators were forced to resign their jobs—one as an agent for the state Gaming Control Board and the other as a newspaper executive.

A comparison of the members of the 1975 and 1993 legislatures shows that over 70 percent of the legislators in each session had occupations in business management, law, or the public sector. The biggest difference between the two sessions was in the "retired" category, with eight retirees serving in the 1993 session compared to only one in 1975. The legislators were not representative of the occupations of the vast majority of Nevadans. For example, only two—a casino owner and a casino dealer—represented the state's largest industry. However, the gaming industry has tremendous influence as an interest group.

Given the explosive increase in the state's population since World War II, it is not surprising that only 30 percent of the legislators in 1975 and 22 percent in 1993 were native-born Nevadans. As is generally true in a representative democracy, Nevada's legislators are better educated than the electorate. As the number of students enrolled in higher education in the state skyrocketed in the 1970s and 1980s, the percentage of legislators who held college degrees went up substantially. Whereas only a little over half of the 1975 legislators were college graduates, 71 percent of the members of the 1993 session had at least a bachelor's degree.

The legislature has also underrepresented women, although recent elections have given Nevada more female legislators than most states. Through the 1991 session, a total of only sixty-two women had served as legislators in the state's history. However, eight new women legislators were elected in 1992, and there were another nine females in the freshman class at the 1995 session. A record total of seventeen women were members of the 1995 legislature—five in the senate and twelve in the assembly. Women won 47 percent of the assembly seats in the two most populous counties of Clark and Washoe in the 1994 election. Although women made up only 27 percent of the 1995 legislators, this proportion was a huge improvement over the two women who served in the last legislature prior to the major reapportionment of 1965 and bodes well for further increases in the future.

Historically, the relatively low percentage of minorities in Nevada's population is mainly responsible for the small number elected to the legislature. Prior to 1995, only eight African Americans had served in the legislature, and all were elected from Clark County, where over 90 percent of the blacks in Nevada reside. Joe Neal, the first African American to be elected to the senate, was tied for seniority in the upper house in the 1995 session with William Raggio and served as minority leader in the 1989 session and as president pro tempore of the senate in 1991. Since the 1971 legislature carved out a black senate seat and two black assembly districts, three African Americans from Clark County have served in the legislature each session.

Blacks made important breakthroughs in the 1994 election. Bernice Martin-Mathews became the first black woman elected to the legislature, and Maurice Washington became the first Republican African American elected to the senate. The two senators and Assemblyman Thomas Batten, all from Washoe County—where African Americans constitute about two percent of the population—were the first black legislators from outside Clark County. Blacks held 9.5 percent of the legislative seats in 1995, compared to less than 2 percent in 1971. African Americans made up slightly under six percent of the state's population in 1970, 1980, and 1990. The large increases in the number of Hispanics and Asian Americans residing in Nevada by 1990 may also have some impact on legislative elections in the future.

LEGISLATIVE SESSIONS

Nevada is among the seven states that meet in regular session only every other year. Many Nevada legislators have favored annual sessions since the 1950s, citing the problem of estimating the revenues and needed expenditures of a fast-growing state more than two years into the future in the biennial budget.

In 1958 voters approved a constitutional amendment proposed by the 1955 and 1957 legislatures to allow annual sessions, which at the time were limited to sixty days. However, a group of people launched a petition drive to repeal annual sessions immediately after the 1958 election. This constitutional amendment was placed on the ballot for the November 1960 general election. The conduct of the 1960 legislative session turned out to be influential in convincing the electorate to repeal the annual-sessions amendment. In 1959 incoming governor Grant Sawyer had submitted a number of proposals to the legislature, most of which were enacted; therefore, Sawyer, who favored a limited budget session of thirty days in the even-numbered years, did not press the legislature for much new legislation when it met in annual session in 1960.[7] Many of the journalists covering the session thought that the legislators did not have much to do and that they had stretched out the session so that it would extend for the full sixty days. Newspaper editorials following the session called for a vote in favor of the ballot question to restore the biennial regular sessions. The people responded with 57.6 percent voting to repeal the amendment that 59 percent of the voters had approved two years before. Ten years later, another attempt by the legislature to gain approval of annual sessions was rejected by a 2-1 margin. However, many legislators continue to support annual sessions, which received editorial support from some major newspapers during the 1991 and 1993 sessions.

In addition to the biennial regular session, the governor may call a special session in which no legislative business may be transacted other than what the governor proposes. As of 1994, Nevada governors had called sixteen special sessions during the state's history. The largest concentration of special sessions occurred from 1954 through 1968, when there were seven special sessions—one more than the number of such sessions during the ninety-year period prior to 1954.

The population explosion that took place during the 1950s and 1960s was the main reason for the increase in the number of special sessions during that period. Partial solutions to the problems that developed because of unforeseen increases in the school population and the demand for additional services were found by the legislature in the late 1960s with the passage of the school support tax and creation of the Interim Finance Committee. The Interim Finance Committee is given an allocation of funds in the biennial budget and may then dispense such funds to take care of financial emergencies between regular legislative sessions.

The original state constitution limited the length of regular and special sessions to sixty and twenty days, respectively; however, the sixty-day limit on regular sessions was not, strictly speaking, observed by the legislature in the post–World War II period. The device the Nevada legislature and some other state legislatures used to get around the constitutional limitation was "stopping the clock" at 11:59 P.M. on the sixtieth day. The legislature often conducted business, including the critical approval of the biennial budget, for several days afterward; all such business was officially included in the journals of the two chambers as having taken place on the sixtieth day.

Some legislators worried that legislation passed after the actual sixtieth day might be challenged in the courts. Hence, the legislature proposed in 1955 and 1957 a constitutional amendment removing the limit on the length of regular and special sessions. In order to make the proposal more palatable to the voters, the legislature also included a companion amendment that limited legislative salaries to sixty days for a regular session and to twenty days for a special session. The voters approved both measures by better than 2-1 margins. The length of the regular sessions has increased steadily over the years, with the 1995 session lasting a record 169 days.

Organization

The goal of the major political parties in Nevada's legislative elections is to win a majority of the seats in each of the two houses and thus be able to control the organization of the chambers, including the committee chairmanships. Historically, the control of the two houses has been fairly evenly divided between the two major parties. Including the 1995 session, the Republicans have organized the senate during forty-one regular sessions, while the Democrats have done so during twenty-one sessions. In 1939 there were eight Republicans, eight Democrats, and one independent in the upper house, and the two parties decided to split the committee chairmanships. The Democrats hold the edge in the control of regular sessions in the assembly, electing the Speaker thirty-seven times to twenty-five for the Republicans. In the five regular sessions from 1893 to 1901, inclusive, the Silver party controlled the organization of both houses.

In 1994 twenty-one Republicans and twenty-one Democrats won assembly seats. Assembly rules did not stipulate how a tie vote should be settled. After prolonged negotiations, the two parties agreed to alternate the leadership and committee chairmanship positions. Thus, each party caucus chose a cospeaker and a cochair for each committee to serve every other daily session.

Each of the major political parties has had a period of strong legislative control. From 1864 through 1891, the Republicans controlled each of the houses in thirteen of the fifteen regular sessions. From 1965 through 1983, the Democrats continuously controlled the upper house and organized the assembly in all but two of the regular sessions. The Democrats hold the record for consecutive regular sessions controlled by one party in either house, having organized the assembly for eighteen straight regular sessions from 1933 through 1967. The Republicans maintained the leadership of the senate for a record thirteen consecutive regular sessions from 1941 through 1963. The record for the most consecutive regular sessions in which one party controlled both houses is six, set by the Republicans from 1921 through 1931 and tied by the Democrats from 1973 through 1983.

Outside of the organizational vote, party is not an important factor when a Nevada legislator is deciding how to vote on most bills. Constituent pressure is more important. In the senate, especially, there is a long tradition of respect for individual senators who are conscientious and place the interests of the state above their own, regardless of party. For example, in the 1975 and 1977 senates, the Democrats outnumbered the Republicans 17-3; yet the three Republicans—Carl Dodge, William Raggio, and Clifton Young—were among the most influential senators.

The organizational process is usually routine in the two houses, with the majority-party members voting for the caucus candidate for Speaker of the assembly and majority leader of the senate. However, party defections can lead to unexpected results. In 1953 and 1981, a minority of the majority party caucus combined with the other party to elect the Speaker. In 1979, a similar combination forced the Speaker-designate to change a committee chairmanship.

In contrast to the practice in the U.S. House, where the Speaker has historically been able to retain his position as long as his party retains the majority of the seats in the chamber, the speakership of the Nevada Assembly, until recently, was "up for grabs" at each regular session. Only four individuals have served two or more consecutive terms as Speaker of the Assembly: Joe Dini (1987, 1989, 1991, 1993, and co-Speaker in 1995); Lem Allen (1895, 1897, 1899); William Kennett (1935, 1937); and Keith Ashworth (1973, 1975). Dini holds the record for most terms as Speaker with six, having also served in the position in 1977. Candidates for the speakership use the other two leadership positions (the majority floor leader and the Speaker pro tem), the committee chairmanships, and membership on key committees, such as Ways and Means, Judiciary, and Taxation, as bargaining chips to gain the support of a majority of the members of the majority-party caucus.

On the Senate side, prior to 1945 the president pro tem also acted as floor leader for the majority party and controlled the committee assignments, which were usually approved routinely by the caucus. Since 1945 the majority leader has become the more powerful position because of control of the majority-party committee assignments, including chairmanships, and the floor debate. The president pro tem mainly fills in as presiding officer when the lieutenant governor, who holds the title of president of the senate, is not present.[8]

Since 1965 the tenure of the Nevada Senate majority leader has been similar to that of the U.S. Senate's majority leader, with the individual holding the post staying in office until he retires or his party loses control of the body. Thus, Mahlon Brown served six consecutive terms as majority leader of the Nevada Senate from 1965 until his retirement in 1976. Brown was replaced by James Gibson, who served as majority leader from 1977 until the Democrats lost control of the upper house in 1987. In 1987 William Raggio became the first Republican majority leader of the senate in twenty-four years and served two terms before being replaced by John Vergiels when the Democrats regained control after the 1990 election. The GOP's recapture of the senate in 1993 returned Raggio to the leadership. The minority-party caucus in each house chooses the minority leader, who controls the committee assignments of minority-party members. In 1993 Dina Titus became the first woman to serve as minority leader. Raggio and Titus retained their positions in the 1995 senate.

Procedures

The U.S. Constitution contains few provisions concerning the procedures that Congress must follow in considering a bill; thus most of the details are covered in the rules of the two houses. However, similar to the basic law of most other states, the Nevada Constitution goes into greater detail about procedures.[9] Each house of the Nevada legislature also adopts its own standing rules in addition to joint rules that apply to both houses. The senate and the assembly have traditionally designated the parliamentary rules contained in *Mason's Manual of Legislative Procedure* as governing when such rules are not in conflict with the standing rules of the two houses.

Committee consideration is even more crucial to the fate of a bill in the Nevada legislature than it is in the Congress. Given the normal length of a regular biennial session in Nevada, there is comparatively little time for debate on individual bills. Thus, great deference is given to committee recommendations, which are seldom defeated on the floor and often are approved unanimously. If there is little committee support, the bill may be ignored, especially if the majority party leadership shows no interest in it. However, if the bill concerns a matter of great public interest, such as a major new tax proposed by the governor, extensive hearings may be scheduled by the committee.

If a majority of the committee members favor the bill, the measure will be reported to the floor of the house with a "do pass" or "do pass as amended" recommendation. If a majority of committee members oppose a bill, the measure will normally be killed in committee. However, if there is strong pressure from the majority-party leadership or the governor—as was the case with the proposed Equal Rights Amendment in the senate in 1977—a bill may be reported out with a "do not pass" recommendation or no recommendation. A tie vote in committee usually kills a bill; however, the compromise between the parties for the 1995 session not only provided for equal party membership on committees but for bills to go to the floor on a tie vote.

The committees that decide how the state's money is spent, the Senate Finance Committee and the Assembly Ways and Means Committee, are by far the most powerful. The money committees hold hearings throughout the regular session, and the length of the session usually depends on how soon the two committees agree on the state's budget. The governor's budget recommendations carry great weight with the committees. An increase in the governor's request for an agency will normally necessitate a cut somewhere else.

The Judiciary Committee is also a choice assignment in the two houses because it has jurisdiction over gaming and proposed constitutional amendments. The Taxation Committee in each of the two houses takes on more importance when tax questions are on the legislative agenda. The taxation committees must act before the Ways and Means and Finance Committees can finalize the budget.

Once a bill is passed in one house, it is sent to the other house for consideration. If the two houses cannot agree on the content of a bill, each house appoints members to a conference committee, which attempts to fashion a compromise bill. In the closing hours of a legislative session, bills are sometimes killed because of a failure of conference committees to find compromises acceptable to both houses.

When a bill passes both houses with exactly the same wording, the measure is forwarded to the governor. During the session, the governor has five days (Sunday excepted) in which to sign or veto a bill; after five days, the bill becomes law without his or her signature. Unlike the president of the United States, Nevada's governor does not have the pocket veto. The governor has ten days after adjournment to veto a bill, in which case the measure is presented to the legislature at its next session for a possible override. A vetoed bill must receive a two-thirds vote of all members *elected to each house* in order to override the governor's veto and become law.

To be effective, a legislator must abide by certain informal norms of behavior that are generally shared by fellow legislators. Likewise, if a legislative body is to be effective in representing the people, a large majority of the members must abide by such norms. In an orientation talk to new legislators in January 1981, former state senator Carl Dodge, who was considered one of the most effective legislators during the twenty-three years he represented Churchill County in the upper house, listed in alphabetical order the following norms as the most important in the legislature: (1) apprenticeship, (2) gracefulness in defeat, (3) honoring commitments, (4) institutional patriotism, (5) integrity and honesty, (6) interpersonal courtesy, (7) keeping confidences, (8) reciprocity, (9) self-restraint, and (10) willingness to work and cooperate. The authors agree with Senator Dodge's list and rank numbers 5 and 3, which are closely related, as the most important norms, followed by number 10 and then numbers 9 and 3, which are also closely related.

Integrity and honesty are very important if a legislator is to have the respect of colleagues. If one's word cannot be trusted, how can such a legislator's arguments on a bill be accepted at face value? A promise to support another legislator's bill should not be broken without getting that legislator's release.

The late Senator James I. Gibson of Clark County was an example of a legislator whose integrity and willingness to work and cooperate made him a powerful force for thirty years in the legislature. During his early years sitting on the Assembly Ways and Means Committee, Gibson gained the respect of his colleagues because he did his homework on the budget and asked witnesses informed and intelligent questions. When he moved to the senate in 1967, Gibson's reputation gained him a seat on the powerful Finance Committee. Long before he assumed the positions of majority leader in 1977 and chair of the Finance Committee in 1985, he had become the informal leader of both the committee and the senate as a whole. As one longtime lobbyist confided in the 1970s, "Jim Gibson is the ball game." Even after the Democrats lost control of the senate in 1987, Gibson continued to be the glue that made the senate work. Indeed, he was probably the most effective and powerful legislator in the history of the state.

An example of how violation of the legislative norms can work to the disadvantage of a legislator occurred in the 1971 session. A freshman assembly-man did not exercise self-restraint in debate and was not honest about self-serving legislation that he introduced. Not only was this legislator ineffec-tive and ignored by members of both parties during the session, but in the 1971 reapportionment, he was placed in the same district with a popular leg-islator of the same party.

LEGISLATIVE REFORM

In the wake of the Watergate scandals, reform legislation was a large item in state legislatures as well as in Congress in 1975. Nevada's legislature passed a conflict-of-interest law that also established an Ethics Commission with the power, but not much operating money, to enforce the legislation. The law concerning the disclosure of business and professional interests by pub-lic officials and the prohibition of participation in decisions involving such interests was declared unconstitutional by the Nevada Supreme Court in 1976 as being too vague.[10] The 1977 legislature responded by passing a statute that spelled out specific conflict-of-interest prohibitions on public officials.

Pressure from Common Cause and other reform groups was a factor in causing the 1991 legislature to toughen the law. The words *may not* were re-placed by *shall not* in the stipulation that "a public official or employee shall not seek or accept any gift, service, favor, employment, engagement, emol-ument or economic opportunity which would tend improperly to influence a reasonable person in his position from the faithful and impartial discharge of his public duties."[11] The 1991 amendments also prohibited Ethics Com-mission members from being "actively involved in the work of any politi-cal party or political campaign" or being a paid lobbyist at a legislative session.[12]

THE LEGISLATIVE COUNSEL BUREAU

A Nevada legislator today might well wonder how legislators prior to 1945 were able to function without the help of an agency similar to the Legislative Counsel Bureau (LCB). Although legislators are sometimes critical when a pet bill is not drafted expeditiously, the LCB provides professional and secre-tarial assistance that is vital if Nevada's part-time legislature is to serve effec-tively as a check on the executive branch.

The Legislative Commission, which is made up of six members from each house, supervises and decides the policies to be implemented by the Legislative Counsel Bureau. The commission normally meets once a month between the regular legislative sessions, although the amount of business may dictate whether a particular monthly meeting is held. It supervises the work of the interim study committees and hears the reports of these committees prior to the next legislative session. The commission also appoints the director of the LCB, who has the authority to employ the staff of the bureau, including the heads of the four major divisions (legal, fiscal analysis, research, and audit). The director serves as head of the Administrative Division and as secretary to the Legislative Commission and the Interim Finance Committee.[13]

The chief of the Legal Division has the title of legislative counsel. The counsel and the staff of attorneys in the division compile and update the *Nevada Revised Statutes* and provide legal advice to legislative committees and subcommittees. The most time-consuming task of the Legal Division is the drafting of bills and resolutions requested by members of the legislature, the governor, executive departments and other state agencies, and the judiciary. By law, the legislative counsel may issue legal opinions, although such opinions are in the same legal category as those from the attorney general—they are advisory only and do not have a binding effect in a court of law.[14]

The Fiscal Analysis Division of the Legislative Counsel Bureau was established by the legislature to provide budgetary and fiscal advice that is independent of advice from the state budget director, who is the governor's key adviser on such matters. Fiscal analysts are often enticed by higher salaries to leave the state budget office after gaining experience there.

The senate and assembly fiscal analysts attend the presession meetings at which representatives of the various agencies and departments make their presentations to the budget director. The senate fiscal analyst sits with the Finance Committee and the assembly fiscal analyst sits with the Ways and Means Committee during a legislative session. Their recommendations can often be critical in the decisions of those two bodies, although the governor's position as represented by the budget director or a staff person perhaps carries more weight overall. During legislative sessions in which taxation is a major issue, as it was in 1991, the fiscal analysis staff that advises the two taxation committees can be influential.

The Research Division of the Legislative Counsel Bureau performs a wide variety of research tasks for public officials and private citizens. For example, a legislator may request information on what types of legislation other states have enacted to deal with a particular problem. The division also conducts surveys and performs research for the interim committees.[15] Between the 1989 and 1991 legislative sessions, not only did the division do extensive research on reapportionment in support of the interim committee that had been set up by the 1989 legislature, but the staff issued a periodic newsletter on reapportionment that was sent to members of the legislature for a year and a half prior to the passage of the 1991 reapportionment act at the end of the session. The library of the Research Division is used by the other units of the bureau, and the division, in turn, uses the resources of the State Library and the State Division of Archives and Records in order to fulfill its informational responsibilities.

The Audit Division of the LCB provides the legislature with its principal means of performing oversight of the executive branch. The main duty of the legislative auditor is to oversee the postauditing of the financial records of "all state departments, agencies and officials using or managing public funds."[16] The division also recommends changes in the financial practices of audited agencies.

The 1969 legislature created an Interim Finance Committee to operate between legislative sessions. The committee handles budgetary shortfalls that result from rapid population increases or from other financial emergencies, thus making a special session of the legislature unnecessary. Its membership consists of the members of the Senate Finance Committee and the Assembly Ways and Means Committee at the previous regular legislative session. The Senate and Assembly fiscal analysts play an even more important role in the work of the interim committee because the legislators usually meet for just a few hours on a request from an agency. Originally, the interim committee was given a contingency fund of $1 million to disburse between sessions; however, the amount of the funding has increased considerably over the years due to inflation and the demands for increased services that have accompanied the large population increases. The purpose behind the creation of the Interim Finance Committee seems to have been achieved; from 1969 through 1994, only three special sessions were called by Nevada governors, with none being called to consider budgetary matters.

EVALUATION OF THE LEGISLATURE

In 1969 the Ford Foundation gave the Citizens Conference on State Legislatures a grant to conduct a comparative study of the operation of the fifty state legislatures. The study's report gave Nevada's legislature an overall ranking of thirteenth in the nation.[17] The timing of the ranking in 1971 was fortuitous because the legislature had just moved into a new building, which had a positive impact on the ranking.

The Citizens Conference ranked the legislatures in five broad areas: functionality, accountability, informedness, independence, and representativeness.[18] Nevada ranked highest (tenth among the fifty states) in the accountability category, with "adequacy of information and public access to it" being an especially strong area. The new facilities, including spacious committee meeting rooms and auditoriums for hearings, made the legislature more accessible to both the public and the media.[19]

Representativeness was the only category in which the Citizens Conference ranked Nevada in the bottom half of the states. The main reason for the low ranking (thirty-second) was the lack of diversity in the background of legislators, with inadequate compensation and biennial regular sessions being mentioned as contributing factors.[20]

Since the 1971 study was published, the legislature has enacted several of the recommendations of the Citizens Conference. The legislature established single-member assembly districts in 1971 and mandated the regulation of lobbyists in 1973. The recommendation that each legislator be given an office was gradually realized over a period of twenty years, with the removal of the Research Division of the LCB to a facility across the street from the Legislative Building finally providing for the additional space to complete the project.

The legislature has not implemented the recommendation to support a constitutional amendment to allow annual sessions. Such an amendment has been introduced at almost every session of the legislature since 1971, but the memory of the resounding defeat of the amendment in the 1970 election and the opposition of some legislative leaders have foiled each such attempt. The recommendation that the constitution be amended to delete the limitation on the number of days for which legislators may receive a salary met the same fate. The voters overwhelmingly rejected a proposed amendment to increase the number of paid days from sixty to one hundred in 1976.

How effective has the Nevada legislature been in providing public policy leadership in the last forty years? In many areas, such as the financing of education, collective bargaining for public employees, and family courts, stronger leadership has come from the legislature than from the executive. Legislators were willing to take leadership roles in promoting the sales tax and the school support tax when certain governors were not willing to take the heat. However, the legislature did not enact effective lobbying and campaign finance reform until the 1990s, despite the efforts of dedicated reformers such as Sue Wagner, Jean Ford, and Thomas "Spike" Wilson in the 1970s and 1980s.

CONCLUSION

Nevada's legislature has become much more professional in the last half of the twentieth century. The state's generally prosperous economy during the 1960s, 1970s, and 1980s, when biennial budget surpluses were the rule, provided the setting for substantial increases in staff support and much better facilities for both legislators and staff.

Most Nevada legislators mirror their constituents' belief in an individualistic ethic. Also, the moderate conservative label fits both the average Nevadan and the average legislator.

The informality that is a hallmark of relationships among legislators and between lobbyists and the lawmakers during legislative sessions is a positive factor in the arrangement of compromises during a session. However, as in Congress and in most states, Nevada's legislative process is subject to the whims of floor leaders and committee chairs who sometimes play "hard ball" and refuse to allow legislation that would otherwise be approved by a majority in both houses to come to a vote. Fortunately, such instances are not common.

Traditionally, the assembly has been a more partisan body than the senate. However, since the death of Jim Gibson, the senate has become more partisan than it had been in the past. Both Republican majority leader Bill Raggio and Democratic minority leader Dina Titus call frequent party caucuses. Titus has been frustrated by the power wielded by Raggio, who became the dominant legislative leader in the mid-1990s. The 1995 assembly was forced to be less partisan because of the 21-21 party division. With Democratic governor Bob Miller pledging to be nonpartisan in his approach, compromise will continue to be more important than partisanship in legislative decision making.

CHAPTER SEVEN

The Governor and the Executive Branch

Nevada's governors have exemplified the emphasis on individualism and informality in Nevada politics. They have not been, with few exceptions, political party leaders as much as individuals who have tried to appeal to the average Nevadan as "one of them." This common touch has been evident in Mike O'Callaghan's willingness to throw out the first ball in Little League baseball openers, in Bob Miller's eagerness to participate in charity basketball games, and in Paul Laxalt's and Richard Bryan's mastery at "working the crowd" at various happenings.

Unlike the U.S. president, Nevada's governor must share executive power with other elected executive officials, who, under the state's constitution, are elected directly by the people and thus may be members of the opposite political party. The early state constitutions provided for this multiple executive system as a reaction to the rule of colonial governors; later state constitutions followed this pattern. Nevada's constitution and statutes do provide a framework for a governor with leadership abilities to be a strong chief executive. Certainly in the latter half of the twentieth century, the governor became the focal point for state government and the one who received most of the praise or blame for the general well-being of the state.

QUALIFICATIONS OF THE GOVERNOR

The constitution requires candidates for the offices of governor and lieutenant governor to be at least twenty-five years old and to have resided in the state for the two years preceding the election. The original constitution provided for a four-year term with no limit on the number of terms. In 1970 the voters approved an amendment to limit the number of years served by a governor.

The 1970 amendment states that no person shall be elected governor "more than twice" and that "no person who has held the office of governor, or acted as governor for more than two years of a term to which some other person was elected governor shall be elected to the office of governor more than once."[1] By tradition, a Nevada lieutenant governor who assumes the office upon the death or resignation of a governor uses the title of "acting governor." Governor Bob Miller, who served the last two years of Richard Bryan's term after Bryan was elected to the U.S. Senate, was elected in his own right in 1990 and filed to run again in 1994. The State of Nevada Employees Association filed suit against Miller, stating that he had actually served four days more than two years as acting governor. The Nevada Supreme Court ruled that Miller's candidacy was in keeping with the intent of the framers of the amendment, and Miller was reelected.

In twenty-five of Nevada's thirty-four gubernatorial elections, voters have chosen the governor and lieutenant governor of the same party. Also, in each of the six cases in which the lieutenant governor became acting governor following the resignation or death of the lieutenant governor, the individuals involved were of the same party. A problem can develop when a lieutenant governor of the opposite party acts in place of a governor during the latter's brief absence from the state, as has been the situation in six of the last twelve elections.

In a case involving Democratic governor Grant Sawyer and Republican lieutenant governor Paul Laxalt in 1966, the Nevada Supreme Court ruled that the governor's absence from the state for five hours on a Sunday to attend a meeting in Sacramento did not give the lieutenant governor the power to take such *nonemergency* action as the impanelment of a grand jury to investigate the Highway Department.[2] Richard Bryan, then attorney general, referred to this 1966 decision in a 1979 advisory opinion "in which he stated that Lieutenant Governor Myron Leavitt was not entitled to a salary for days in which Governor Robert List was absent from the state, unless as acting governor he had taken some significant and required action."[3]

There was an unusual case in the 1980s in which a lieutenant governor changed parties within a year after being elected. Robert Cashell, former chairman of the Board of Regents of the University of Nevada system and hotel-casino owner, considered a run for the Democratic nomination for governor in 1982 but decided on the lieutenant governor's race after his polling showed Attorney General Bryan with a substantial lead. Bryan and Cashell did not cooperate during the general election campaign; indeed, some of the Bryan people charged that Cashell was actually working behind the scenes for List's election, which would have cleared the way for a Cashell run for governor in 1986, given the two-term gubernatorial limit.[4]

With his strong base of support in populous Clark County, Bryan was able to defeat List, while Cashell, with an imposing campaign fund for a candidate for lieutenant governor, was able to win by an even larger margin. During the 1983 legislative session, Cashell complained that the governor was ignoring him, and openly opposed Bryan on some key issues. Given this background, it was not surprising that Cashell, after strong encouragement from Senator Paul Laxalt and President Ronald Reagan, announced in 1983 that he was switching to the Republican party. A possible Bryan-Cashell gubernatorial race in 1986 did not come about because Bryan's popularity rose with the state's rising economy, and his performance during the legislative session in 1985 was widely praised in the media.[5] Cashell retired from elective politics at the end of 1986 after serving out his term as lieutenant governor.

GUBERNATORIAL PROFILES

There have been twenty-six governors in the history of the state, including four who served as acting governor upon the death or resignation of a governor and were not elected to the office itself. The governors have been, for the most part, split between the two major parties. However, at the end of Governor Bob Miller's term in 1998, the Democrats will have controlled the governor's chair for thirty-two of the preceding forty years.

The backgrounds of the governors have differed over time. Of the first ten governors, who served between 1864 and 1908, all had a background in mining, cattle ranching, or both. Of the six most recent governors going back to 1959, five were attorneys and four had also been county district attorneys. From 1908 through 1958, three journalists, two attorneys, two engineers, two bankers, and a businessman served as governor. Only four—Emmet Boyle, Charles Russell, Grant Sawyer, and Richard Bryan—were graduates of the University of Nevada; seven were native-born Nevadans: Boyle, Fred Balzar, Morley Griswold, Richard Kirman, Edward P. Carville, Russell, and Paul Laxalt. (Bryan was born in Washington DC, where his father, a legal resident of Las Vegas, was attending law school.)

Of the twenty-six governors, only six had served in the legislature and only three of those—Bryan, Russell, and Balzar—had served in both houses. Bryan and Bob List are the only ones who used the attorney general position as a stepping stone. The only person to use the lieutenant governor's office as a springboard to the governor's chair—outside of those who inherited the office due to death or resignation—was Laxalt in 1966.

Scholars have sometimes examined the American presidency in terms of constitutional and extraconstitutional roles.[6] Some of those presidential roles based on constitutional powers, such as chief executive and chief legislator, are also important gubernatorial roles; others, such as chief diplomat and commander-in-chief, are not significant roles for the governor, although the state's chief executive is head of the state militia or National Guard until it is called to active duty by the president. The governor's informal roles as economic leader and education leader are important in all states; in addition, the people have looked to the governor in some states as a protector of the environment.

Chief Executive

In one respect, the Nevada governor's executive or administrative powers are considerably less than those of the president. The governor does not appoint and cannot remove the important state officials who are elected directly by the people. However, the state's chief executive does appoint about eighty cabinet-level agency heads and deputies. In addition, the governor is a member of several important boards and commissions.

Although not having the sole pardoning power, as does the president with those who have been convicted of federal crimes, the governor does have a constitutional veto power over a pardon granted by the State Board of Pardons, whose membership includes the justices of the state supreme court and the attorney general. The constitution stipulates that a majority of the seven-member board, "of whom the governor shall be one," must vote in favor for a pardon to be granted.[7] Some justices of the state supreme court have been uncomfortable sitting on the Board of Pardons because they have viewed the power as a strictly executive function. A constitutional amendment proposed by the legislature that would have given the governor exclusive pardoning power was decisively defeated by the voters in 1960.

The appointment power of the governor is considerable. In 1991 the laws provided for the governor to appoint the members of 134 boards, commissions, and committees, including interstate commissions. These boards and commissions range from the very important Gaming Control Board and the

Gaming and Parole Commissions to the minor Junior Livestock Show and Funeral Directors and Embalmers Boards. The governor has an advantage over the president in that such appointments are not subject to approval by the legislature.

The appointment of the Nevada members of the joint Nevada-California Tahoe Planning Commission has been a good indicator of the governor's position on environmental matters. Most of the body's important decisions have involved environmental protection of Lake Tahoe and the surrounding area versus the rights of property holders. More often than not, the governors of the two states have disagreed on the issue, thus producing deadlocks on the commission membership. The only period of accord since 1970 (when Governors Reagan and Laxalt both came down on the property-rights side) occurred in 1975–79 when Governors Jerry Brown and Mike O'Callaghan strongly favored environmental protection of the lake area. Democratic governors in both states have been prone to appoint more environmentalist-minded members to the commission than have Republican governors.

When a newly elected governor is of the opposite party from the outgoing governor, there is likely to be a large turnover in the heads and deputies of the cabinet-level agencies. Between 1950 and 1982, inclusive, all of the gubernatorial transitions involved governors of different parties. An examination of the List-Bryan transition in 1982 showed that even after the two individuals had fought a hard campaign against each other, they were able to cooperate in making a smooth transfer of power.[8]

Bryan had interacted with many of the key agency heads during his ten years in the legislature and his four years as attorney general. In addition to his personal evaluations of the administrators, he relied on the advice of such people as his budget director-designate William Bible, who—as a legislative fiscal analyst and deputy budget director—had also had contact with many of the executive heads, and Thomas "Spike" Wilson, a respected state senator and attorney. Bryan and his aides stated that qualifications and expertise were the most important criteria used in determining whether to retain an administrative head or deputy, although those who played major roles in List's campaign for reelection were not reappointed.[9] The incoming governor received more than two thousand applications for the "unclassified" positions that he could have filled with appointees. Bryan made forty-three new appointments, thus retaining almost half of the administrative heads and deputies who had served under List.[10]

The governor's personal staff is a vital part of the executive branch, especially when a governor such as Bryan or Miller uses the staff to supervise certain departments and agencies. The chief of staff is generally the governor's closest aide. Other positions, all of which have to be approved for budgetary purposes by the legislature, are executive assistants (who may also serve as legal counsel or legislative liaison), press secretary, and appointments secretary.

Morale among state employees often rises and falls according to how much support they believe they are receiving from the governor. Governor Mike O'Callaghan felt that the state employees were "his people." His successful fight for a 15 percent pay increase for them at the 1975 legislature—after the high inflation of 1973–74—endeared him even more to the workers. O'Callaghan was very upset when he became aware of a movement among some legislators to increase the legislative oversight of executive departments and agencies. Over a decade later, in 1988, voters rejected a constitutional amendment that would have authorized the legislature to review administrative regulations. Inasmuch as Governor Bob Miller had been very supportive of state employees, his 1991 veto of a collective bargaining bill for which the State of Nevada Employees Association (SNEA) had fought for many years came as a surprise to many observers. The veto was probably the main reason that SNEA decided to become part of the AFL-CIO in 1994.

With the large number of government departments and agencies that are under the governor's jurisdiction, he or she cannot meet regularly with the department heads as a group. During Bryan's administration, his staff worked with James Roberts, emeritus professor of public administration, to set up workshops and seminars involving all department and agency heads.

Chief Legislator

Similar to the president's constitutional duty to deliver a State of the Union address to Congress, the Nevada Constitution states that the governor "shall communicate by message to the legislature at every regular session the condition of the state, and recommend such measures as he may deem expedient."[11] With the advent of television coverage of the "State of the State" address, Nevada governors have used the occasion not only to spell out their legislative programs but also at times to appeal directly to the people to put pressure on the lawmakers in order to enact key aspects of the program—just as has been the case with presidents from the time of Franklin D. Roosevelt.

Nevada's governor has some advantages over the president in the exercise of power as chief legislator. One advantage is that, as noted in the previous chapter, Nevada has citizen legislators who receive a relatively low salary and are only in session about 160 days every two years. Given the need of a large majority of legislators to work at another occupation, the time they have to devote to legislative matters is limited. Also, the governor has the bureaucracy of the executive branch at his or her disposal and can amass the background material and statistics needed to support his or her legislative positions and initiatives. The legislature has only a smaller number of full-time staff people in the Legislative Counsel Bureau to counteract the executive. Although the legislature's money committees have competent staff, the legislators themselves have only a brief time during the biennial session to hold hearings and digest the large number of individual department and agency budget requests submitted by the governor. Not surprisingly, then, the overall biennial budget passed by the legislature generally does not vary much from the governor's proposals.

The governor has a potent legislative weapon in his power to veto bills passed by the legislature. During Mike O'Callaghan's eight years as governor in the 1970s, he did not have a single veto overridden until after he was out of office. (A bill that he vetoed after adjournment of the 1977 legislature was overridden in January 1979.) However, the Nevada governor does not have the *item* veto. The governors of forty-three states are able to veto items in appropriations bills; without this power, Nevada's chief executive must either accept or reject the omnibus appropriations bill that is passed at the end of a session. In contrast, the governor of California can remove or lower specific items in appropriations bills.

Close contact between the governor and his or her aides and the legislature during a session tends to limit the number of vetoes exercised by the executive. Prior to 1971, when the legislature met in the State Capitol building, there was usually a continuous stream of legislative leaders going down the stairs to the governor's office during the closing days of a session. The threat of a veto was usually enough to cause the legislators to come up with a compromise version of a bill.

The move to the legislative building reduced the personal interaction between the governor and legislators. However, top gubernatorial aides are the eyes and ears of the governor in legislative halls and committee rooms. Bryan held a strategy session each morning with his legislative team, which included his budget director and his chief of staff, prior to its departure to the legislative building. The members of the lobbying team briefed the governor in late afternoon on pertinent information they had gleaned from conversations with legislators and other key figures at the legislature.

The governor also uses the phone and personal meetings in the governor's office to try to convince legislators to support particular legislation. Some recent governors have even turned up in the legislative halls in the closing days of a session to persuade legislators and to negotiate compromises on important bills.

The governor may use individuals outside the government to influence legislators. During the 1985 legislative session, Governor Bryan called his college fraternity brother Frank Fahrenkopf, chairman of the Republican National Committee, to put pressure on Republican Assembly Speaker Byron Bilyeu. Fahrenkopf called Bilyeu, and the governor's bill was passed.

Nevada's governor has two more legislative advantages over the nation's chief executive. One is based on the provision in the Nevada Constitution stating that "each law enacted by the legislature shall embrace but one subject."[12] Thus, the governor is not faced with "riders," which often are added to congressional bills in an attempt to get the president's approval of something that would be vetoed if it stood alone.

The governor also has more control over a special session than the president. The president has the power to call a special session but cannot limit the business that is conducted by Congress in such a session. The Nevada Constitution states that the governor not only has the power to convene the legislature "on extraordinary occasions" but that "the legislature shall transact no legislative business except that for which they [the two houses] were especially convened, or such other legislative business as the governor may call to the attention of the legislature while in session."[13] This power has enabled governors to limit the length of recent special sessions to four hours in 1980, two days in 1984, and two hours in 1989.

Economic Leader

Nevadans look to the governor for leadership in the economic area. The public often blames the governor for a declining state economy or gives him the credit for a thriving economy, even though national or international economic forces over which the governor has no control are mainly responsible. However, some recent Nevada governors have taken initiatives that have affected the state's economic picture.

In addition to the governor's ability to influence the state's economy through the executive budget and tax policies, the executive is expected to protect the state's major economic assets. In view of the importance of gambling to Nevada's economy in the latter half of the twentieth century, some attention should be given to its history in the state.

Nevada's first governor, Henry G. Blasdel, was opposed to gambling, but the legislature overrode his veto of pro-gambling legislation in 1869. Therefore, gambling was legal in Nevada from 1869 to 1909.[14] Although an anti-gambling law was enacted by the legislature in 1909, the law was widely disregarded. Between 1909 and 1931, many stores and gas stations had an illegal slot machine or two, and one club in Reno "operated openly with casino gambling."[15] Thus, gambling was widespread in Nevada, whether legal or illegal, long before its legalization in 1931.

The initiative for the 1931 law came from the legislature and was sparked by the Great Depression, the decline of mining, and a realization that the economic boost from the construction of Hoover Dam was ending. Phil Tobin, a freshman assemblyman from Humboldt County, introduced the bill. In an interview in 1976, Tobin stated that he "was irritated by the fact that a lot of money was being paid to police and other authorities to protect the illegal gambling operations."[16] The Wingfield machine, including developer Norman Biltz and influential lobbyist John Mueller, worked behind the scenes to assure passage of the bill.

Originally, any policing of legal gambling was handled by local officials who had the authority to grant gaming licenses. The State Tax Commission took over the licensing authority in 1945; however, as has been pointed out by James W. Hulse, the regulation of gambling continued to be "casual at best" under the five-year governorship of Vail Pittman, when little concern was shown for the criminal background of many casino owners.[17]

The investigation of national organized criminal activity by a U.S. Senate committee headed by Senator Estes Kefauver in 1951–52 placed the spotlight on the infiltration of Nevada's casinos by mobsters. Kefauver was a presidential candidate at the time, and the hearings over which he presided were the first to be televised nationally. This unfavorable national publicity was a factor in Governor Charles Russell's decision in 1955 to recommend the legislature's approval of a proposal to establish a separate division, entitled the Gaming Control Board, within the State Tax Commission.

Jerome Skolnick charged in the 1970s that the failure of the state to set up a separate control agency before 1955 was a major factor in the ability of organized crime to infiltrate gambling in the state. The 1955 law "grandfathered in" gamblers who had already been granted licenses, including those with questionable backgrounds, without subjecting them to the more thorough investigation set up by the State Gaming Control Board.[18]

The immediate cause of Governor Russell's decision to push the 1955 legislature to pass tougher legislation was the disclosure by an investigative reporter for Hank Greenspun's *Las Vegas Sun* that notorious eastern racketeers had infiltrated the ownership of the Thunderbird Hotel on the Las Vegas Strip.[19] Russell continued to show how important he thought strong regulation of gambling was for the state's economic well-being by vetoing a 1957 "gambler's-day-in-court" bill. The bill would have prevented the "summary closing" of casinos found cheating until they had exhausted their appeals in the courts.[20]

Governor Grant Sawyer, who succeeded Russell in 1959, showed that he, too, believed in strong regulation. He immediately recommended legislation to sever the Gaming Control Board from the Tax Commission and to create a new Gaming Commission. The full-time members of the Gaming Control Board oversee the investigations of potential licensees and the enforcement of gaming regulations. The part-time members of the Gaming Commission set policies on gambling in accordance with state laws and make the final decision on the granting of a gaming license after receiving a recommendation from the control board.

Edward A. Olsen, who served as chairman of the Gaming Control Board from 1961 to 1966, wrote in a published article that the two regulatory agencies "have three primary responsibilities of equal rank. First, gambling must be kept honest or . . . tourist dollars will slow to a trickle. Second, the state must receive its correct share of casino winnings in the form of taxes or it will face bankruptcy. Finally, Nevada gambling must be kept as free as possible from the taint of underworld or face the prospect of federal prohibition of gambling."[21] In order to keep underworld figures out of Nevada gambling, the Gaming Control Board issued, in its early days, a "Black Book" that contained background material and photographs of "persons of notorious or unsavory reputation." Gambling establishments were sent copies, accompanied by a strong admonition to keep these individuals with underworld connections off their premises or face the prospect of losing their gambling licenses.[22]

During Sawyer's administration, two "Black Book" cases received considerable national attention. Johnny Marshall, a Chicago mobster who was included in the book, openly challenged the Gaming Control Board by appearing publicly with singer Roberta Linn at several of the large hotel-casinos on the Las Vegas Strip. Some of the hotels took no action for fear of offending Linn, but the Desert Inn, under pressure from the control board's chairman, ejected Marshall from its premises.[23] Marshall filed suit in federal court, where the judge ruled that the state had acted reasonably in classifying "individuals of notorious and unsavory reputation or extensive police records so that they are treated differently from others."[24] The federal court of appeals upheld the decision, but it warned the state gambling authorities that they should hold a hearing in the future before including someone in the "Black Book."[25]

The other sensational case involved even more famous figures. While driving through Iowa on his return from a vacation in 1963, Gaming Control Board chairman Ed Olsen was tracked down by state troopers with the message that he should call his office in Carson City. Olsen was informed that Sam Giancana, a Chicago mobster who had been included in the "Black Book" from its inception, was being hosted by Frank Sinatra, who was part owner of the Cal-Neva Lodge at Lake Tahoe. Giancana, who was later involved during the Kennedy administration in a plot to assassinate Cuban leader Fidel Castro, was at the Cal-Neva to see his friend Phyllis McGuire perform with the McGuire Sisters. Sinatra thus became the first casino owner to lose a gaming license for entertaining a person included in the "Black Book." (In 1981, Sinatra regained his license and invested in Caesar's Palace Hotel-Casino on the Las Vegas Strip.)

Despite the attempts to strengthen the enforcement arm of the Gaming Control Board and the court decision upholding the legality of the "Black Book," reports in the national media indicated that hidden mob interests in hotel-casinos in Las Vegas were a continuing problem. In 1969 Governor Paul Laxalt asked the legislature to change the gaming laws so that corporations might buy hotel-casinos. Apparently swayed by the argument that corporation ownership would give gaming a cleaner look in Nevada, and thus lessen the chance of federal intervention, the legislature approved Laxalt's proposal. Led by the Howard Hughes organization, a number of large national corporations, including Hilton, MGM, Holiday Inn, and Del Webb, became owners of casinos in Nevada; in so doing, they totally changed the face of gaming and added some respectability to the industry.

One problem that continued to plague the governors and gambling regulators in the 1970s and 1980s was the accuracy of the reporting of casino profits. Federal grand jury investigations in Detroit in 1979 and in Kansas City in 1983, both aided by FBI wiretaps, disclosed the use of "skimming" by some Las Vegas casinos. The practice involved the removal of amounts of money from a casino's daily "take" prior to the official counting for tax purposes. Skimming not only reduced the amount of gaming taxes the casino paid to the state, but, according to the grand jury reports, it also resulted in the unreported money being funneled to underworld figures in the two cities.

Governor Bob List responded to the charges that mobsters still operated in the gaming industry by asking for and receiving large increases in the number of authorized agents for the Gaming Control Board at the 1979 and 1981 legislative sessions. By the time the Kansas City grand jury investigation became public in 1983, Richard Bryan was governor. When investigators for the Gaming Control Board agreed with the federal grand jury about the skimming at the Cal-Neva Lodge at Lake Tahoe and the Stardust Hotel-Casino in Las Vegas, the Bryan-appointed board closed the Cal-Neva and appointed interim supervisors to run the Stardust until it could be sold. Thus, early in the Bryan administration, the gaming industry received the message that regulation under the new governor would be strict and tough.[26]

Even with the substantial increases in the number of gaming control agents in the 1980s, in 1995 Nevada still had far fewer agents to investigate, enforce, and audit gaming regulations in its hundreds of gambling operations spread out over hundreds of miles than had the state of New Jersey with its small number of hotel-casinos within walking distance of each other in Atlantic City. In 1985 Paul Bible, then the chairman of the Nevada Gaming Commission, called for a large increase in the number of agents to police gambling but noted that an increase could probably come about only if the casinos paid the tab for regulation, as is the case in New Jersey.[27] However, the political clout of the gaming industry among legislators continues to be very strong, and legislation that appears inimical to the large hotel-casino operators is not likely to be adopted. As an example of this political clout, the 1991 legislature enacted a law backed by the large operators that restricts new casinos in the state to establishments that have at least two hundred rooms. However, the gaming industry did not succeed completely at the 1991 session, for it failed to get the tax package it favored.

Although gambling and tourism dominate Nevada's economy, the introduction of casino gambling in New Jersey and in special areas in other states—along with the widespread adoption of state lotteries—led Bryan to emphasize the need for economic diversification in his successful campaign for governor in 1982. The 1983 legislature enacted Bryan's proposal to set up commissions for economic development and tourism, although the legislators amended the proposal at the behest of Lieutenant Governor Robert Cashell, who had contributed to the campaigns of many of the lawmakers, to replace an appointee of the governor with the lieutenant governor as chair of both commissions. Many new businesses and tourists have been attracted to the state as a result of the efforts of these two commissions; however, the growth of gaming operations has increased even more, so the dependence on gaming in the mid 1990s was as great or greater than it was ten years earlier.

In 1993 the opening of three mega Las Vegas hotel-casinos featuring family-style entertainment gave the state's economy a large boost. A similar hotel-casino and a large national bowling center opened in Reno in 1995. Only time will tell whether this new emphasis will keep the state's economy healthy in the face of the spread of casino gaming to Indian reservations and tourist meccas such as New Orleans.

Head of State and Ombudsman

Nevadans expect the governor to represent the interests of the state as a whole. This expectation is especially clear when the governor interacts with other governors or with the federal government. Grant Sawyer was the first Nevada governor to be chairman of the National Governors Association (NGA) and the first person to serve simultaneously as chair of the NGA and the Western Governors Association. Governors often go to Washington to testify before congressional committees and meet with the president at the White House. Governor Bob Miller's relationship with President Bill Clinton when they were both governors paved the way for the closest connection between a sitting Nevada governor and a president. The close relationship was probably a factor in Clinton's decision to back off from proposing a federal tax on gambling winnings to help support welfare reform.

The people expect the head of state to speak at special events in the state. In discussions with fellow governors in the 1960s, Sawyer found that he was "doing ten times as much of that as they were in their larger states."[28] Because of the informal nature of Nevada politics, the people expect personal contact with their governor, and most Nevada governors have obliged.

The governor also acts as an ombudsman for people who ask for help with a problem. An aide in the governor's office screens requests and sends them to the appropriate agencies. Depending on the problem, the reply to the constituent may be over the signature of the governor or the agency head. The governor also relies on the Consumer Affairs Division of the Commerce Department to protect the interests of consumers.

O'CALLAGHAN AS AN ARCHETYPICAL STRONG GOVERNOR

Democrat Mike O'Callaghan (1971–78) was probably the strongest and most popular governor in the state's history. One had to see him in action in the governor's office to appreciate how much power he brought to bear on issues of interest to him. On one occasion he called the chairman of a county school board to threaten him with jail time if he did not comply with state law and bargain collectively with the schoolteachers on salaries. A marine veteran who lost part of a leg in the Korean War, he often used colorful language; yet he was compassionate.

Party affiliation did not matter when O'Callaghan believed that a legislator had voted the wrong way on an important bill; that legislator was likely to receive a phone call from him. Freshman Republican Sue Wagner was called off the assembly floor in 1975 to take such a call. O'Callaghan also had a close relationship with Republican senator Bill Raggio, and the two often huddled together at University of Nevada, Reno, sports events. His strong leadership meant that he usually had his way; seldom did he lose a bill that he believed to be important.

O'Callaghan loved being governor. A workaholic, he was usually in his office early in the morning—hours before other state workers reported for duty. (Sawyer and Bryan were other workaholic governors who spent long hours on the job.)

Perhaps because he had been a government bureaucrat himself, O'Callaghan was loyally supportive of his administrative team. With all the power that he exercised, he retained the common touch and the respect of both legislators and the media.

THE GUBERNATORIAL STYLE OF BOB MILLER

The gubernatorial style of Bob Miller (1989–98) is in some ways a sharp contrast to that of O'Callaghan. *Laid-back* is the term most commonly used to describe Miller's style. He has a likable personality and displays competence in a low-key manner.

Miller delegates more responsibility to staff than any of the three Democrats who preceded him in the Governor's Mansion—Bryan, O'Callaghan, and Sawyer. Chiefs of staff Scott Craigie and Patty Becker and budget chief Judy Matteucci deflected some of the heat from the media during the governor's first six years.

As has been true with most Nevada governors, Miller has been a pragmatic problem solver. He has proved to be an effective leader, following up on Bryan's initiatives in the areas of education reform and hospital cost containment, which are discussed in chapter 13. He also acted decisively during the financial crisis that hit the state in 1991 and 1992. In 1993 he proposed an innovative reorganization of the executive branch. The legislature approved most of the consolidations of agencies and departments that he requested, although it refused to go along with the governor's proposal to merge the Department of Education into a super agency. A year and a half later, the governor abandoned one part of his "reinventing government" plan after problems developed with a consolidated audit program.

Democrat Miller is a mainstream Nevadan in his value system, is a strong family man, and is not strongly partisan. Above all, Miller has stated, he is proud that as governor he has represented "all the people" in the state.[29]

OTHER ELECTED EXECUTIVE OFFICIALS

The governor must share executive power with five other elected officials. More often than not, some of the other officials will not be of the same party as the governor. One party has won all six positions in only thirteen of the thirty-four elections for state officers; the last time for such an occurrence was 1946. In 1990 and 1994, Republicans were elected to four of the six offices and thus had a majority of the top elected executive positions for the only times since 1930; however, Democrats won the two most important offices—governor and attorney general—in both elections.

Although a woman has never been elected governor in Nevada, women have been elected to four of the other executive positions: in 1982 Patty Cafferata became the first woman elected state treasurer; in 1986 Frankie Sue Del Papa became the first woman elected secretary of state and four years later became the first female attorney general; and in 1990 Sue Wagner became the first woman elected to the office of lieutenant governor in the state.

Lieutenant Governor

Constitutionally, the lieutenant governor has two main duties: to preside over the senate as its president and to assume the duties and powers of the governor's office in case of the governor's removal from office, disability, or absence from the state. The legislature has added the positions of chair of the Commissions for Economic Development and Tourism. Informally, the lieutenant governor often fills in for the governor at ceremonial events, with the extent of such involvement depending on the relationship between the two individuals and whether they are of the same party. If there is a close relationship between the two officials, such as there was between Governor O'Callaghan and Lieutenant Governor Harry Reid, his former student, in the early 1970s and between Governor Bryan and Lieutenant Governor Miller in 1987 and 1988, the governor is likely to involve the lieutenant governor extensively as an adviser and representative. A poor relationship between the two individuals, whether for partisan or personal reasons, will likely result in minimal, if any, contact between them. Governor Miller and Lieutenant Governor Wagner worked well together, even though they were of different parties. When Wagner retired in 1995 because of injuries from an airplane accident, Miller called her "one of the best, if not the best, public servant I have ever known."[30]

Until recently, the lieutenant governor's position was regarded as a part-time job, with the holder by necessity working at another occupation or profession except during the legislative session. As late as 1957, the lieutenant governor's annual salary was only $600, in addition to receiving the same pay as legislators for a legislative session. The 1991 legislature increased the salary to $20,000, an amount not large enough to make it a full-time job for most individuals, although that is what Wagner made it.

Attorney General

Other than the governor, the attorney general has the most important duties of any elected executive official in the state. However, not until 1978 did the people elect a governor who had served as attorney general. In twelve of the thirty-four general elections, the electorate has split the positions of governor and attorney general between two political parties. Republicans were shut out of the office for nineteen consecutive elections from 1894 to Bob List's election in 1970. In recent decades the voters seemed less interested in the party label. In six straight elections (1966–86), the electorate provided the governor with someone of the rival party as chief legal adviser.

The attorney general oversees a large number of deputies, most of whom are assigned as counsel to state agencies, departments, and divisions. The chief deputy attorney supervises the other deputies on a day-to-day basis. In 1982 the voters approved the creation of a consumer advocate position to represent the people before the Public Service Commission. Since that time, a consumer advocate who is appointed by the governor has represented the general public, while a deputy attorney general appointed by the attorney general has advised the commission.

How strongly the attorney general acts in the area of consumer protection depends on the priorities of the individuals who hold the office. Recent attorneys general—Bryan, Brian McKay, and Del Papa—have strongly supported consumer protection. In the area of protection of the environment, Del Papa went beyond her predecessors and joined as a friend of the court on the side of the Sierra Club in a federal case. Her action angered the mining industry, which believed that she should not have involved the state in the case. The office also represents the state in cases heard before the Nevada Supreme Court and the U.S. Supreme Court. Normally the attorney general will not personally argue such cases unless they are high-profile cases.

The attorney general writes advisory legal opinions at the request of other executive officials or agency heads. A governor of the opposite party from the attorney general may use such advisory opinions sparingly or may choose to ignore them, as they do not have the force of law. In 1994 Attorney General Del Papa's advisory opinion concerning the powers of the Commission on Judicial Discipline vis-à-vis the state supreme court was repudiated by the supreme court itself.

The attorney general has supervisory powers over the county district attorneys and may, in extreme cases, take over the duties of a county district attorney when the latter has been derelict. The attorney general is also constitutionally a member of the Boards of Examiners, Pardons, and Prison Commissioners as well as several other boards and commissions established by law.

Secretary of State

Historically, the public has tended to view the secretary of state as nonpartisan. The last defeat of a sitting secretary of state at the polls occurred in 1910. Democrats held the office for the next eighty years, with only four individuals serving during that period. John Koontz won election seven straight times and provided a historical perspective on the Boards of Examiners, Pardons, and Prison Commissioners from 1946 to 1974.

Perhaps the mainly ministerial duties account for the routine reelection of the secretaries of state during those eighty years. In addition to keeping records of official acts of the legislature and the executive departments, the office issues charters of incorporation to businesses that qualify under state law, regulates securities issued by Nevada-based corporations, and compiles and publishes official election results.

The elections of Del Papa in 1986 and Cheryl Lau in 1990 as secretary of state changed the public perception of the office. Del Papa was a political activist who had served on the staffs of U.S. senators Alan Bible and Howard Cannon in Washington and had been an elected university regent. Her lobbying was the key factor in the passage of the motor-voter bill. Lau was also active in politics and had a high-profile position at the 1992 Republican National Convention. She supported a Democratic postcard registration bill that was enacted by the 1991 legislature. After Lau gave up the position to run for governor in 1994, Republican assemblyman Dean Heller carried all 17 counties in a landslide election to the office. At the 1995 legislative session, Heller's strong effort to reduce the threshold for reporting campaign donations from $500 to $100 failed.

Treasurer and Controller

The public still views the state treasurer and controller as nonpolitical. The treasurer is the official receiver and disburser of state funds. While most of the staff is engaged in routine duties, the most important discretionary responsibility of the office is the investment of state monies deposited in the state treasury. A treasurer's performance may well be measured by how well she or he handled the state's investment portfolio.

The controller performs the state's bookkeeping function. State monies are disbursed by the state treasurer on the basis of warrants issued by the controller. The offices of controller and treasurer receive little media attention during an election.

CONCLUSION

Taken as a whole, the governors during the last half of the twentieth century could be classified as conservatives on fiscal matters and moderates on social issues, making them mainstream Nevadans in both areas, according to recent polls.

During the first half of Nevada's existence, a strong governor was probably not a necessity in the nation's least populated state. However, legalization of gambling in the 1930s and the large population increases following the Second World War have made strong executive leadership an imperative. The early twenty-first century promises to be a volatile time for Nevada economically. Governors need to think in terms of long-range policies and should use their influence as head of state to educate the people about the critical issues facing Nevada.

Many political scientists argue that the single executive, such as the president of the United States, is superior to the plural executive that is present in almost all states. The former system does concentrate responsibility in one person. However, in Nevada, the people have usually concentrated praise or blame on the governor even though there are other elected executive officials over which the governor has little control.

The greater danger of the plural executive system is the election of an attorney general or a lieutenant governor of the opposite party who constantly opposes the governor openly. That situation might cripple the chief executive's effectiveness as a leader. Fortunately, this type of partisan clash has not been the norm. Democrats O'Callaghan and Bryan each served with a cooperative Republican attorney general.

A constitutional amendment would be necessary to change the method of selecting any of the elected executive officials. The voters did approve the removal of state superintendent of schools as an elective position in 1956. However, the electorate would probably disapprove any attempt to remove the attorney general and lieutenant governor as elective offices.

Two possible constitutional amendments might gain approval by the voters and would strengthen the hand of the governor. One would provide for the governor and lieutenant governor to run as a single ticket, as is the case in almost half the states. This change would create a team relationship between the two positions and prevent the reoccurrence of the Sawyer-Laxalt and Bryan-Cashell situations in which the two officials were hardly on speaking terms. The other amendment would make the treasurer and controller positions—or a combined position as recommended by state treasurer Bob Seale during the 1994 election campaign—appointive rather than elective. Because most of the duties and responsibilities of these two offices are routine, an appointive system would more likely produce individuals qualified by training and experience to perform these duties. The legislature could decide on the qualifications for the positions.

CHAPTER EIGHT

The State Bureaucracy

When the average person hears the word *bureaucrat*, he or she is likely to think of a nameless person who is paid by the federal, state, or local government to sit behind a desk doing routine, unexciting tasks. Yet individuals in the various government bureaucracies perform vital functions that affect the daily lives of millions of people across the nation. In Nevada, bureaucrats, among other duties, provide the expertise to facilitate the making of the state and local government budgets—both in the executive and legislative branches—to advise the part-time legislators, and to implement and enforce the laws.

Bureaucrats are not confined to the government. Linda and Ken Henderson are young professionals working in Las Vegas. Linda is a loan officer at First Interstate Bank in their headquarters on Paradise Road. Ken is a supervisor in the Department of Motor Vehicles in the state office building on East Sahara Street. Ken and Linda are professionals, but they are also bureaucrats. The term is often used to describe Ken's occupation because he is a state employee, but people do not think of Linda as a bureaucrat because she is in the private sector.

The word *bureaucracy* often has a negative connotation. It is used to imply inefficiency, unresponsiveness, and generally bumbling administration. The term, in its true meaning, should have a neutral connotation. A bureaucracy is an organizational structure that includes specifically defined jobs, a hierarchy with specific lines of authority, and written rules and regulations. A bureaucracy may also be evaluated as efficient or inefficient; it may function well or poorly.

Bureaucracies may be public or private. A large organization must operate through a bureaucratic structure. Bureaucracies include public organizations, such as the Department of Defense and the Nevada Department of Human Resources, but large private organizations, such as General Motors and IBM, also have bureaucratic structures. Church organizations, such as the Roman Catholic Church and the Church of England, and nonprofit organizations, such as the American Red Cross and the Salvation Army, have bureaucratic organizations. In short, positions, organizational charts, rules, and regulations that are found in any large organization comprise its bureaucracy.

In government, a merit or civil service system is usually an integral part of the bureaucratic structure. The term *merit* is used to differentiate a personnel system that attempts to appoint individuals to jobs on the basis of merit (i.e., on the basis of education and experience) from a system that does not. Historically, many governments used patronage rather than merit to appoint individuals to jobs. The reform movement of the late nineteenth century urged the adoption of merit systems.

PERSONNEL ADMINISTRATION IN NEVADA

The Nevada Constitution has little to say about the state's personnel system. Article 5 establishes the governor as the head of the executive branch, identifying him or her as the "supreme executive power of the state." The governor appoints the head of many executive agencies. The constitution also provides for the voters to elect five other executive officials. The state bureaucracy consists essentially of the people who work in the agencies headed by these six officials.

As a small state whose development has come later than in most other states, Nevada created a formal state personnel system comparatively recently with the passage of the Personnel Act of 1953. The act established the Department of Personnel "to provide all citizens a fair and equal opportunity for public service" and "to increase the efficiency and economy of the governmental departments and agencies."[1]

The growth of the state bureaucracy reflects, in part, the rapidly growing state population. As table 10 shows, the number of state employees has grown dramatically in recent decades. Although the growth in state employment since 1957 has been dramatic, it has not been as rapid as the state's population growth; indeed, Nevada still has one of the smallest numbers of state employees even though it ranked thirty-ninth in the nation in population in the 1990 census. In 1989 only two states employed significantly fewer people than Nevada; the state of Wyoming employed only 12,212 and South Dakota employed 12,619.[2]

Table 10: State and Local Employment in Nevada in Selected Years

Year	Full-Time Equivalent Employees (Percent Increase)	
	State	Local
1957	2,151	6,863
1962	3,529 (64.1)	9,840 (43.4)
1967	5,657 (60.3)	15,115 (53.6)
1972	7,920 (40.0)	21,276 (40.8)
1977	10,675 (34.8)	26,255 (23.4)
1982	12,346 (15.7)	34,872 (32.8)
1987	15,275 (23.7)	38,434 (10.2)

Source: U.S. Bureau of the Census, Census of Governments. The census of governments is taken in years ending in 2 and 7.

Table 11: State and Local Employment in Nevada, 1987

	Full-Time Employment Per 10,000 Population	Rank among the States
State	152.6	36
Local	361.7	15
State and Local	514.3	24

Source: U.S. Bureau of the Census, Compendium of Public Employment, 1987 Census of Governments.

Table 12: State Employment by Function in Nevada in 1989

Function	Number of Employees
Higher Education	4,102
Other Education	263
Hospitals	856
Health	556
Social Insurance Administration	1,330
Highways	1,374
Police Protection	352
Corrections	1,785
Natural Resources	866
Judicial and Legislative	278
Finances and Government Administration	1,125
Public Utilities	744
Other	1,471
Total	15,938

Source: U.S. Bureau of the Census, Public Employment in 1989.

Because states vary greatly in population, it is perhaps more accurate to view state and local employment in relation to the number of citizens being served. Table 11 shows that in 1987 Nevada ranked substantially higher in per capita local employment as compared to state employment, indicating that Nevada may provide more of its public services through local governments than most other states.

There is no evidence that Nevada's conservatism has any major effect on the amount of its public employment. Other factors, such as federal mandates and the number of school-age children and senior citizens, probably affect state and local employment more than the general political attitudes of the people.

Table 12 indicates the various areas in which state employees were working in 1989. These figures do not include employees of counties, cities, school districts, and other local governments.

STATE DEPARTMENT OF PERSONNEL

The Department of Personnel is responsible for administering the personnel system for departments throughout the executive branch. The department is headed by a director who is appointed by and serves at the pleasure of the governor. An individual who wants a job in the Department of Highways applies through the Department of Personnel. The department administers examinations and assists in writing position descriptions for every state job. A survey by the Council of State Governments reported in 1990 that Nevada had a total of 1,200 different job classifications, including such diverse occupations as accountant, prison guard, secretary, and highway engineer.[3] This number compares with 7,300 in New York and 4,400 in California. Nevada's neighboring state of Arizona had 1,450 classifications and Utah had 2,100.

The Department of Personnel also administers the state's affirmative action program through its Equal Employment Opportunity section. This program is designed to encourage the recruitment and promotion of women and minorities in state employment. In 1991 the ethnic breakdown of all Nevada state employees (with figures for the percentage of the total state population in 1990 given in parentheses) was as follows: White, 86 percent (78.2 percent); Black, 5 percent (6.6 percent); Hispanic, 5 percent (10.4 percent); Asian/Pacific, 2 percent (3.2 percent); and American Indian, 2 percent (1.6 percent).[4] Department of Personnel data show that minority hiring has been stable through the last four administrations, with the percentage being 13 percent during the O'Callaghan and List administrations and 14 percent during the Bryan and Miller administrations (through 1990).[5]

Two issues have been raised concerning the state's affirmative action program. First, there is disagreement as to whether the program should be located administratively within the Department of Personnel. Some affirmative action advocates urge that the program's director should report directly to the governor. Second, the goal of the state to "promote from within" often conflicts with its affirmative action goals. Governor Miller has urged state agencies to recruit more broadly for staff, but the state's largest employee organization, the State of Nevada Employees Association (SNEA), advocates promotion from within.

PUBLIC EMPLOYEE UNIONS

In recent years public employee unions have grown in size and activity. Government employees have been joining unions for over a century. The National Association of Letter Carriers, the International Association of Fire Fighters, and various police associations were established in the nineteenth century. The National Federation of Federal Employees and the American Federation of Government Employees were founded in the twentieth century. In the states, the American Federation of State, County, and Municipal Employees (AFSCME), founded in 1936, has become the largest public employee union. The National Education Association and the American Federation of Teachers represent large numbers of public employees in education, most of whom work for local school districts.[6]

Public employee unions operate somewhat differently from unions representing private sector employees. First, public employees are both workers and voters. Thus, the employees have the opportunity at the ballot box to help select the people with whom they will be negotiating—a situation that does not exist in the private sector. Second, many public employees do not have the right to strike—a situation that changes the manner in which the employees engage in collective bargaining. Third, public employee bargaining takes place under the close scrutiny of the media and the public. The process takes place in what might be compared to a fishbowl because of the great public interest in the salaries and benefits accorded to teachers, police, firefighters, and other public employees.

In Nevada, SNEA, established in 1954, counts about half of the state government's employees among its members. Some might argue that SNEA is not technically a union because it is not engaged in collective bargaining with the state; furthermore, SNEA recognizes that Nevada's employees do not have the legal right to strike. It does, however, perform many functions of a union.

SNEA performs four major services for state employees. First, it engages in informal negotiation and discussions with state budget officials concerning salary and benefit issues. Before each session of the legislature, SNEA officials meet with the governor's budget staff to attempt to gain inclusion of the best possible compensation package in the governor's budget proposal to the legislature. Prior to the 1983 legislative session, for example, SNEA representatives realized that the 1982 recession had caused serious problems for the state budget and that there would be little, if any, money for salary increases. Therefore, they worked out an agreement with Governor Bryan in which they accepted a budget with no salary increases in return for the governor's promise not to solve the state's budget crisis by laying off state employees. The willingness of SNEA's leaders to enter into such an agreement did not please all of its members, but the bargain was probably in the best interest of the state and those employees who might otherwise have lost their jobs. SNEA was not willing to consider a similar arrangement in 1991; subsequently, in January 1992 Governor Miller laid off 266 state workers.

A second function performed by SNEA is the representation of state employees in hearings involving termination, discipline, or grievances. The organization provides a representative to accompany employees to such hearings upon request.

Third, SNEA endorses candidates for public office, especially for the legislature. The organization interviews candidates during the campaign and supports those who seem most sympathetic to its concerns. Other public employee organizations, such as the Nevada State Education Association and the Service Employees International Union (SEIU), also engage in this activity. A candidate who gains the endorsement of such groups can count on a bloc of votes—and perhaps financial contributions and campaign workers as well.

Finally, SNEA lobbies the legislature very aggressively during the legislative session. The compensation package for state employees is usually the organization's first priority in lobbying, but it also gets involved in other bills of concern to its members. For example, SNEA usually opposes efforts to contract out state services to private businesses for fear that some state employees might lose their jobs.

State law enforcement officers, university faculty, social workers, and other workers employed by the state also have organizations that work on their behalf. None of them, however, is as large or as broadly based as the State of Nevada Employees Association.

THE STATE RETIREMENT SYSTEM

One benefit the state provides for its employees is an excellent retirement system administered by the Public Employees Retirement Board, which consists of seven members who are appointed by the governor and serve staggered four-year terms.[7] The Public Employees Retirement System (PERS) is financed from employer contributions, employee contributions, and investment income. The state now pays the full retirement contribution for most state employees. In 1995 PERS administrators estimated that 84 percent of each retiree's pension came from investment income.

The state retirement program is not just a single system. Most state employees are part of PERS and are vested after five years of service. The amount of the retirement benefit is based on 2 1/2 percent per year of service and the average annual salary of the highest thirty-six consecutive months. The full benefit is payable at age sixty or after thirty years of service. A person whose average salary was $40,000 and who had served for thirty years would receive a retirement benefit of $30,000.

PERS personnel also administer the retirement fund for police and firefighters. Because of the stress and higher level of risk of these occupations, participants in this fund can retire after twenty years of service at age fifty with full benefits.

ADMINISTRATORS AS POLICYMAKERS

In a democracy, it is assumed that public policy is made by officials elected by the public. In reality, many of the people who compose the public bureaucracy also are involved in policymaking. Such involvement does not mean that something wrong or illegal is occurring. Permanent professional staff members of state agencies have an appropriate role to play as policymakers, and this role is performed in several different ways. Public employees become policymakers because of at least four characteristics that they possess—expertise, experience, institutional memory, and political insulation.

Many state employees are experts in a professional field. To cite a few examples, some have been educated as civil engineers, accountants, mental health professionals, and law enforcement officers. These professionals know their particular fields far better than the legislature or the governor; this knowledge gives them influence on policy at both the lawmaking and the law implementation stages. When the governor or a legislator recommends legislation, it is common for the relevant committee to ask staff members in the agencies involved to comment and make suggestions about the proposed law.

Professional staff members also influence policy by the manner in which they implement policy. The legislature often enacts laws containing general language with the intention of leaving staff members some discretion in implementation. Legislation may be written to require only that implementation be "reasonable" or "fair" or "rational"—thus leaving it to professional administrators to interpret the meaning of the terms.

Because Nevada had a relatively small population during its first hundred years and was influenced by a relaxed western frontier mentality, many agencies do not have extensive records, statistics, and historical documents that describe how they operated in the past. In such cases, state officials and legislators often rely on the memories of those who have worked in an agency for a long time. These individuals provide what is called the agency's "institutional memory."

Finally, professional staff members are often influential because they have the advantage of political insulation. Governors, legislators, and other elected officials are never anxious to make unpopular decisions, such as the enactment of new taxes. In some cases, however, laws can be enacted with sufficiently general language so that the hard decisions are left up to professional staff members. Examples of such cases are the determination of who qualifies for probation or parole and who is eligible to receive workers' compensation, unemployment compensation, or welfare payments. It is better that these decisions be made by individuals who do not have to stand for election every two or four years.

THE BUREAUCRACY AND "PICKET FENCE" FEDERALISM

Federalism has sometimes been compared with a layer cake, with the three layers representing the national, state, and local governments. Deil Wright and Terry Sanford, former governor of North Carolina, have suggested that federalism now resembles a picket fence.[8] In their metaphor, each vertical stake in the fence represents a single governmental function (e.g., education, law enforcement, and welfare). The top portion of the stake represents the federal government, the middle portion represents the states, and the lower part represents the local governments.

The point that Wright and Sanford make is that in a federal system, close working arrangements develop among specialists in a given field even though they work for different governments. The professional employee in the Nevada Department of Education gets to know people in the local school districts and also becomes familiar with officials at the U.S. Department of

Education in Washington or at the regional offices. Thus, such an employee may become better acquainted with counterparts in local and federal agencies than with the professional staff people in other state agencies, such as highways. The picket fence symbolizes this relationship.

THE BUREAUCRACY AND PUBLIC ACCOUNTABILITY

If the state's professional staff (i.e., its bureaucracy) influences public policy, then there should be ways to ensure its public accountability. How can voters and taxpayers be sure that their government is doing what they want it to do? The public can hold the governor, state legislators, and other elected officials accountable by the threat of "throwing the rascals out" at the next election. In addition to the regular election process, the Nevada Constitution provides an additional method by which irate citizens can recall an elected official during his or her term of office, as explained in chapter 5.

Regular full-time state employees, however, are not elected and are not subject to recall. How are they held accountable? First, the professional staff employees are responsible to elected officials. Whereas staff members bring experience and expertise to bear in making recommendations to the governor, legislators, or the attorney general, the individual elected official involved is responsible for the ultimate decisions. The merit system also ensures a certain amount of accountability, as it should prevent incompetents from gaining covered state jobs and should provide for disciplinary action against those who ignore personnel rules or state laws or policies.

The budget process is perhaps the most effective means of ensuring accountability. The governor and legislature decide on the budget and establish the purposes for which the revenues are to be expended. The state bureaucrats must function within those budget policy guidelines; otherwise, they are subject to severe discipline and possibly removal from their posts.

Legislative oversight is also an effective—although sometimes controversial—means of attaining bureaucratic accountability. This oversight refers to the process whereby legislators attempt to monitor state agencies to be sure they are implementing state laws and policies in accordance with legislative intent. Legislative oversight is accomplished in a variety of ways, including committee hearings, the budget review process, and periodic audits by the legislative auditor's office.

The legislative oversight process is sometimes controversial because of conflict with the activities and responsibilities of the governor. Most state agencies are part of the executive branch of government and are under the direction of the governor or one of the other elected executive officials. The governor might be upset if legislators, especially of the opposite party, appear to be interfering too much with the administration of executive agencies. In 1975 Governor Mike O'Callaghan, who was quick to respond to what he considered to be unfair attacks on his administrators, was angered when certain legislators were thinking of introducing a bill that would have given the legislature more specific oversight powers. A decade later the 1985 and 1987 legislatures did propose a constitutional amendment that would have authorized the legislature to review administrative regulations, but a slight majority of the voters in the 1988 election rejected the amendment. Nevertheless, legislative as well as executive oversight continues to be important in assuring the accountability of the bureaucracy.

Finally, another way to assure that state employees reflect the public's preferences is to see that they are a cross section of the public at large. If state employees come from all areas of the state, they will be more likely to reflect the attitudes and interests of this cross section. It is also important that the gender and ethnic mix of the state's bureaucracy reflect the mosaic of the state's population. Through its statewide recruiting activities and affirmative action program, the Nevada Department of Personnel attempts to assure that the bureaucracy is reflective of the state's citizenry.

Assuring that a public bureaucracy is responsible is a never-ending process. Public employees will sometimes confuse their private interests with the public interest. They may seek additional staff or dollars for their agency in the name of better public service, although their main motivation is power and status. Their efforts to protect their employees from interference by politicians may make it more difficult to remove truly incompetent employees. They may present a variety of reasons for opposing privatization of government services without mentioning that their real motivation is to protect public jobs.

Public employees, though not directly elected themselves, will often respond to pressure from an elected executive official, legislators, the press, and the public. Given an economic system that emphasizes the pursuit of self-interest and the Nevada political culture that strongly embraces individualism, it is not surprising that public bureaucrats sometimes place their private interests above the public interest. In the case of Linda and Ken, mentioned at the beginning of the chapter, the profit motive and the bottom line will help provide a discipline for Linda because she is in the private sector. The types of checks and balances on the bureaucracy discussed above help to assure that Ken is responsible to the public he serves.

An alert press and a well-informed public that is capable of occasionally becoming outraged are also important factors in keeping the bureaucracy accountable. Although the figures noted above suggest that Nevada's conservatism and individualism do not seem to have a major effect on the number of public employees in the state, these characteristics may cause the state's citizens to be particularly vigilant and skeptical in viewing the activities of their public servants.

PRIVATIZATION

Some observers of state government believe that money could be saved and services provided more efficiently if the state turned some functions over to private business. Privatization is controversial, and there are good arguments on both sides. Advocates argue that private managers will be more efficient and that requirements for bidding and the competition of the market place will keep costs down. They suggest that administration that is free from the rules, regulations, and red tape of the state can operate more effectively. On the other hand, critics are concerned that profits can become more important than service and that private managers may not be as responsive to the policy preferences of the public. Public employee unions tend to oppose such efforts as a threat to the jobs of public employees, even though when private administrators take over, they sometimes hire the employees who have been providing a service.

The privatization movement, ironically, has created the need for a new class of public administrators. Governments that privatize services need administrators who know how to set the price level on services, negotiate contracts, monitor contracts, and serve as a liaison between the public and private sectors.

In 1991 the privatization issue arose when the Las Vegas Chamber of Commerce debated a broad-based business tax to provide the state with additional revenue. A majority of the members supported an effort to lobby the legislature to enact such a tax. However, a minority of the members—mainly those representing small businesses—opposed the effort and argued that the privatization of more state functions would eliminate the need for more state revenue.

Prison administration, public works, and waste disposal are three areas in which several states have experimented with privatization. In a May 1991 editorial, the *Las Vegas Review-Journal* urged state and local governments to consider experimenting with the privatization of state parks, school bus systems, school lunch programs, and motor vehicle registrations.[9] Governor

Bob Miller has indicated a willingness to consider private administration of prisons.

Some private administration already occurs in the state. Food service on both of the university campuses is provided by private companies that bid for the right to the business. In Clark County, the county commission contracts with a private management firm to administer the county-owned hospital, and the private security forces employed by major hotels and casinos supplement the law-enforcement efforts of the police departments in Reno and Las Vegas. When the Thomas and Mack Center and the Lawlor Events Center were built on the two university campuses, the Board of Regents initially gave serious consideration to having private firms manage the facilities before ultimately deciding to retain control.

It is likely that students of state bureaucracies will continue to see privatization as one alternative to increases in the size of state government. It is unlikely, however, that this will prove to be a panacea for state problems.

CONCLUSION

Bureaucracies will continue to grow in states, such as Nevada, with a fast-growing population. These states will then face the problem—as they have in the past—of how best to assure that state professionals and other employees are competent, efficient, and responsive to the demands of citizens. The issues of budget stringency, accountability, and privatization will continue to be major personnel policy issues in Nevada.

The financial downturn of the early 1990s caused the state to face the problems of serious budget shortfalls and personnel reductions for only the second time since World War II. The budgetary problems make it difficult for states to retain employees and find revenues for increases in salaries and benefits. These problems also cause the public, faced with possible tax increases, to focus attention on public programs and employees. Accountability has become an important concept in government, as the public demands that public employees be held responsible for efficient and effective job performance.

The decision of SNEA to affiliate with the AFL-CIO may presage a more militant position by the state employees' organization in the future. The decision in 1993 to have state employees pay a much higher proportion of their dependents' health-care insurance costs also reinforced SNEA's arguments for collective bargaining.

CHAPTER NINE

The Court System

In the 1980s and early 1990s, controversies among members of the Nevada judiciary frequently made the front page of newspapers around the state. Coverage of the personality clashes between justices of the supreme court was a departure from the previously anonymous inner workings of the court. Individualism, the dominant feature of Nevada's political culture, had come to the fore to damage, at least temporarily, the public's respect for the state's highest court.

Clashes between supreme court justices Elmer Gunderson and Noel Manoukian sometimes marred deliberations in the late 1970s and early 1980s. In 1992, three of the five justices went public with their attempt to push Chief Justice John Mowbray, who had become blind, to retire from the court. They complained that Mowbray was not able to carry his share of the court's load. Mowbray resisted, and the feud continued. The chief justice's son finally convinced him not to file for reelection.[1]

In late 1993 and 1994, the state's highest court became involved in a dispute over the powers of the state Commission on Judicial Discipline. Charges filed with the commission against Washoe County district judge Jerry Whitehead were leaked to the press, which had a field day covering statements issued by the attorney general, individual members of the supreme court, and Whitehead's attorney. Two of the five justices recused themselves from the case—one voluntarily and one under duress. The temporarily reconstituted supreme court then ruled that it had the authority to decide whether the commission could investigate the charges against Judge Whitehead.

Despite this publicity, which had a negative impact on the court's public image, the legal community still generally respects the supreme court for the quality of its decisions. The disputes did raise again the question of how judges should be selected.

JUDICIAL REVIEW

Acceptance of the concept of judicial review is perhaps the main reason why the American judiciary is a more powerful branch of government than in most democratic countries. The origins of the doctrine that judges may declare actions of the legislative and executive branches unconstitutional go back at least to the early seventeenth century and to the writings of Sir Edward Coke, the English barrister. The judges who incorporated the English common law into colonial and early state governments were influenced by Coke's writings.[2] As one scholar has noted, the judges "of the Founding Era" seemed to have accepted the concept "so fully that it was taken for granted."[3] Prior to the Constitutional Convention of 1787, state courts in New Jersey, Virginia, New York, and Massachusetts had struck down certain enactments of their legislature as unconstitutional.[4]

Alexander Hamilton endorsed judicial review in the *Federalist* (no. 78), but the U.S. Constitution of 1787 did not mention such a power. Chief Justice John Marshall, who shared Hamilton's conservative political views, set the official precedent for judicial review in the famous *Marbury v. Madison* (1803) decision of the U.S. Supreme Court.[5]

All state judiciaries exercise the power to declare acts of the other two branches unconstitutional. This power has become an important part of the checks and balances system of the states as well as that of the federal government. However, Nevada's supreme court has used the power sparingly, in part because the attorney general frequently issues advisory opinions on the constitutionality of certain acts of the legislature or executive. The various state courts have also declared actions unconstitutional on the basis of a conflict with U.S. Supreme Court decisions and the U.S. Constitution.

STRUCTURE OF THE COURT SYSTEM

State courts operate separately from the federal courts. A case can start in a federal court or be appealed to one only if a question of federal law is involved. Well over 95 percent of the court cases in the United States begin and end in state courts.

The court of last resort in Nevada is the supreme court. As of 1995, Nevada was one of only eleven states that did not have an intermediate appeals court or courts between the trial courts and the highest court in the state.[6] Until the population booms after World War II, Nevada's supreme court had been able to handle the appeals from the lower courts without difficulty. However, by 1990 the number of cases filed in the state's only appeals court had increased by almost 2000 percent over the number of 1955 filings. Six legislatures proposed a constitutional amendment to create an intermediate criminal appeals court between 1969 and 1991, but the voters turned down the amendment in 1972, 1980, and 1992. Thus, as of 1995, the Nevada court system consisted of the supreme court, district and family courts, and the justice and municipal courts.

The supreme court has responded to the huge workload by disposing of most cases without hearing an oral argument. Of the 1,057 cases disposed of by the court in 1990, only 162 involved a written opinion following a hearing in the judicial chambers. The other cases are decided on the basis of written briefs presented by the two sides.

SELECTION AND REMOVAL OF JUDGES

In the 1830s Alexis de Tocqueville wrote in his brilliant analysis of American society, "If I were asked where I place the American aristocracy, I should reply without hesitation that it is not composed of the rich, who are united together by no common tie, but that it occupies the judicial bench and bar."[7] In making this statement, Tocqueville was thinking of the lifetime appointment of the federal judiciary and its power of judicial review. Having been born into an aristocratic family in France, he was appalled at the tendency of some of the newer states in the Union to elect judges to fairly short terms of office and predicted that "these innovations" would "sooner or later" have "fatal consequences" for the republic.[8]

The framers of the Nevada Constitution were probably not acquainted with Tocqueville's observations when it came to the judicial article; they were more concerned with the charges of fraud and bribery against the territorial judges. The fact that these judges had been appointed and not elected was not lost on the drafters of Nevada's fundamental law. Not only were Nevada's judges elected from the time of statehood, but they ran as members of a political party until a 1915 law made all judicial officers nonpartisan.[9]

Election versus Appointment

Nevada is among the minority of states that still elect all their judges. Eleanore Bushnell, among many scholars, has argued for the superiority of judicial appointment over the election of judges. She contends that some persons who would make effective judges may not have the personality to campaign successfully for the office. She adds that a judge "must be able, when necessary, to make a widely unpopular decision without jeopardizing his (or her) future on the bench."[10]

Seventeen states have adopted a modified Missouri Plan in order to combine appointment with approval by the people. Under this system, a judge is first appointed by the governor from a list submitted by a commission; thereafter, at the end of each term, the judge runs unopposed in an election in which the people vote on whether to retain the incumbent for another term.

The proposed omnibus judicial amendment that was rejected by the electorate in 1972 contained a modified Missouri Plan. State Senator William Raggio continued to press for adoption of the plan, and the 1985 and 1987 legislatures approved another constitutional amendment and placed it on the ballot for ratification. Only 44.4 percent of the voters approved the Missouri Plan amendment at the 1988 election, showing that the electorate was still unwilling to give up the power to elect judges in the first instance. A 1989 survey conducted by Michael Bowers showed that 76 percent of the members of the Nevada Bar Association favored a merit system for selecting members of the supreme court and district courts.[11]

The Missouri Plan may not be dead in Nevada, in part because the 1992 television campaigns of two Clark County district judges, Miriam Shearing and Charles Thompson, to replace the retiring Mowbray on the supreme court did not reflect well on the judicial system. After the election, the two judges apologized to the public for what Shearing characterized as an "incredibly nasty and rancorous" campaign, and they were both admonished by the Commission on Judicial Discipline for the "tone and conduct" of the campaign. Shearing became the first woman elected to the state's highest court, with 42.7 percent of the vote to 39.5 percent for Thompson. Perhaps a significant number of the 17.8 percent who voted for "none of these candidates" were indicating their displeasure with the campaigns of both candidates.

Although all state and local judges are still elected in Nevada, judges are often appointed to fill vacancies. They then run for election, often unopposed, when their term expires. All eight justices who sat on the supreme court from 1957 through 1970 had first been appointed by the governor to fill vacancies. However, from 1970 to 1994, five of the seven justices gained their seats through election. Incumbent justices seldom lose when running for reelection. Since the change to nonpartisan elections in 1915, 95 percent of the incumbents who ran for reelection to the state's highest court were victorious, and 72 percent of those were unopposed. Thus, the election process does not ensure the people a choice in judicial races.

Prior to the 1976 constitutional amendment, the governor had the sole power to fill a vacancy on the supreme court or a district court. The 1976 amendment established a Judicial Selection Commission, made up of a member of the supreme court, three members of the State Bar of Nevada, and three nonlawyers appointed by the governor.

In order to fill a vacancy on the supreme court, the governor must choose from among three nominees recommended by the selection commission. For a district court vacancy, an expanded commission that includes a member of the State Bar of Nevada and a nonlawyer—both of whom must be residents of the judicial district involved—recommends three names to the governor. Vacancies in justice courts are filled by the relevant board of county commissioners, and a municipal judge vacancy is filled according to the city charter.

Removal of Judges

The original state constitution provided two methods for removing a supreme court justice or a district judge during a term of office: impeachment and removal "for cause" by the legislature. All of the states except Oregon use impeachment as a method of removal. The Nevada Constitution states that "the governor and the other state and judicial officers, except for justices of the peace, shall be liable to impeachment for misdemeanor or malfeasance in office."[12]

Most of the early state constitutions provided for impeachment of executive and judicial officials, and the U.S. Constitution contains similar procedures. The impeachment procedures in the Nevada Constitution are basically similar to the federal procedure. The assembly decides whether to impeach a judge, and the trial on the charges is held in the senate.

As noted above, the delegates at the Constitutional Convention of 1864 were concerned about whether some territorial judges had accepted bribes. Therefore, the delegates added another, quicker way to remove from office a justice of the supreme court or a district judge: "for any reasonable cause" by a two-thirds vote of members elected to each house of the legislature.[13] During the convention, some delegates mentioned the need for such a provision because of the urgency to act quickly in the event that a judge might become mentally incapacitated and refuse to resign.[14] When a case did arise early in the state's history in which a judge was deemed to be insane and was sent to an asylum in California, the legislature was not convened to take action to remove him from office. In a resulting court case, the Nevada Supreme Court stated that impeachment and legislative removal for "cause" were "exclusive" and, therefore, the only two legal ways to remove a judge from office.[15]

This exclusivity of the two original methods of removing a state official or judge from office lasted until 1912, when the electorate approved a constitutional amendment to add recall by the people. Recall is applicable to every elected public official in the state and, therefore, applies to justices of the peace, who were exempted from the original methods of removal.

A fourth method of removal was among the judicial amendments approved by the voters in 1976. The amendment created a Commission on Judicial Discipline with the power to censure, retire, or remove a supreme court justice or district judge. The commission consists of two justices or judges appointed by the supreme court, two members of the State Bar of Nevada appointed by its board of governors, and three nonlawyers appointed by the governor. The commission elects a chairperson from among the nonlawyers. An advantage of the method of removing a judge by action of the Commission on Judicial Discipline is that a judge who is not performing well can be encouraged quietly to retire from the bench without the accompanying publicity that would be involved in the use of the first three methods. The discipline commission has generally been able to operate without much publicity; however, the Whitehead case shattered that privacy.

THE SUPREME COURT

The original constitutional provision for a six-year term for justices of the supreme court has never been changed. The 1976 omnibus judicial amendment provided that when the legislature increases or diminishes the number of justices, it must "provide for the arrangement of their terms so that an equal number of terms, as nearly as may be, expire every 2 years."[16] If the constitutional amendment—proposed by initiative and approved by the voters in 1994—is approved again in 1996, supreme court justices and all other judges in the state would be limited to two terms.

Size

The size of the Nevada Supreme Court was one of the matters debated at the first state constitutional convention in 1863. The key issue was whether there should be three or five justices. One of the arguments in favor of five justices was that it would be more difficult to bribe the larger number. However, James A. Banks, a delegate from Humboldt County, doubted that there were five qualified jurists in the Nevada Territory, arguing, "For if we have five, in all probability there will be one or two blockheads among them, while if the selection is confined to three, there will be a greater probability of our securing not only a pure but an able Supreme judiciary."[17] The delegates finally agreed on a compromise, with the constitution providing for a three-justice supreme court along with a proviso allowing the legislature to increase the number to five without a constitutional amendment.

The supreme court functioned for over one hundred years with only three members until the 1967 legislature took advantage of the power to add two justices. One of the five judicial amendments approved by the voters in 1976 gave considerable latitude to the legislature in determining the size of the supreme court. Section 2 of Article 6 now reads: "The supreme court consists of the chief justice and two or more associate justices, *as may be provided by law*." The legislature now can increase the number of associate justices without limit. In the future, if it increases the size of the court beyond the present five members, the court may sit in panels of three or more justices on certain types of cases, as specified by the legislature. With its heavy caseload, the legislature might consider adding four new justices in the future; the court then could be divided into three panels which could sit at the same time and considerably increase the number of oral arguments heard in the chambers.

Another 1976 amendment allows the supreme court to hear oral arguments outside the state capital. Hence, the court schedules a period of time during each session in which it meets in Las Vegas. This procedure saves time and expense, especially when a large percentage of the court's cases involve parties and witnesses who live in Clark County. Special cases have also been heard in Washoe and other counties.

Selection of the Chief Justice

The constitution states that the "senior justice in commission" shall serve as chief justice.[18] With three justices, the rotation was normally very simple, with the senior justice in commission being the justice who was serving the last two years of the six-year term. The addition of the two justices in 1967 meant that in two of every three elections for the supreme court, there would be two justices with the same date of commission. Although the constitution states that when two justices have the same date of commission, the chief justiceship is decided by lot, in practice the two justices have at times split the two-year chief justiceship into two one-year terms.

In 1992 63 percent of the voters rejected an amendment to allow the justices to select the chief justice. The media gave little attention to the amendment, and some voters may have mistakenly thought that the change would take away the public's power to select the chief justice.

Jurisdiction

The Nevada Supreme Court, similar to its federal counterpart, has both original and appellate jurisdiction. Very few cases actually begin in the state's highest court, although it does have original jurisdiction to issue certain writs.

Almost all of the cases that reach the Nevada Supreme Court come on appeal from one of the state district courts. During recent court sessions, approximately 50 percent of its caseload involved criminal appeals. When the court holds an oral hearing, it normally gives each side in the case fifteen minutes to present its legal arguments. After the hearing, the court holds a conference to enable the justices to exchange their opinions on the case before they vote. More often than not, there will be a unanimous decision, and only one opinion will be written. If one or two justices disagree with the majority's decision on a case, the justice or justices may write a dissenting opinion.

If a justice decides not to sit on a case because of conflict of interest or illness, the chief justice normally asks a retired justice or a district judge to sit with the court for that case. The constitution specifically designates the chief justice as the administrative head of a unified court system; in that capacity, the chief justice may assign district judges, including those who have retired, to sit in other judicial districts when problems arise, such as overload, conflict of interest, or illness.

Federal Constitutional Issues

The U.S. Constitution declares that state judges are bound by the federal Constitution and the laws made thereunder. However, the Tenth Amendment's provision that "the powers not delegated to the United States by the Constitution, nor prohibited by it to the states, are reserved to the states respectively, or to the people" has left some leeway for judges supporting states' rights to disagree with judges who stress national supremacy.

One of the most controversial decisions of the U.S. Supreme Court in the last thirty years was *Miranda v. Arizona* (1966).[19] A few months after the landmark decision regarding defendants' rights, a conference of Nevada and Utah judges was held in Las Vegas to discuss the implications of the decision. Given the conservative and states' rights political attitudes that prevailed in the two states, similar responses could have been expected from the two delegations. The justices of Utah's supreme court were outspoken in opposition to the decision; all stated that they would not apply it and that the U.S. Supreme Court could overrule them if it wished. However, the Nevada justices—all of whom had been originally appointed to the supreme court by Governor Sawyer, an ardent supporter of civil rights—stated just as strongly that state judges were bound to enforce the decision.

Two recent decisions of Nevada's highest court involving interpretations of the state and federal constitutions received national attention. In 1977, after investigating the basketball program at the University of Nevada, Las Vegas (UNLV), the National Collegiate Athletic Association (NCAA) ordered UNLV to suspend basketball coach Jerry Tarkanian for a year. Tarkanian then brought suit against the NCAA, claiming that he had been denied due process. A district judge ruled in Tarkanian's favor, and the state supreme court unanimously agreed, stating the "action of NCAA, requiring state university to suspend basketball coach, was discipline of state university employee, and therefore exercise of traditionally exclusive prerogative of state, and thus constituted 'state action' for purposes of due process analysis."[20] The NCAA appealed to the U.S. Supreme Court, which overruled the Nevada court in a 5-4 decision.

The Nevada Supreme Court's decision in the Tarkanian case was based on the state constitution's Declaration of Rights rather than on the Bill of Rights of the U.S. Constitution. The state's highest court has not been among the state courts to assert the "new judicial federalism." However, as John Kincaid has written, "to the extent that rights were protected in the United States from 1776 to 1925 (150 years), they were protected almost entirely under the state bills of rights."[21]

In 1992 a former law professor and a political science professor petitioned the state supreme court to issue a *writ of mandamus* to order the secretary of state to remove from the ballot an initiative that would place limits on the number of terms a U.S. congressman or senator may serve. The professors argued that such a limitation could only be accomplished by amending the

U.S. Constitution and not by actions of individual states. The Nevada Supreme Court voted 3-2 to issue the writ and therefore to remove the initiative from the ballot.[22] Justices Charles Springer and Robert Rose, both former state chairmen of the Democratic party, voted on the majority side. In their dissent, Justice Thomas Steffen, originally appointed to the court by Republican Governor List, and Justice Clifton Young, a former Republican officeholder, agreed that the constitutionality of the initiative was questionable. However, they argued that no harm would be done by allowing the people to express their views on the issue. District Judge Mark Handelsman, sitting in for the ailing Mowbray, cast the deciding vote. In 1994 the court allowed a similar initiative to go on the ballot, despite having questions about the constitutionality of limiting judicial terms.

LOWER COURTS

The state district courts have a six-year term of office and original jurisdiction to grant the same writs as does the supreme court. The constitution also gives district courts original jurisdiction "in all cases excluded by law from the original jurisdiction of justices' courts."[23] The legislature sets the limits on the civil and criminal jurisdictions of the justice courts; the more serious cases must begin in the district courts.

District courts have appellate jurisdiction in cases that begin in the justice and municipal courts. Thus, a person may appeal a misdemeanor conviction from the courts of limited jurisdiction; however, the appellate jurisdiction of the district court is final in such cases.

After her 1985 bill creating a family court was questioned on constitutional grounds, state senator Sue Wagner introduced a constitutional amendment to establish family courts in 1987. The amendment was approved with only one dissenting senate vote in both the 1987 and 1989 sessions and then ratified by the voters by almost a 2-1 margin in 1990.[24]

The family court judges handle child support and custody cases, as well as divorces (if the couple has children), child abuse and neglect cases, underage marriages, and other civil cases involving children. The goal of the new system is to provide a court that will focus on the best interests of the children, as opposed to the previous system in which a child abuse case could be heard in one court, a parental rights termination case in another court, and a dispute over custody in yet a third court—all involving the same child.

The justice and municipal courts are the two courts of limited jurisdiction in Nevada. Justices of the peace are elected to six-year terms by the voters in a township to handle minor civil and criminal cases. Since Nevada is such a large state geographically, the justice courts allow a person to have a hearing closer to home than the county seat.

Much of the work of the justices of the peace involves holding preliminary hearings to determine if there is enough evidence to bind over for trial in the district court those individuals accused of committing a felony. The preliminary hearing is used in over 95 percent of the felony cases in Nevada, with the remainder coming to trial through indictment by a county grand jury.

Each incorporated city in Nevada must have a municipal court presided over by a municipal judge. However, in deference to the smaller cities that may not have the finances to support a full-time municipal judge, the legislature has provided that the justice of the peace whose territory includes the city may be an *ex officio* municipal judge with the consent of both the county commission and the justice of the peace. Minor traffic cases dominate municipal court dockets, although other misdemeanor violations of city ordinances are heard, too.

APPLICATION OF THE LAW

In state cases involving a question of federal law or a conflict with federal law, the U.S. Constitution is the ultimate authority, followed by the laws passed by Congress that have not been declared unconstitutional by the U.S. Supreme Court. If a federal question is not involved, the highest authority in the state is the Nevada Constitution. If the state constitution does not address the question involved, laws passed by the state legislature are next in the hierarchy of law. County or city ordinances come into play if no higher law is applicable.

If no written law at any level is applicable, a Nevada judge may apply common law. The English common law is used in forty-nine of the fifty states, with Louisiana using a combination of the Napoleonic Code—going back to its French roots—and the common law. English common law goes back to the twelfth century, when kings sent individuals to various parts of the kingdom to decide disputes on the basis of the traditions of the people in the particular area of the country. Later, decisions of previous judges in similar cases were used as bases for the settlement of disputes. A Nevada judge may refer to opinions of previous judges in Nevada or other states to support a decision in a case.

The omnibus judicial amendment ratified in 1978 made it possible for equity cases to originate in a lower court in addition to the district court. The legal concept of equity also originated in England when it was discovered that strict application of common law might not provide justice in a case.

CONCLUSION

In late 1992 the Nevada Supreme Court moved into its new three-story building in the Capitol Complex in Carson City. The new structure, which is more than triple the size of the court's old space, should take care of the court's facility needs well into the twenty-first century. The supreme court now has the space to handle an expansion to nine members and the creation of three panels that could meet in separate chambers. Governor Miller proposed to the 1995 legislature that the number of justices be increased to seven and included funding in the budget for the new positions.

The 1994 election appeared to place the voters on the side of the Commission on Judicial Discipline and the attorney general in their dispute with a majority of the members of the supreme court. They reelected Attorney General Del Papa and Justice Bob Rose, who had recused himself after siding with the judicial discipline commission in the dispute. The voters also supported a legislative proposal to amend the constitution to extend the jurisdiction of the commission and to expand the forms of discipline it may impose.

CHAPTER TEN

Political Parties, Elections, and Interest Groups

Throughout Nevada's history, political parties (including the political leaders and machines), elections, and the dominant interest groups have been intertwined. One reason for the close interaction among these three elements is that Nevada's politics is conducted on a personal basis. The phenomenal growth in population may eventually change this personal relationship, but governors and legislators have normally been much more accessible than is true in most states.[1]

POLITICAL PARTIES

In the first three general elections after statehood in the 1860s, all the elected executive officials were members of the Union (Republican) party, and all but two members of the first legislature elected in 1864 carried the Union party label. With the 1870 election of a Democrat as governor, Nevada became a two-party state and has remained so ever since, except for the domination of the Silver party in the 1890s.

Other than the Silver and Populist parties around the turn of the century, the Socialist party, which elected a state senator in 1912 and an assemblyman in 1914, is the only minor party that has elected members to the legislature. However, legislators have been elected as independents, including Douglas Tandy, who served twice as Speaker of the assembly. Emerson Titlow, whose vote allowed the Democrats to organize the state senate in 1965, was the last legislator to be elected as an independent.

A minor party may qualify for the ballot by obtaining the required number of signatures on petitions. It remains on the ballot if one of its candidates received at least three percent of the number of votes cast in the last general election, or if three percent of the registered voters have designated that they are members of the party.[2] In recent decades the Independent American party (1968, 1970, 1974, 1976, 1992, and 1994), and the Libertarian party (1976–94) have qualified for the ballot.

Precinct Meetings and Conventions

Party precinct meetings had their origin in early New England when a small group of community leaders met to choose party nominees to go on the ballot. Throughout the nineteenth century, the common method of nominating party candidates for the general election was through the precinct or "mass" meetings and the county and state party conventions. The party was considered a private group. As V. O. Key pointed out, "it was no more illegal to commit fraud in the party caucus or primary than it would be to do so in the election of officers of a drinking club."[3]

The first attempt to regulate party meetings by law was made by California's legislature in 1886. Wisconsin's legislature enacted the first statewide direct-primary statute in 1903. The move toward nomination by direct vote of the people around the turn of the twentieth century was an outgrowth of the populist movement, which believed that party caucuses and conventions were too easily controlled by bosses and big business. Nevada enacted a direct-primary law in 1909; the state has used the direct primary ever since, with the exception of the 1916 election.

Even with the direct primary, certain political leaders have been able to control the party organization by "packing" the precinct meetings where the initial selections are made for the delegates to the county, state, and national party conventions. Prior to the 1960s, turnout for the precinct meetings was traditionally low in Nevada. Therefore, it was easy for a party boss to get his people to the precinct meetings and to control the election of delegates up the line. Senator Pat McCarran spelled out this process explicitly in a letter to Pete Petersen, who was in charge of the senator's personal organization in Nevada. Anticipating possible opposition in the 1950 Democratic primary from former governor Edward P. Carville and Reno attorney Albert Hilliard, McCarran wrote,

> I think something should be done toward controlling the precincts, one occupied by Carville and the other by Hilliard. I don't want them to get a single delegate out of either of those places. I don't want those birds to have a chance to show their noses in the State Convention, or any of their friends. This can be done if we just get the matter arranged as to a favorable place to hold the mass

meetings and then have our friends so organized that they will fill the places plumb full so that nobody else can get in and then have the motions all ready to put over and adjourn P.D.Q. with all the delegates nominated and elected. It may be necessary to rent five, ten or twenty busses so as to have them loaded up and take them to the respective mass meetings where they can take over. We want to do this thing and do it right.[4]

After the senator's death in 1954, McCarran's people continued to use various tactics to control the precinct meetings and the election of delegates to the county conventions, such as informing only their backers about the location of the homes where the meetings were held. However, in 1958 Grant Sawyer ran against machine politics in his successful gubernatorial campaign and promised reform. The 1960 legislature passed reform laws governing the calling of precinct meetings and the election of delegates to the county and state conventions of the major political parties. Not only were the times and locations of precinct meetings to be publicized, but the election procedures for the members of county and state central committees were specified in the legislation.[5]

Although a political boss is not likely to control precinct meetings in the future, the absence of general citizen interest makes the meetings fair game for control by special interests or party factions. In 1968 anti–Vietnam War Democrats turned out in large enough numbers in Washoe County precincts to get a peace plank in the county platform. The anti–Vietnam War plank, which was a slap at President Lyndon B. Johnson, also was adopted in the closing hours at the Democratic state convention in Reno after many conservative Clark County delegates had left to catch their return flights to Las Vegas. However, the Nevada delegation at the national convention in Chicago—at the behest of Senators Howard Cannon and Alan Bible, strong supporters of President Johnson—renounced the state peace plank by voting overwhelmingly against such a plank in the national party platform.

An example of a party faction that packed the precinct meetings was the group supporting television evangelist Pat Robertson for the Republican nomination for president in 1988. The Robertson supporters, most of whom had never been involved in partisan politics, turned out in large numbers. These Robertson people then elected enough delegates to the county and state conventions that one of their own was elected state chairman at the state convention. This takeover of the party leadership by an evangelical group did not work out well because it alienated many longtime party workers. The chairman was ultimately unseated in midterm by the Republican state central committee. However, the GOP in Nevada is still split between the traditional Republicans and the Christian Right.

The realistic functions of the county and state conventions are to elect the party officers, including the Nevada members of the national committees of the two major parties, and the delegates to the respective national conventions during presidential election years. There was a modification of the latter function in 1976 and 1980 after the 1975 legislature passed a presidential primary law that was repealed six years later. In those two presidential years, the state conventions selected slates of delegates pledged to the various candidates and an uncommitted slate. The vote at the presidential primary determined the number of delegates from each slate that went to the national convention. Every candidate who carried at least five percent of the total vote received at least one delegate.

After the experience of two presidential primaries, in 1984 Nevada returned to selecting delegates to the national conventions by the method in effect prior to 1972. However, now there is a secret ballot at each level (precinct, county convention, and state convention) to determine the delegates to the next level, with presidential preference or uncommitted status being crucial in the process.

ELECTIONS

Nevada voters have usually paid more attention to individuals than to party labels when casting their votes for president, state executive officers, members of Congress, and legislators. From 1932 until recently, the individual candidate who classified himself or herself as a moderately conservative Democrat had some advantage. However, a December 1994 University of Nevada poll showed that Nevadans preferred the Republican party over the Democrats by a three percent margin.[6]

Voter Registration

To vote in Nevada, a person must be a U.S. citizen and at least eighteen years old. A person who registers as having "no preference" or as a member of a minor party cannot vote in a party primary; consequently, until recently over 90 percent of those who registered indicated a preference for one of the two major parties. Table 13 shows that there was an increase in "No preference" and minor party registrations in the 1980s and early 1990s. By 1994 the "No preference" category itself made up 14 percent of the total registrations.

Since the 1930s, Democrats have held a registration edge over Republi-

Table 13: Voter Registration in Presidential Years, 1968–1992

Year	Democrats	Republicans	Misc.+	Total	% Democrat	% of VAP*
1968	111,390	65,302	12,119	188,811	58.9	66.5
1972	133,278	80,199	17,568	231,045	57.6	63.0
1976	149,397	83,474	18,181	250,953	59.5	54.9
1980	158,617	115,182	23,519	297,318	53.3	49.6
1984	184,199	146,553	25,653	356,405	51.7	51.6
1988	209,048	188,571	47,314	444,933	47.0	57.0
1992	295,111	255,897	98,905	649,913	45.4	64.3

+ Includes "No preference" and Independent American and Libertarian parties.

* Voting age population.

Source: Secretary of State Cheryl Lau, Carson City.

cans, with the former reaching a peak of 64 percent of the total registration in 1966. In the late 1970s and the 1980s, the revitalization of the Republican party organization in Clark County and the popularity of President Ronald Reagan and U.S. senator Paul Laxalt led to an increase in the Republican percentage of the state's voting registration. The large number of retirees from southern California with Republican party leanings who migrated to the state in the late 1980s and early 1990s further reduced the Democratic edge to less than 2 percent in 1994.

Registration activities are among the top priorities of both major parties during election years. Also, nonpartisan groups, such as the League of Women Voters, register new voters at shopping malls and at university and college campuses. With the recent growth of in-migration, registration at motor vehicle license offices has expanded the voting rolls.

Even with substantial improvement in the percentage of people registered to vote, the state's percentage was the lowest in the nation from 1976 through 1988. For example, in 1992 79 percent of the registered voters across the country turned out to vote, but the number of registered voters was only 64 percent of those who were eligible to register. The turnout at the polls in Nevada was 50.8 percent of the voting-age population, which was sixth lowest among the fifty states. However, the 1992 turnout was an improvement over 1980 and 1984, when the state ranked next to the last in the nation.

The low registration figures are generally blamed on the relatively high percentage of transient residents in Nevada. The casino industry employs a substantial percentage of the state's workers, many of whom have no roots in the state and are in low-paying jobs with little job security. Thus, there is likely to be a more substantial segment of the population that is not informed or interested in voting than in most other states.

Primary Elections

Similar to most other states, Nevada has a *closed* primary. Only voters who have registered as Democrats or Republicans can vote in that particular party's primary election. Supporters of the closed primary claim that it promotes party responsibility and does not allow "raiding" by voters who are really supporters of the other party. Voters in the eleven states that have an *open* primary can wait until they go to the polls on election day to decide in which party's primary they will vote. Three of those states—Alaska, Louisiana, and Washington—have *blanket open* primaries in which all the parties are on the same ballot and voters can vote, for example, in the Democratic primary for governor, the Republican party for U.S. senator, and the Libertarian party for state attorney general. Supporters claim that the blanket open primary is the most democratic system.

The first Nevada *presidential* primary in 1976 attracted most of the major candidates of both parties, with Governor Jerry Brown and former governor Ronald Reagan of California winning the Democratic and Republican primaries, respectively. However, by the time the 1980 Nevada primary was held in late May, the party nominations of President Jimmy Carter and Reagan had already been decided by earlier primaries, and the frontrunners did not show up in the state. Therefore, the 1981 legislature buried the *presidential* primary with little fanfare.

The 1975 legislature enacted a law that set up a "none of these candidates" ballot option in all statewide elections. Perhaps not wanting to be embarrassed themselves, the option does not apply to state legislative elections. The option received national attention in 1976 when the two candidates for the GOP nomination for Nevada's lone seat in the U.S. House ran behind the votes for "none of these candidates." Voters expressed their unhappiness with the choice they had; however, the live candidate who received the highest number of votes won the primary.

Regulation of Campaign Finance

The 1975 legislature, caught up in the Watergate reform movement, passed legislation mandating disclosure of contributions and limiting campaign spending in Nevada elections. The next year, the U.S. Supreme Court declared that campaign spending limits interfered with the freedom of speech guarantee of the First Amendment.[7] Consequently, the Nevada Supreme Court declared the spending limitation portion of the Nevada law unconstitutional.[8] The 1977 legislature salvaged the sections on campaign contributions and expenditures, although only contributors who gave over $500 had to be disclosed by name. A 1991 law placed caps on donations from both individuals and groups and prohibited a candidate from utilizing unspent campaign funds for personal use.[9]

VOTING BEHAVIOR

From 1912 through 1992, Nevada has been a "bellwether" state in presidential elections. Nevadans supported the national winner in twenty of the twenty-one elections. The only exception was 1976, when the state preferred Gerald Ford to Jimmy Carter.

In accordance with its individualistic culture, presidential candidates have had coattails to carry congressional candidates to victory in Nevada in only a few instances. In 1932 Franklin D. Roosevelt won 69 percent of the vote in Nevada and undoubtedly was a factor in Pat McCarran's close win over Senator Tasker Oddie. Then, in 1952, Dwight Eisenhower's 61 percent of the vote helped Senator George Malone (with 51.7 percent) gain reelection and Cliff Young (with 50.5 percent) defeat incumbent Congressman Walter Baring. President Richard Nixon's landslide (63.7 percent) victory in 1972 was perhaps the most important factor in little-known David Towell's (52 percent) election to the U.S. House of Representatives over James Bilbray. Those who ran well ahead of the presidential candidate of his party to win election to one of the houses of Congress include Alan Bible (1956 and 1968), James Santini (1976 and 1980), Richard Bryan (1988), and Harry Reid (1992).

County Voting Patterns

Sharp differences have developed in the voting patterns of the small rural counties and the large counties of Clark and Washoe in recent elections for the U.S. Senate. Reid carried only two counties—Clark and Mineral—in his 1986 win over Santini; Bryan won only three counties—Clark, Washoe, and Storey—in his 1988 unseating of Senator Chic Hecht; Reid carried only Clark, Washoe, Carson City, and three rural counties in his reelection in 1992; and Bryan won Clark and Washoe Counties, Carson City, and six rural counties in his reelection in 1994. These differences are a departure from the past and can be partially explained by the tendency of the two Democratic candidates to concentrate their campaigning and especially television advertising in the state's two metropolitan areas.

From 1932 to 1982, only one winning U.S. Senate candidate—Howard Cannon in 1958 and 1964—failed to carry a majority of the seventeen counties. Cannon relied heavily on his vote-rich home county of Clark and its strong Democratic vote, as did Bryan and Reid later. Ten counties in the state voted for the winning candidate in over 80 percent of the forty-four presidential, U.S. Senate, and gubernatorial elections held during that fifty-year period. Douglas, the most Republican county, was the only county to support the winning candidate less than 70 percent of the time. In nine of the thirteen presidential, fifteen of the nineteen U.S. Senate, and eleven of the twelve gubernatorial elections during the period, twelve or more of the counties supported the winning candidate. This consensus among the counties is highlighted by sweeps of all seventeen counties by four presidential (1932, 1936, 1972, 1980), one U.S. Senate (1980), and two gubernatorial (1962, 1974) candidates.

In the seven elections from 1982 through 1994, Ronald Reagan and George Bush won all the counties in 1984 and 1988, as did Governors Bryan and Miller in 1986 and 1990. In all four gubernatorial sweeps from 1962 through 1990, a popular incumbent won a second term against weak opposition. In the entire period from 1932 through 1994, Storey (Virginia City) comes closest to being a bellwether county; it supported the winning candidate in 88 percent of the elections for the three positions.

As table 14 indicates, the voting patterns of a majority of the counties changed markedly in the period from 1982 through 1994. The biggest changes in the direction of higher Democratic voting percentages in the ten elections took place in Carson City, Washoe, Lyon, Douglas, and Storey Counties. The largest changes in the direction of lower percentages of Democratic voting were in Lincoln, Elko, Esmeralda, Lander, Eureka, and Nye Counties. The increase in mining activity and the controversy between the mining industry and environmentalists are obvious reasons for the changes in party voting. Recent Democratic candidates have tended to come down on the side of the environment, whereas Republican candidates have been more concerned with promoting mining and protecting cattle ranchers. The five counties in the first group are in or close to the Reno–Lake Tahoe area, where environmentalists are strong. The six counties in the second group depend heavily on mining.

Table 14: Rankings of Counties by Percentage of Democratic Vote in Presidential, U.S. Senate, and Gubernatorial Elections

County	1932–1980 (47)	1982–1944 (12)	Difference
Clark	1	1	0
Lincoln	2	10	−8
Mineral	3	3	0
White Pine	4	4	0
Nye	5	8	−3
Esmeralda	6	13	−7
Storey	7	2	+5
Elko	8	15	−7
Lander	9	14	−5
Humboldt	10	11	−1
Pershing	11	8	+3
Washoe	12	5	+7
Lyon	13	7	+6
Eureka	14	17	−3
Churchill	15	16	−1
Carson City	16	6	+10
Douglas	17	12	+5

Source: Election Returns, Secretary of State, Carson City.

The voting pattern of Nevada counties in presidential elections changed beginning with the 1968 election. Reacting to the antiwar and social protests of the 1960s, conservative Democrats in large numbers joined Republicans in voting against the more liberal Democratic candidates. All seventeen counties have voted for Republican candidates for president in a majority of the seven elections from 1968 through 1992; eleven of those counties went for the GOP in all seven races. Douglas County has voted Republican in every presidential election since 1936, and Lyon County has not voted Democratic since 1940.

In gaining 26 percent of the total vote in 1992, Ross Perot carried Storey County, lost Esmeralda County by one vote to George Bush, and finished second to Bush and ahead of Bill Clinton in five other counties. The independent's presence on the ballot allowed Clinton to win Nevada's four electoral votes, even though the latter carried only Clark and White Pine counties.

In U.S. Senate races from 1932 through 1994, two counties gave the majority of their votes in almost every election to the candidates of one party. In the twenty-four Senate races, Clark gave a majority to only one Republican, Paul Laxalt in 1980. During the same period, Douglas gave a majority to only one Democrat, Howard Cannon in 1976. Eight counties supported GOP candidates in each of the five Senate elections from 1980 through 1992.

Legislative Elections

The state conventions of both major parties have used three caucuses— Clark County, Washoe County, and the fifteen rural counties—to provide geographical representation on national convention delegations and certain state party offices. The same breakdown of voting patterns of the counties in legislative elections from 1932 through 1992 shows sharp differences among the groups.

Clark County elected a majority of Democrats to its assembly delegation in all thirty-two legislative elections during the sixty-two-year period. From 1932 through 1950, Clark elected only one member of the GOP to the assembly, and the highmark of Democratic dominance occurred in 1976 when the party won all twenty-two seats. Following that debacle, the Republicans— led by Senator Laxalt and state chair Frank Fahrenkopf—raised the money to hire a full-time executive director for Clark County. The GOP organization was successful in improving both the recruitment of candidates and the running of the campaigns. By the 1984 election, the Republicans, aided by the popularity of President Reagan and Laxalt, were able to elect eleven of the twenty-four-member Clark County assembly delegation. The GOP surge reawakened Clark County Democrats, who regained a huge 21–3 margin in 1986. By 1994, however, the GOP had increased its percentage of the registration in Clark and picked up six seats to increase its members to eleven in the twenty-six-member county delegation.

During the 1932–92 period, Democrats also won a majority of the Clark County delegation to the senate in every election. Chic Hecht, who served two terms, was the only Republican elected to the upper house between 1932 and 1982. GOP senate candidates participated in the party's revival in the 1980s. Their capture of four of the twelve Clark County seats in the 1987 session, five seats in the 1989 and 1993 sessions, and seven of the county's thirteen seats in the 1995 session allowed the party to gain control of the upper house in those four sessions after twenty-two straight years of Democratic control.

Although Washoe County's population has grown steadily since the 1965 reapportionment, it has not come close to matching the growth of Clark. Thus, the county's representation has gone from twelve members of the assembly and six senators in 1967 to nine members of the lower house and four-senators in the 1995 legislature; in addition, a fifth senate district includes a portion of Washoe County and three other counties. The GOP has an edge in registration in Washoe, but most of its legislative districts are competitive. From 1972 through the 1994 election, the county's voters elected seventy-five Republicans and seventy-two Democrats in legislative races.

From 1932 through 1966, the fifteen smaller counties showed their voting independence. The rurals elected a majority of Democrats to the assembly in every election with the exception of 1950, when they elected fourteen members of each major party. (Many of these legislators were conservative McCarran Democrats.) However, from 1940 through 1964, those same counties elected a majority of Republicans to the senate in every election. The fifteen counties elected slightly more Democrats than Republicans to both houses in the 1970s, but the mining boom and the anti-environmentalist sentiment in many of the counties led to a Republican upsurge in the 1980s. In the legislative elections from 1980 through 1994, the rural counties elected seventy-three Republicans and only twenty-one Democrats to the two houses. In October 1994 the GOP had 54.4 percent of the major party registration in the fifteen counties.

INTEREST GROUPS

During the early years, Nevada politics was dominated by the mining and railroad interests; during the next fifty years, the most influential interests were those connected with the Wingfield, McCarran, and Biltz-Cord machines, which exercised considerable political clout because of the effectiveness of lobbyist John Mueller. In the 1960s, the gaming industry began to operate more responsibly and became the dominant interest group. Then, in the late 1980s and early 1990s, the influence of the Nevada State Education Association with both Governor Bob Miller and the legislature allowed the NSEA to challenge gaming for the position of the most powerful group.

Aiding Political Campaigns

Financial contributions to political campaigns are used by interest groups to gain access and influence at all levels of American politics. In Nevada, the gaming industry has been the major player in making contributions. In some gubernatorial campaigns, gaming has contributed more than half of the funds expended by the candidates. It is common practice for the major hotel-casinos to contribute to both major party candidates in such elections, although the amounts will vary. Gaming also contributes heavily to the campaigns of key legislators.

NSEA and the State of Nevada Employees' Association (SNEA) contribute to legislative candidates who have supported their causes in the past or pledge support in the future. However, the large number of teachers who are willing to campaign door-to-door for endorsed candidates is NSEA's most effective contribution. Having one strong friend in the legislature, especially if that friend has a leadership role on a key committee, can often make the difference between victory and defeat on a critical piece of legislation for an interest group.

Lobbyist John Mueller, a former state engineer, used his knowledge of the politics of the small counties and personal cultivation of the senators representing them to dominate the upper house from the late 1920s until his death in 1962. At that time, each county had one senator, and the fifteen rural counties were in complete control of the senate. Political ally Norman Biltz has described Mueller's relationship with the rural senators: "He was working twenty-four hours a day, thirty days a month, and year after year, giving assistance to these men, whether they were in financial trouble, or mental trouble, or whatever their problems were."[10]

Mueller was respected for his integrity. Contrary to most lobbyists, he did not expend money on the entertainment of senators. In 1954 he stated that he had "never bought a lunch for or spent a dime on a legislator"; yet he was a major player in the legislative process for over thirty years.[11]

Mueller helped in the reelection campaigns of "his" senators.[12] It was not just coincidental that the small counties elected a majority of Republicans to the senate in each election during the last twenty-two years of Mueller's life, while the same counties were electing a majority of Democrats to the assembly.

In the 1970s, Jim Joyce, a former aide to Senator Cannon in Washington, became the most powerful lobbyist in Carson City and retained that position until his untimely death in 1993. Joyce's original power base was his Las Vegas public relations firm, which ran the political campaigns of many of the Democratic legislators.[13] Thus, he had instant access to those legislators when he put on his other hat as a lobbyist.

Lobbying

Because politics inside the legislature is conducted on a very personal basis, it is not surprising that legislators have been friendly toward most lobbyists throughout the state's history. Especially when individual lobbyists have shown that they have integrity and can help furnish information and do favors, they are likely to be treated as old friends. Joyce's strength as a lobbyist was reinforced by his reputation for being honest and straightforward in dealing with legislators and for displaying concern for the best interests of the state as a whole. At every legislative session, Joyce was a voluntary lobbyist for the University of Nevada system or another public cause. He represented a variety of interests, including gaming, and seldom lost a bill for which he lobbied.

Lobbyists use many techniques to influence legislators. In 1971 Faun Dixon conducted a survey of legislators and lobbyists as to what they considered the most effective techniques. The two groups agreed that the four most important techniques were personal presentation of arguments, presenting research results, testifying at hearings, and contact by a constituent.[14] These techniques would still be ranked highly in the 1990s, with perhaps the addition of "contributing work in a political campaign" to the list. Joseph Crowley, who has testified at nine legislative sessions as president of the University of Nevada, Reno, has listed the following words as being important guidelines to effective lobbying: *preparation*, *persistence*, *patience*, *credibility*, and *access*.

Prior to 1979, when the rule was changed, favorite lobbyists often sat on the floor of the chambers with legislators. Because of the general trust that had been established over the years, the legislators were very reluctant to pass any legislation requiring registration and reporting by lobbyists. Finally, the 1973 legislature, under threat of an initiative petition drive by Common Cause, enacted a registration law for lobbyists. A year later, California voters approved an initiative prohibiting expenditures by a lobbyist of more than ten dollars a month on entertainment of each legislator. Fearing that Common Cause might initiate a similar law in Nevada, veteran Nevada lobbyists in 1975 drew up an amendment to the 1973 law providing for the filing of monthly reports by lobbyists during a legislative session. The reports must include the amount of money expended on entertainment, gifts, and loans for legislators.[15] A 1979 amendment requires lobbyists to wear identification badges. By 1995 lobbyists had to list the individual legislators who were recipients and how much was spent on each one. This last requirement seemed to have an effect on some legislators who now decline to accept luncheon and dinner "gifts."[16]

In the 1995 legislative session, 642 lobbyists registered under the 1973 act. A national study in 1991 disclosed that Nevada's legislature was the sixth "most lobbied" state legislature in the nation, with nine lobbyists for every legislator.[17] In addition to those who registered as representatives of private businesses, public employees, and local government entities, some lobbyists were members of public interest groups, such as Common Cause and the Sierra Club, and some were representing only themselves as they attempted to "educate" the legislature on certain issues.

In a survey of members of the 1983 legislature, the interest groups rated "most influential" were two gaming industry groups. The Nevada Resort Association, which represented the large hotel-casinos in Clark County at the time, was ranked first, with the Gaming Industry Association, representing northern Nevada casinos, being a close second.[18] Not surprisingly, the three lobbyists who were considered "most effective" by the legislators during the session—Jim Joyce, Harvey Whittemore, and Sam McMullen—all represented gaming interests.

Ranking third in the survey of influential groups at the 1983 session was the State of Nevada Employees Association (SNEA). However, for eighteen years SNEA failed to gain passage of a collective bargaining bill for state employees before finally succeeding in 1991. Then, Governor Bob Miller vetoed the measure after the legislature had adjourned. Miller had been pressured to use the veto by the American Federation of Labor (AFL), which believed that the bill favored SNEA over other public employees' unions. The 1993 legislature refused to override the veto.

By the 1990s, the ranking of the influential interest groups had changed. As one veteran lobbyist remarked after the adjournment of the 1993 legislature, "The schoolteachers owned the session."[19] At a time when the governor proposed a "hold-the-line" budget after the shortfalls of the previous biennium, the Nevada State Education Association did much better than any other group. John Cummings, executive director of NSEA, led an effective contingent of eleven lobbyists at the session.

The gaming industry was the second most influential group at the 1993 session. Jim Joyce died during the 1993 session, and Harvey Whittemore, a member of the powerful Lionel, Sawyer, and Collins law firm, assumed the mantle of the most effective lobbyist at the 1993 and 1995 sessions. During the 1995 session, Whittemore and Richard Bunker, another gaming lobbyist, were informal advisers to Governor Miller and helped him in the legislature. The NSEA, with a lobbying team that included Whittemore, continued to be a potent force, despite a new Clark County Republican contingent that opposed it on many issues.

Lobbyists who have formerly served in the legislature have obvious advantages of access. In 1995 thirteen former legislators registered as lobbyists, with former Speaker Bob Barengo representing the most clients—twenty.

A close observer of the legislative process in Carson City is likely to be struck by the large number of state agency and department heads who testify and talk to legislators. In many instances, these leaders from the executive branch and the institutions of higher education are asked to testify in order to defend their proposed budgets and legislation. In other instances, these individuals act in the same manner as the lobbyists for private interests in trying to prevent the passage of legislation that they believe to be inimical to their agencies.

Given the legislature's power to enact legislation directly affecting local governments, Clark and Washoe Counties and the cities of Las Vegas and Reno have been represented by full-time lobbyists at recent legislative sessions. Other counties and cities either have part-time lobbyists or are represented by lobbyists for the Nevada Association of Counties or the Nevada League of Cities. Representatives of Clark and Washoe County governments were major figures in the battle between the two entities over the "fair share" division of the state sales tax during the 1991 session.

As most legislators would quickly point out, lobbyists play a vital role in the legislative process. Just as in the case of the individual legislator, an individual lobbyist cannot be effective unless his or her word can be trusted. In an incident that took place in the 1970s, Bob Guinn, a longtime, respected lobbyist for the transportation industry, discovered that he had inadvertently given inaccurate information in testimony before a legislative committee. He did not wait until the next day to act; he tracked down every legislator on the committee the evening of the testimony and corrected the information he had given them. He did not want to lose the reputation he had established for honesty and integrity among the legislators. Thus, while some lobbyists may attempt to mislead the legislators from time to time, such individuals are not likely to be effective in the long run.

CONCLUSION

Continuing explosive population growth—especially in the Las Vegas area—for the foreseeable future will increase candidate reliance on the mass media in future elections. Thus, in high-profile elections, voters will still make decisions based more on individual candidates than on party identification. Recent elections also indicate that instead of a north-south division among voters, the Reno–Carson City metropolitan area may find more common ground on various issues—such as education, crime, welfare, and the environment—with the Las Vegas metropolitan area than with the neighboring rural counties.

Jim Joyce, who can be ranked with Henry M. Yerington, Black Wallace, and John Mueller as one of the greatest lobbyists in Nevada history, is gone. However, because of its sheer size and dominance in the economy of the state, the gaming industry will continue to be a powerful influence in elections and the legislature. Also, for the foreseeable future, the state will need large increases in the number of schoolteachers each year in order to keep pace with population growth and to follow the ongoing directive to decrease class size. These increases will add to the already potent political clout of the NSEA.

CHAPTER ELEVEN

Budgeting and Taxation

Just as certain leaders and interest groups have dominated Nevada politics through most of its history, certain individuals have been key players for long periods in state financing. Howard Barrett was the state budget director from 1960 through 1982, serving two Democratic and two Republican governors. None of the governors had as much influence in determining the budgets of the various agencies during that period as Barrett. Budget directors Bill Bible and Judy Matteucci also wielded considerable power and acted as lightning rods for Governors Bryan and Miller in the twelve years after Barrett's retirement.

Nothing identifies a state's policies and priorities more than its budget. A budget shows where a government wants to spend its money and how it chooses to raise that money (i.e., what taxes it chooses to levy). Although state expenditures tend to rise each year, the rate of growth in spending has varied among the states. From the 1940s to the mid-1970s, state and local spending grew rapidly throughout the nation; however, that growth slowed significantly in the late 1970s.

Following the inflation engendered by federal expenditures for both the Great Society programs and the Vietnam War in the 1960s and early 1970s, taxpayers across the nation were in a mood to oppose additional taxes. As direct protest against federal taxes is difficult, taxpayers directed their frustration at state and local taxation. The protest was most evident in California, where the voters adopted Proposition 13 in 1978. Proposed by popular initiative, the constitutional amendment placed limits on property taxes, but the "message" of lower spending and taxes was heard by political leaders across the nation.

The sharp economic recession of 1981–83 impacted every state budget. Nevada, where many people thought the state was immune to recessions, discovered during the early 1980s that the Silver State, too, was vulnerable to downturns in the business cycle. Following the recovery in 1983, state expenditures in Nevada and most other states resumed their annual growth through the rest of the 1980s.[1] The 1990–91 national recession affected various areas in the country differently; Nevada was still booming in 1990, but the recession hit in 1991, and the drop in state revenues raised havoc with the 1991–93 budget.

Each state budget is unique and reflects the differences in revenue sources. For example, Nevada has no individual or corporate income tax. Nevada relies more heavily than most other states on gaming and sales taxes to support state government.[2]

SALES AND USE TAXES

Most states rely heavily on the sales tax. The tax is relatively easy to administer and collect and produces large amounts of revenue. The use tax is similar to a sales tax, except that it is levied on items purchased outside the state and then brought into the state for use. As a practical matter, the state finds it impossible to collect the tax on most purchases, but it can be enforced on purchases of larger items that must be registered in the state, such as cars, motorcycles, or boats. Some states have tried to pressure mail-order companies to collect the use tax from customers. The sales tax is also attractive because the federal government has refrained from levying it or the value-added tax (VAT), which is widely used in Europe, thus leaving the tax to the states. People pay the tax, for the most part, in small doses—except for "large ticket" items such as cars—and thus prefer it over the property tax that is collected in larger amounts four times a year. Also, the sales tax is more palatable to Nevadans because tourists pay about 28 percent of the tax.

Critics argue that the sales tax is regressive (i.e., lower-income individuals pay a higher portion of their income in sales taxes than do higher-income individuals). In order to partially alleviate this problem, many states, including Nevada, exempt food and prescription drugs from the tax. Most states levy a sales tax only on goods and not on services, such as those rendered by physicians, attorneys, beauticians, and architects. In 1987 the Florida legislature enacted a sales tax on services, but public and business protest caused the legislature to repeal the tax less than six months later. The attempt of Assemblyman Bob Thomas to engender legislative support for a tax on services in Nevada in the early 1980s went nowhere, and a 1988 public opinion poll in the state showed that only 25 percent of the respondents favored a sales tax on services.[3]

Although a majority of states had adopted a general sales tax by the end of World War II, such a tax was not seriously considered in Nevada until 1949. Many legislators believed the new revenue source was needed to supplement gaming and property taxes—especially in view of the need to fund a growing school population—but many of them had also promised to oppose a sales tax in their election campaigns. The 1949 assembly killed the proposed tax by a vote of 22-20.[4] Educators were again thwarted in 1951 and 1953 because Governor Charles Russell had given the people a "no new taxes" pledge during his 1950 campaign. However, a financial crisis in the schools, which led to a special legislative session and a study of school funding by an outside group, resulted in passage of a 2 percent sales and use tax by the 1955 legislature.

The approval by the people of the sales tax referendum in 1956 prevents the legislature from making any changes in the 1955 law. As the needs of education continued to outstrip the revenues in the 1960s, state senator Carl F. Dodge and his study committee came up with the "key to unlock the sales tax."[5] The 1967 legislature passed a 1 percent "school support" tax to be collected at the same time as the general sales tax. After the Nevada Supreme Court upheld the constitutionality of the "school support" tax, Governor Paul Laxalt recommended, and the 1969 legislature passed, an optional one-half percent tax to be used for the "relief" of city and county governments in the counties that decided to add the tax. Thus, in the 1970s, most consumers in Nevada were paying a 3 1/2 percent sales tax, although only 2 percent went into the state general fund.

The electorate made two changes in the sales tax in the 1970s, approving the exemption of prescription drugs in 1970 and food (although not restaurant food) in 1979. State senator Mary Gojack, the main sponsor of the resolution to place the food exemption on the ballot, based her argument on fairness. She was able to show that low-income families paid a much higher percentage of their income on food than did higher-income families.[6] The voters approved of the food exemption by better than a 3-1 margin at a special election in June 1979.

The legislature and Governor Robert List reduced the maximum property tax rate in 1979 and promised further reductions in 1981 in order to convince the people to turn down the controversial constitutional amendment (Question 6, a clone of Califonia's Proposition 13) in 1980. The 1981 legislature adopted List's "tax shift" recommendation, which called for a further reduction of the property tax to be balanced by an increase in the school support tax from 1 to 1 1/2 percent and the addition of a supplemental city-county relief tax of 1 3/4 percent. The basic city-county relief tax of 1/2 percent was restricted to counties having two or more incorporated cities, with the funds going to the cities; the state general sales tax remained the same, because a change would have necessitated a vote of the people. The 1981 legislature also provided another optional 1/4 percent addition to the city-county relief tax to be earmarked for local transportation needs, upon the approval of the voters in the county. After voters in Washoe and Clark Counties had agreed to the optional tax, taxpayers in those counties were effectively paying a 6 percent sales tax. As Glen W. Atkinson and James Newman later wrote: "The combined effects of the 1979 and 1981 packages were detrimental to both local and state governments. These effects were exacerbated by the severity of the national recession which followed and the continuing reduction in federal aid. Sales tax revenues are more sensitive to swings in the business cycle than many other taxes, such as that on real property."[7]

As a result of the depletion of the state treasury during the 1981–83 recession, the 1987 legislature commissioned a study of Nevada's tax system by the Urban Institute and Price Waterhouse. The study showed that "35 percent of the sales tax is paid by Nevada residents in their roles as retail consumers of taxable goods and services, 28 percent of the retail sales tax is directly paid by visitors, and 37 percent is collected from other sources— primarily by business firms in their purchase of taxable items that are used in their operations."[8] The study recommended that the legislature "broaden, on a revenue-neutral basis, the general sales tax base to fully include hotels and lodging, food for home consumption, drugs (prescription), household fuels and other utilities (including telephone service), and services to persons (e.g., dry cleaning, beauty and barber shops) and newspapers." The study estimated that the base of the sales tax would be broadened by about 70 percent by such actions and that the sales tax rate could thus be reduced by over 40 percent. The study also recommended that to offset the regressivity of the sales tax, the legislature enact a "variable vanishing sales tax credit (such as is now used in eight other states) designed to target special tax relief to low-income residents."[9]

The Price Waterhouse study warned that because of a projected shortfall by the mid-1990s, Nevada needed a broader-based tax. However, the leaders of the 1989 legislature stated that the study was published too late for the members to digest it fully. The projected shortfall was already occurring by the time the 1991 legislature convened. Although the Assembly Ways and Means Committee decided to follow the advice of the tax study by proposing a broadening of the tax base to the extent of levying a 6 percent tax on some services, the new levy did not survive in the conference meeting with the Senate Finance Committee.

With the shortfall in revenues, there was no thought of cutting the sales tax as recommended by the tax study; instead, the legislature increased the school-support portion of the state sales tax by 3/4 of one percent in order to decrease the pupil-teacher ratio in the lower elementary grades. The increase brought the total sales tax to 6 3/4 percent in Washoe County and 7 percent in Clark County, which had added another 1/4 of one percent for tourism. (Shortly after the end of the session, the Washoe County Commission announced that another 1/4 of one percent would be needed to help make up for the "fair share" redistribution of the sales tax from Washoe to Clark County.)

Nevada now has one of the highest sales taxes in the nation. In 1991 California raised its state sales tax to 8 percent and thus replaced Connecticut, which lowered its sales tax at the same time that it adopted a state income tax, as the state with the highest levy. Five states still do not levy a sales tax.

TAXES ON GAMBLING

Gaming taxes constitute the major source of revenue to the state general fund in Nevada. The largest of these taxes is the levy on gross gambling receipts, which accounts for between 65 and 70 percent of all state gaming revenue.[10] The tax on gross receipts, first assessed in 1945, began at 1 percent of gross casino receipts or winnings and was increased to 2 percent in 1949. The 1955 legislature made a substantial change in the method of levying the tax, applying a graduated percentage rate from 3 to 5 1/2 percent, and the rate remained the same until the 1981 legislature increased the maximum rate to 5 3/4 percent.[11] In the face of an attempt by Senator Don Mello to increase the rate by 1 percent, the gaming industry agreed at the 1987 legislative session to a 1/4 of one percent increase in each of the next two bienniums. Thus, by 1991 the maximum percentage rate for the casino gross receipts tax was 6 1/4.

Between 1965 and 1979, the second highest gaming tax revenues came from the casino entertainment tax, which the legislature enacted in 1965 to replace the 10 percent federal cabaret tax that was repealed by Congress that year. The tax applies to the sales of food, beverages, admission charges, and any other material during the periods when entertainment is taking place;[12] it is now the third largest source of gaming revenues.

The second highest gaming revenues now come from the $250 annual tax on each slot machine in the state. In 1971 a coordinated effort of a few Nevada legislators, led by longtime assemblyman William Swackhamer, Governor Mike O'Callaghan, and the congressional delegation, persuaded Congress to return 80 percent of the $250 federal slot machine tax to the state, with the understanding that the revenue would be used for education.

The slot machine rebate was revisited later in the 1970s, as athletic boosters at UNLV were looking for funding for a new basketball facility to support the institution's application for membership in the Western Athletic Conference. A resolution was introduced at the 1977 legislature at the behest of the UNLV boosters to earmark an additional 15 percent slot machine rebate to pay for an events center, if the boosters could convince Congress to increase the rebate by that much. The athletic boosters at the University of Nevada, Reno, with the strong support of Don Mello, the chair of the Assembly Ways and Means Committee, convinced the legislature to add an events center at the northern Nevada campus. Fortuitously, Senator Paul Laxalt, a close personal friend of President Reagan, was a member of the Finance Committee of the U.S. Senate, which considered the additional rebate; the committee and the Congress as a whole were willing to go farther than the additional rebate. The federal tax on slot machines was repealed in its entirety in 1978. The 1979 Nevada legislature enacted a replacement $250 tax.

In addition to the above three gaming taxes, which account for well over 90 percent of the state's gambling revenues, a gaming table tax is collected by the state and then distributed equally among the state's seventeen counties. This distribution was enacted by the 1957 legislature after many rural legislators, who held fifteen of the seventeen senate seats at the time, complained that only Washoe and Clark Counties were benefiting financially from legalized gambling in the state. The equal distribution of the tax on gaming tables has been an especially important source of income for the smallest-population counties.

Until 1978 Nevada was the only state receiving tax revenue from casino gambling, although several states received more revenue from gambling because of horse racing. When New Jersey legalized casino gambling, Nevada officials were concerned about its effect on the state's gaming revenues. However, due to construction of several new showplace hotel-casinos on the Las Vegas Strip and in the new boom town of Laughlin along the Colorado River, the gaming revenues have continued to grow.

SELECTIVE TAXES

In contrast to sales taxes that are levied on nearly all retail purchases of goods, selective taxes are levied only on specific items. Such taxes are sometimes called excise taxes; examples are the taxes on motor fuel, liquor, and tobacco. While general sales taxes are generally levied as a percentage of the product's price, selective taxes are often imposed on some other basis, such as a given amount of motor fuel (gallon), per pack (cigarettes), or per pint or liter (liquor).

Advocates justify selective taxes in three ways. First, such taxes tend to provide reliable sources of revenue, even though the amount collected tends to be a small portion of total state revenues. Second, the taxes are sometimes related to a specific use of the funds. Taxes on motor fuel are used to support road construction and repairs and other transportation projects, while tobacco taxes are earmarked in some states for medical research. Finally, some argue that excise taxes should be used to discourage the purchase of certain products, such as liquor and tobacco. A variation of this latter argument is that the use of such products is immoral or unhealthy; therefore, users should be punished through the imposition of a high "sin" tax.

Opponents contend that taxes on liquor and tobacco, similar to the sales tax, are regressive. Critics also argue that many purchasers of liquor and tobacco are addicted to those products and, therefore, should not be taxed for using them.

The tax on motor fuel is viewed by tax experts as one of the fairest taxes, based on the benefit theory of taxation, in that the people who use the roads are paying the taxes for the construction and upkeep of the highways and city streets. All fifty states (as well as the federal government) levy a tax on motor fuel, and almost all earmark the revenues for a special highway fund, as Nevada does. In the 1970s and 1980s highway construction and maintenance suffered in Nevada and many other states because the inflation rate in construction costs exceeded even the high inflation rates that plagued the general economy.

With Nevada roads deteriorating badly by the late 1970s, the 1981 legislature doubled the state motor vehicle fuel tax from six to twelve cents a gallon in a two-step increase. During the 1980s many states increased their motor vehicle fuel taxes, using the argument that higher fuel costs would cause people to conserve fuel and thus make the nation less dependent on imported oil. However, when the 1991 Nevada legislature added five cents to the motor vehicle fuel tax with another two-step increase, the principal argument used by the State Department of Transportation officials was the need to upgrade and rebuild roads.

THE PROPERTY TAX

Through most of Nevada's history, the property tax provided the major source of support for state government as well as for schools and local governments. With the enactment of state gaming taxes in 1945 and the general sales tax in 1955, the state relinquished all but five cents (out of the maximum $5 per $100 of assessed valuation allowed by the state constitution) of the property tax.[13] The 1963 law that set the assessed valuation at 35 percent of real market value is still binding on county assessors. As part of the tax package to bail out the state general fund after the 1982 recession, the 1983 legislature added five cents to the state's portion of the property tax. After voters in May 1989 approved an amendment increasing the bonding capacity of the state, the 1989 and 1991 legislatures increased the state's portion of the property tax to pay the interest on the state's construction bonds.

The possibility that Question 6 would be approved a second time in 1980 caused Governor List and the legislature to reduce the property tax drastically. The 1979 legislature enacted a provisional tax-reduction package that included placing a limit of $3.64 for each $100 of assessed value and eliminating the tax on household goods and furniture in single-family residences. The provisional aspect was that the package, along with the elimination of the sales tax on food, would "self-destruct" if the electorate approved Question 6, which would have rolled back property values to the 1975–76 assessments for tax purposes and limited the property tax to 1 percent of market value.[14]

Governor List had promised the voters that he would recommend even further reductions in the property tax if the people voted down Question 6. Thus, List recommended a "tax shift" to the 1981 legislature. Increases in the sales taxes allowed for a reduction in the property tax by placing caps on the amount of revenues the local governments could collect. (School districts were already limited as to the amount of revenues they could collect.) Even though the property tax limit was increased each session between 1981 and 1991, inclusive, Nevada still had one of the nation's lowest property taxes.

NEVADA'S BAN OF A STATE INCOME TAX

Over one-third of all general fund revenues for the fifty states comes from the individual and corporate income taxes, with all but six states (as of 1995) levying such taxes. Income taxes are considered progressive, inasmuch as the income of the wealthy is assessed at a higher rate than that of the poor. The Price Waterhouse study argued that "the personal income tax can be used to offset the regressive nature of other taxes, such as the sales and property taxes."[15] Another argument for the tax is that it grows with the economy; therefore, in a state with an expanding population, the increased amount of the tax would help to meet the costs of providing services for the new residents.

The personal income tax has long been anathema to Nevada politicians and the general public. One of the main arguments against the tax has been that it would be paid almost entirely by Nevada residents; thus, there has been an inclination for the people to support higher gambling taxes that are paid mainly by tourists and for the politicians to prefer an increase in sales taxes that are partially paid by nonresidents rather than the personal income tax. Nevada, along with Alaska and Hawaii, has been among the most successful states in "exporting" its tax burden to others—mainly tourists and visitors. Nevada uses the "no income tax" appeal to attract businesses from other states, especially California. This appeal may also have been an important factor in the large number of retirees who have moved to the state from California in recent years.[16]

A constitutional amendment prohibiting a state personal income tax was placed on the ballot through initiative petitions and overwhelmingly approved by the voters in 1988 and 1990. In other states, the prohibition of a personal income tax would severely hamper the ability of such states to fund basic services. Nevada has the luxury of not having such a tax because gaming revenues in fiscal year 1994 were about equal to the revenue that would have been produced by a three percent personal income tax.

THE BUSINESS TAX

The business tax enacted by the 1991 legislature was a reaction to an initiative petition that placed on the 1990 general election ballot a proposal for a corporate profits tax. Petitions were circulated by members of the Nevada State Education Association (NSEA) after the teachers' organization had been frustrated in its attempts to secure a larger tax base for education at the 1985 and 1987 legislative sessions. The proposal would have levied an 8 percent tax on net corporate income between $20,000 and $120,000 and 10 percent on any higher income; in addition, each corporation would pay an annual $500 license fee. With public opinion polls showing strong support for the proposed law, a coalition of business leaders proposed a gross payroll tax as an alternative. Governor Bob Miller then talked NSEA into withdrawing support for the initiative, promising that he would propose an alternative business tax at the 1991 legislative session if the initiative were defeated at the 1990 election. The educators, afraid that support for education might be hurt at the next legislative session if they opposed such an alternative, then urged the people to vote down the ballot issue, which 77 percent of the voters proceeded to do.

Governor Miller proposed a business activities tax that included a 1 percent tax on wages, plus a 1 percent tax on proprietary compensation that exceeded $35,000 in a calendar year. The 1991 legislative taxation committees were concerned that the governor's proposed tax on proprietary compensation for individuals, such as doctors and lawyers, might be interpreted as an income tax by the courts—an interpretation that would cause the courts to declare the law unconstitutional in the face of the 1990 constitutional amendment prohibiting a personal income tax.

The legislature then came up with its own measure: a payroll tax applied on a graduated scale ranging from $100 annually for one employee up to $400,000 a year for 5,042 or more employees; the law exempted sole proprietorships. The cap of $400,000 benefited the state's seven largest employers, six of which are hotel-casinos. The 1993 legislature removed the cap and set a flat rate per employee. The gaming industry viewed the change positively, for the increased taxes on large gaming operations removed the threat of an increase in overall gaming taxes.[17]

The adoption of the first direct tax on businesses in Nevada leaves only Alaska and Wyoming as states that do not impose a general business tax. Nevada is one of only five states that do not levy a corporate income tax; of these five states, Texas levies a capital stock franchise tax and Michigan has a modified value-added tax.[18] Nevada levies a net proceeds tax on mining; a constitutional amendment allowing the taxing of minerals at a rate different than other property was approved by the voters in the midst of the 1989 legislative session. The legislature then raised the tax rate on minerals from 2 percent of net proceeds to 5 percent on mines with revenues of $4 million or more.

NEVADA'S TAX EFFORT

Are Nevada's taxes too high? According to a study by the U.S. Advisory Commission for Intergovernmental Relations, Nevada's overall tax burden is among the lowest in the nation.[19] The low taxes provide an important selling point as the state attempts to attract new businesses.

Will the tax burden of Nevadans increase in the future? If the recent past in Nevada and in other states is any indication, the answer is almost certainly yes. Population growth has brought the demands for more schools, roads, parks, police protection, and other services. While most state leaders in Nevada have considered population growth to be a positive factor, a Catch-22 aspect of growth is that in the short run, new residents often do not pay their own way for public services. People moving to the state will pay taxes to support public services eventually, but the problem is that schools and streets must be in place *when they arrive*. This lag means that current residents must pay the short-run costs of growth.

In 1994, 78 percent of the voters supported a constitutional amendment to require at least a two-thirds vote of both houses of the legislature "to pass a measure which generates or increases" any form of public revenue. The amendment will go into effect if it is approved again at the 1996 election. Therefore, while taxes may rise in coming years, they will continue to be low in comparison with most other states.

BORROWING AND DEBT

Nevada ordinarily operates with two budgets: the operating budget, which includes expenditures on items and services that will be used in the current year, and the capital budget, which includes items such as buildings. Like most states, Nevada is required by its constitution to have a balanced operating budget. During the 1970s, when there were consistent operating budget surpluses every biennium, much of the capital budget was funded by the surpluses. The 50 percent growth in population during the 1980s taxed the resources of both budgets.

Borrowing for capital construction projects, such as highways, is justified because the people who will benefit in the future will be helping to pay off the bonds over a period of twenty or thirty years. Also, construction will be paid off with cheaper dollars toward the end, if there has been substantial inflation. In growth periods, such as Nevada has had in recent decades, sufficient bonding capacity is needed to meet the demands for new schools and roads at the time the growth occurs. Thus, the aforementioned approval of the 1989 amendment doubling the bonding capacity of the state was a crucial decision.

Table 15: 1990 Per Capita Long-Term Debt of the Forty-One States with Debt

Highest: Hawaii	$1,917.30
Second Highest: Oregon	1,898.90
Average	312.40
Nevada (rank: 28)	170.10
Second Lowest: Michigan	21.20
Lowest: Kentucky	19.20

Source: "The Fifty States Sixth Annual Financial Report, *City and State,* 22 April 1991.

Table 15 indicates that Nevada's long-term debt is well below the national average. However, the table does not reflect the additional borrowing authorized by the 1991 legislature after the doubling of the state's bonding capacity in 1989.

THE BUDGET PROCESS

The budget process in Nevada consists of four stages: executive preparation and presentation, legislative review and adoption, implementation, and review. The four stages are not discrete; they overlap as some activities occur simultaneously. While the current budget is being implemented, the governor's office will be preparing the budget for the next biennium and a legislative committee may be reviewing some aspect of an agency's budget from a prior biennium.

Executive Preparation and Presentation

The first step is budget preparation, which is the responsibility of the governor. Early in the spring of the even-numbered years, the state budget director, who is one of the governor's most important appointees, asks the state agencies to prepare their budget requests. The timing of this request means that the agencies must estimate their needs three and one-half years ahead of the end of the biennial budget. The budget director may also provide some guidelines for the requests. If the governor wants to be conservative or is faced with bleak economic prospects, he or she may have the budget director inform the agencies that they may not request more than a 3 or 4 percent increase. The guidelines may also incorporate the governor's priorities for the next biennium; for example, recent governors Richard Bryan and Bob Miller emphasized education, especially elementary education. Miller encouraged educators to budget for a lower pupil-teacher ratio in the early grades. Alternatively, the governor may send a message through the budget director to the agencies that there will be "no new taxes," as Governor Mike O'Callaghan did in his four biennial budgets and as Bryan did in 1985 and 1987. Their message to the agencies was "hold the line."

All "departments, institutions and other agencies of the state government" have a 1 September deadline for submitting their biennial budget requests to the budget director.[20] The budget director and staff will then spend the final months of the year examining the budget requests, meeting with each agency head, estimating how much revenue will be available for the biennium, and trying to put together a set of budget recommendations that will be acceptable to the governor. Because of the requirement of a balanced budget, the executive budget must also indicate the sources of revenue to pay for the requested appropriations.

The budget director normally informs each agency head in December of the office's preliminary budget for the agency. If the agency head believes the figures are too low, an appeal may be made to the governor. It is not unusual for the governor to raise the proposed appropriation after meeting with an agency head and the budget director. In January 1995 Governor Miller agreed to increase the proposed funding for public schools and for the colleges and universities after meeting with educators.

Recent governors have given a general outline of their budget and priorities for the next biennium in their State of the State messages during the first week of the biennial legislative session. The executive budget is delivered to the legislature shortly afterward; in recent years, the budgets have consisted of two volumes, each of which is about two inches thick.

The governor's budget proposals carry great weight with the legislature. It is ordinarily an uphill battle to convince the legislature to add money to the governor's request for a particular agency. The public schools and the university have been more successful than most other agencies in gaining such increases, perhaps because the spokespersons for the education establishment do not report to the governor.

Overly optimistic revenue projections by Governor Miller and the legislature's money committees in putting together the 1991–93 budget caused Senate Majority Leader William Raggio to sponsor a 1993 law to shift responsibility for revenue forecasts from politicians to economists. The governor appoints three economic experts to the panel, and the senate majority leader and the Speaker of the assembly each appoint one. The law, which is similar to laws enacted in a majority of states, requires the panel to issue a report on its revenue projections by 1 December of the even-numbered years. The state budget office first used the panel projections in preparing the 1995–

97 biennial budget. The 1993 legislature also authorized an interim committee to study establishing a legislative budget office, similar to the Congressional Budget Office, which would put the legislature on a more even footing with the executive branch in budget making. The 1995 legislature moved a step in this direction by funding more legislative fiscal analyst positions.

Legislative Review and Adoption

As important as the executive budget is, it is still just a set of recommendations. The legislative review process is centered almost entirely in the Senate Finance Committee and the Assembly Ways and Means Committee. Because of the power of these committees, a legislator appointed to one of them will likely try to stay on as long as possible. Thus, there are usually some senior members of the money committees who are well informed about budget matters; James Gibson, the powerful and highly respected legislator who was a member of one of the money committees during his entire thirty-year tenure in the legislature, had great knowledge of past budgets and testimonies by agency heads. During the 1970s and 1980s, Gibson's influence on the Senate Finance Committee was enhanced by his remarkable memory of past budget presentations.

All of the issues that divide citizens over public policy are to be found in the budget debates. There will be differences over the budget that reflect the northern part of the state versus the southern part, urban versus rural residents, Democrats versus Republicans, those who want higher spending versus those who want lower taxes, and so on. While the legislative hearings are important, they are by no means the only places where budgetary decisions are considered. Representatives of various interests, including private lobbyists and officials of public agencies, meet one on one with legislators in attempts to persuade them to support particular budget items. Legislators discuss the budget among themselves, make compromises, engage in give-and-take or what some people call "logrolling," and eventually make final decisions on the budget.

As mentioned in chapter 6, the procedure for bringing the two houses together to work out differences on measures is handled differently when it comes to the budget. The reconciliation takes place between the two money committees prior to the budget going to the floors of the two houses for approval. Therefore, consideration by the full houses is almost always perfunctory.

Implementation

After the legislature has approved and the governor has signed the budget, which usually consists of several bills rather than just one, its implementation becomes the responsibility of the executive branch. One criterion used to evaluate how well agency heads are doing their jobs is their ability to accomplish the agency's goals within the budget.

No state official can predict with certainty what will happen to state revenues during a biennium because the revenues often depend on what happens to the national economy. When revenues fall short of estimates in the budget, the governor may freeze new hiring for a time or order an across-the-board spending reduction. Only Governors Bob List (1982) and Bob Miller (1992) in recent decades resorted to laying off state workers.

Review

The process of reviewing past budget activities is dispersed among several agencies. The state controller audits claims against the state; the attorney general may get involved if there is a question about the legality of a particular state expenditure; and the legislative money committees review past budget actions as they consider a new budget request. The credibility of an agency head will be called into question if the agency has spent money in a manner inconsistent with the intent of the money committees; indeed, such an agency can expect a tongue-lashing and perhaps a reduction in its budget at the next legislative session. The legislative auditor's office also conducts periodic audits of the financial records of the various agencies.

In addition to the above checks, the state's professional budget staffs carefully review past spending patterns. The budget director and the legislative fiscal analysts review past budgets when they prepare recommendations for the future. These staff people especially are concerned with past spending and economic trends that may have implications for future budgeting. For example, enrollment figures for the elementary schools are good barometers for projecting secondary school enrollment, while past secondary school enrollments can be used to anticipate enrollments in higher education in the state.

Overall, the budget process is at the heart of the political process. Where a state spends its dollars gives an indication of the state's priorities and policy preferences. Understanding a state's budget process is an important key to understanding how government and politics operate in that state.

CONCLUSION

Nevadans have learned that their economy is not immune to the business cycle. The governor and legislature should think in terms of the long view and give priority to broadening the state's revenue base. One approach would allow cities and counties to exceed the property tax cap when voters approve of increases to fund certain projects. With their strong individualistic ethic, Nevadans are conservative on fiscal issues, especially on taxation. If they are convinced a moderate tax increase is needed, polls have consistently shown that tax increases on cigarettes, liquor, and gaming are by far the most popular. However, the large gaming corporations in the state have been investing heavily in operations in other states, including Indian reservations, and can be expected to argue that significantly higher gaming taxes would induce them to place even more of their investments in opportunities outside Nevada.

CHAPTER TWELVE

Local Governments:
Powers and Politics

Tip O'Neill, the longtime Speaker of the U. S. House of Representatives, is perhaps best remembered for his statement that "all politics is local." He never forgot that his main responsibility was to his constituency in Cambridge, Massachusetts. In Nevada, local politics does not receive as much attention as it does in larger states because all politics in the state is "local." The interested citizen has no problem interacting in some way with her or his governor, U.S. senator, legislator, county commissioner, or mayor.

The relationship between a state and its subdivisions is not the same as that between the federal and state governments. The states existed prior to the federal government, which was created by the U.S. Constitution; that document defines the relationship between the two entities. The states retained many of their powers under the Constitution, and the federal government cannot unilaterally abolish states or diminish their powers.

In contrast, local governments within a state—such as counties, cities, and school districts—are creatures of the state and have only those powers that the state has given them. Under its unitary form of government, a state could theoretically provide all government services and activities directly from the state capital and create no local governments. In the real world, such an occurrence is a practical impossibility.

STATE-LOCAL RELATIONS

The Nevada Constitution directs the legislature to "establish a system of county and township government, which shall be uniform throughout the state."[1] The constitution also includes a long list of local government functions and activities about which the legislature is prohibited from passing special or local laws.[2] Special or local laws are laws that pertain to one specified county or city. Having been written in the middle of the nineteenth century, the Nevada Constitution was the product of an era that had seen much corruption in state legislative enactments to favor a particular county or city. In many cases, local political officials had bribed state officials to pass special laws granting favors to their communities. It is not surprising, then, that the writers of the Nevada Constitution followed the example of other states in prohibiting the state legislature from enacting local laws applicable to only one local government.

As states became more populous and urbanized, legislatures often provided different laws for government units in different population categories. For example, the Nevada legislature can pass laws that apply to all counties with a population of 200,000 or more as a way of circumventing the prohibition against passing special legislation. In practice, such laws would apply only to Clark and Washoe Counties. Federal and state courts have generally ruled that classifying governments by population size when passing legislation does not violate constitutional prohibitions against special or local laws. The reasoning is that legislation written in this fashion would become applicable to other counties if their populations increased enough. On the other hand, a law that specifically stated that it applied only to Clark and Washoe Counties would violate the constitution.

During most of the nation's history, states have maintained tight control over their local governments. This control is illustrated by the position courts have traditionally taken in interpreting state-local relations. In a famous Michigan case, Judge John F. Dillon, in what became known as Dillon's Rule, defined the powers of local government as follows:

> It is a general and undisputed proposition of law that a municipal corporation possesses and can exercise the following powers and no others: First, those granted in express words; second, those necessary or fairly implied in or incident to the powers expressly granted; third, those essential to the accomplishment of the declared objects and purposes of the corporation—not simply convenient, but indispensable. Any fair, reasonable, substantial doubt concerning the existence of power is resolved by the courts against the corporation, and the power is denied.[3]

The most important part of the rule is the last sentence, which establishes that if there is any doubt as to whether a governmental power is a state or municipal power, the courts will rule in favor of the state and against the local government.

The Nevada courts have followed the pattern of other states; one of the early Nevada Supreme Court decisions on state-local relations stated: "The municipality is created mainly for the initiative, advantage, and convenience of the locality and its inhabitants; a county is created almost exclusively for the convenience and advantage of the state and its government."[4] This ruling illustrates another characteristic of state-local relations—the tendency to grant more authority to cities (municipalities) than to counties. Cities are usually referred to as municipal corporations, whereas counties are commonly called quasi-corporations, indicating that they have less flexibility and independence from the state government.

In practice, the relationship between states and local governments has varied from one period of history to another. Although states attempted to maintain tight control over their local governments, they apparently were not very effective as "parents" in assuring the good behavior of their offspring. In 1887 James Bryce published his classic book, *The American Commonwealth*, in which he called American city government the one conspicuous failure of the American governmental system.[5] Soon after the turn of the century, Lincoln Steffens made the same point in his muckraking book, *The Shame of the Cities*.[6] Another observer of that era referred to county government in the United States as the "dark continent" of American government.[7]

The twentieth century has seen a tendency to grant somewhat more flexibility to local governments. The reform movement that swept state and local governments soon after the turn of the century and that urged such reforms as the short ballot, nonpartisan local elections, at-large city elections, the council-manager plan, and local home rule had the effect of giving more freedom of action to local governments. The New Deal in the 1930s, when federal programs expanded local government involvement in welfare and public housing, increased local authority even more. After World War II, the rapid population growth in urban areas required that local governments provide additional services and exercise more authority.

Local governments often reflect areas of the nation in which they develop. For example, in New England in the early days of the nation's history, local communities created a form of direct democracy called the town meeting. All citizens would gather at the meetings on a regular basis and participate directly in local government. As a result, the town (or township) emerged as the most important unit of local government. Counties were a much less significant government in New England. In the southern states, counties developed as very powerful government units.

As southerners and midwesterners moved west, Nevada came to reflect the pattern of strong county government found in those regions. The large amount of sparsely populated territory in Nevada also made the use of counties very practical. Even today, the state's most populous region is governed in large measure by a county government, with only about one-third of the people in Clark County residing within the city limits of Las Vegas. For example, the world-famous Las Vegas Strip and the area around UNLV are in the county, not in the city.

STATE-LOCAL FINANCIAL RELATIONS

Most local taxes are imposed by a local legislative body, such as the county board of commissioners or the city council. In some cases, however, the legislature imposes a state tax that is then shared with local governments.

As noted previously, the approval of the 2 percent sales tax in a referendum in 1956 restricted the legislature from making any changes in the tax. Therefore, the 1967 legislature passed the school support tax, and the 1969 legislature enacted the city-county relief tax, both of which were collected at the same time as the state sales tax and then returned to the school districts, cities, and counties.

The "Fair Share" Controversy

As noted in chapter 11, the "tax shift" proposed by Governor Bob List and enacted by the 1981 legislature involved a massive shift of the tax burden from property taxes to sales taxes. With the restriction on the 2 percent state sales tax, the increases were made in the school support tax and the city-county sales tax. As part of the tax-shift measure, the legislature devised a complex formula for returning additional revenues to local governments to replace the lost property tax revenue. Because property values at that time were comparatively higher in the Reno area than in the Las Vegas area, Washoe County and its local governments lost more revenue from the plan than did Clark County. To compensate for this shortfall, the distribution formula for the revenue from the supplemental city-county relief tax returned relatively more to Washoe County than to Clark. As a result, Washoe County received more sales tax revenue than it paid in each year, and Clark County paid in more revenue than it received back.

This distribution plan became very controversial in Clark County in the mid-1980s, and politicians from the area started referring to the tax shift as the "tax shaft." Soon, Clark County legislative candidates were running on a platform promising a "fair share" of the state's revenue for their county. "Fair share" was later expanded to refer to the state's largest county's right to the major share of the state's expenditures on items such as highways, new state buildings, and prisons.

Although Clark County has had a majority of the seats in both legislative houses since 1973, attempts to pass "fair share" legislation in the 1987 and 1989 legislatures were thwarted by GOP control of the state senate for the first time since 1963. A majority of the senate Republicans were from northern Nevada; consequently, Clark County legislators were unable to get their "fair share" bill through the upper house, where the majority leader was William Raggio from Washoe County. In 1990 the Democrats regained control of the senate, so the stage was set for an all-out effort by the Clark County delegation to pass a bill to give the county its "due" on revenue distribution.

"Fair share" was the most divisive and emotional issue during the 1991 legislative session. Both Clark and Washoe Counties hired lobbyists to protect their interests. With the numbers on their side, the Clark County legislators were not inclined to compromise after ten years of what they believed to be unfair treatment. However, the legislature did decide to phase in the new plan for distributing the supplemental city-county tax revenue over five years, 1991–96. By 1996 both Clark and Washoe Counties will receive revenue equal to 97 percent of what was collected in each of the counties, with most of the rural counties receiving slightly more in the distribution than what they paid into the city-county fund.

Expenditure and Revenue Caps

During the late 1970s and the 1980s, the legislature looked for ways to place limits or caps on local government expenditures. With the rising property values, especially in the Reno area, the legislature thought that some local governments were gaining a property tax windfall that was then spent for various purposes. Partly as a result of the effort to convince the voters to turn down Question 6 in 1980, the 1979 legislature placed limits on the expenditures of local governments.

The 1983 legislature went even farther with the limitations by extending the caps to revenue as well as expenditures. The legislature limited the amount that could be raised by the sales and property taxes combined to an annual increase of not more than 80 percent of the Consumer Price Index. Local governments protested the combining of the revenues into a single total. If sales tax receipts increased more than expected in a given year, the local government would have to reduce the property tax to bring the total amount collected from the two taxes in line with the limit. The cap on revenue had the potential for making the property tax rate very unstable; thus, the 1987 legislature corrected the procedure by placing a cap on each tax separately so that the receipts from one tax had no impact on whether the receipts from the other tax went up or down.

The control exercised by the legislature over local revenue extends beyond the city-county sales tax and the property tax. As Atkinson and Oleson have noted, "Every significant source of local revenue is controlled in one or more of the following ways: the rate which may be levied; the base on which the rate may be levied; the total revenue which can be raised; the use of the funds or the distribution of the funds.[8]

The tax shift and the expenditure and revenue limitation issues illustrate the importance of state-local relations in Nevada. The policies in these areas were all established by the state government. The impact of the policies, however, was primarily on the local governments. County boards of commissioners, city councils, and school boards all had to develop policies within the limits imposed on them by the state.

State Mandates

A closely related issue concerns unfunded state mandates. Such mandates occur when the state enacts a law or regulation that requires local governments to take actions or provide services but fails to provide funding. The most onerous recent unfunded mandates were contained in the federal Clean Water Act, Solid Waste Management Act, and the medically indigent program. The state has tended to send these mandates to the local governments. In Nevada, the two urbanized counties are able to handle the financial cost better than some of the small rural counties.[9]

In 1992 the Nevada Association of Counties placed an advisory referendum on the ballot in every county. It read as follows: "Should the Nevada legislature be permitted to enact legislation or state agencies be allowed to issue regulations which mandate counties to provide new services, expand services, or to conduct activities without the legislature appropriating sufficient funding for these services, expanded activities or programs?" The vote was overwhelmingly negative in every county; overall, 82 percent voted against allowing the state to implement unfunded mandates. The referendum was only advisory, but the 1993 legislature responded by enacting a law requiring a source of funding for any mandates on cities or counties in the future.

Although local governments are legally subdivisions of the state, they are the political entities closest to the people. They often are more concerned with everyday problems encountered by the people than are the federal and state governments. Local governments often overlap jurisdictionally and territorially with other local government entities. The five basic types of local government in Nevada are county, city, school district, special district, and regional organization.

The "quasi-corporation" status of counties means that they function primarily as units to carry out duties assigned to them by state government. Counties also carry out duties requested by their own residents, but this function has traditionally been secondary to their role as administrative arms of the state. As some counties have become urbanized, they have responded more to the demands of their citizens. Thus, these counties have taken on many of the characteristics of cities.

Nevada has seventeen counties or, more specifically, sixteen counties and the consolidated city-county government of Carson City. The voters amended the constitution in 1968 to permit the legislature to consolidate Ormsby County and Carson City, so that Carson City today performs the functions of both city and county governments. The legislature also has the power to create new counties. The last time it used this authority, other than the brief existence of Bullfrog County in the late 1980s, was in 1919, when the legislature created Pershing County.

County Functions

The functions of Nevada's counties, similar to those in other states, include law enforcement, administration of the courts, public works, administration of elections, certain health and welfare responsibilities, culture (mainly libraries) and recreation, and the administration of records and information on such matters as marriage licenses and property ownership. As urban areas in the United States have grown, many counties have been called upon to provide virtually all the services normally provided by cities.

When large urbanized areas are not within the boundaries of any incorporated municipality, the county becomes the primary local government for those areas. Clark County in southern Nevada is a good example of this type of urbanized county. The county, which contained 61.7 percent of the state's population in 1990, has five incorporated municipalities—Las Vegas, North Las Vegas, Henderson, Boulder City, and Mesquite. Nevertheless, 48 percent of the county's population in 1990 lived outside the limits of any of the cities. In addition to the famous Strip, the communities of Jean and Stateline and the rapidly growing gambling mecca of Laughlin on the Colorado River are all unincorporated. Clark County is the main provider of urban services for the residents of these areas. Among these services are a large public hospital, a university medical center, and McCarran International Airport.

The revenues for county expenditures come from a variety of sources, with the two major being the supplemental city-county relief tax (the 2.25 percent sales tax that was discussed in chapter 11) and the county portion of the property tax. In the 1989–90 fiscal year, these two sources accounted for 68.9 percent of the revenues in Washoe County and 54.3 percent of Clark County's revenues. Other income sources are business and nonbusiness licenses and permits, intergovernmental revenues such as federal grants and motor vehicle privilege and fuel taxes, charges for services, fines and forfeitures, and interest.

County Officials

The Nevada Constitution mandates the election of a board of county commissioners as the county's legislative body. The commissioners are elected to four-year terms on a partisan ballot. The legislature sets the number of commissioners on each county's board: Clark County has a seven-member board; Douglas, Lyon, Nye, and Washoe Counties have five members; and the other counties have three members. The consolidated Carson City government has a five-member board of supervisors.

Two characteristics of governmental structures are found in most American counties, including those in Nevada: the use of the "long ballot" (i.e., direct election of several administrative officials in addition to the election of the county's major policymakers) and the lack of a single elected chief executive. Not only do the voters in Nevada counties elect the board of commissioners, but they also vote for the sheriff, district attorney, county clerk, assessor, recorder, treasurer, auditor, public administrator, and district court judges. (The legislature has allowed some counties to combine some of these positions.) The election of so many officials creates problems of supervision and coordination. Although the county board approves budgets, it is difficult for the commissioners to exercise control over the other officers because they can claim that they are responsible only to the voters.

The problem of coordination is also seen in the lack of a single elected chief executive. The board of commissioners elects one of its own members to serve as chair and preside over meetings, but that person is not regarded as the chief executive officer of the county. The mayors of Las Vegas and Reno are much better known to their constituencies than the chairs of the Clark and Washoe county boards of commissioners.

A city manager has become a popular approach to the problem of a county executive. Six Nevada counties—Clark, Washoe, Carson City, Elko, Churchill, and Mineral—employ county managers. The manager is appointed by and is responsible to the board of commissioners. If the manager has the board's support, he or she can do much to provide administrative direction and coordination to county matters. However, being appointed rather than elected, the manager does not have the visibility or authority that derives from being chosen by the voters. The manager also does not have legal authority to supervise the directly elected county officials. Nevertheless, an effective manager can do much through persuasion and negotiation to bring about increased coordination and direction to county government.

In the more urbanized counties, the manager can also play a strong role in supervising the many agencies and departments that do not have directly elected heads. The exact role of the manager varies, depending on the job description and the amount of support given by the commissioners. The Clark and Washoe County managers are given broad powers to oversee the budgets and the administrative activities of the county. In the smaller counties, where government activities are more limited, there is a tradition of greater involvement in administration by the commissioners. The role of the manager is thus defined by both the law and the traditions that have evolved in each county.

Bullfrog County

No discussion of county government in Nevada would be complete without at least a mention of Bullfrog County, as it is destined to be an amusing footnote to Nevada's history. Opposition to the construction of a nuclear waste site at Yucca Mountain has been strong among politicians as well as the public. However, there has been the expectation that if the repository did come to Nevada, it would be accompanied by large amounts of federal dollars. Some political leaders became concerned, however, that the federal dollars would go mainly to sparsely populated Nye County, where Yucca Mountain is located. In 1987 lawmakers enacted legislation to solve the problem. The law took twelve square miles around Yucca Mountain from Nye County and named it Bullfrog County. The county had zero population; therefore, it would have no need for any public funds or services.

The legislation provided that any federal funds designated for the county in which the waste repository was located would go to Bullfrog County. The law created a three-member board, appointed by the governor, to govern the county and to distribute the funds to the various counties in the state on the basis of a formula devised by the legislature. One estimate placed the amount of the federal funds that might be available to the new county as high as $25 million annually.[10]

The obvious loser in this legislative plan was Nye County. Some state leaders also became concerned that Bullfrog's creation might give federal officials an impression that the state was not really opposed to the nuclear waste repository and that it would be acceptable if the price were right.

The Nye County commissioners asked Governor Bryan to call a special session of the legislature to repeal the act, but the governor refused to do so. Nye County then filed suit against the state, charging that the legislation was unconstitutional because it violated the state constitutional prohibition against special legislation that was applicable to only one county. A state judge declared the law unconstitutional, and there was no appeal. In 1989 the legislature repealed the act creating Bullfrog County. Thus, for a brief time in 1987 and 1988, Nevada had 18 counties.[11]

CITY GOVERNMENT

City governments, or incorporated municipalities, are general-purpose governments that can exercise general governmental authority within their boundaries. They function mainly as agents of their residents in contrast to counties that serve primarily as agents of the state. In 1995 Nevada had nineteen municipalities; it is likely that the booming town of Laughlin in Clark County will become the twentieth incorporated city.

City Charters

State legislation provides that cities may be organized under general or special charters. Prior to 1927, Nevada cities were incorporated under special charters that reflected the particular requirements of the community involved. Most incorporated cities in Nevada, including all large municipalities, operate under special charters approved by the legislature. The statutory general charter applies to six smaller cities, ranging in population (in 1990) from 1,871 in Mesquite to 6,438 in Fallon.

Many states have granted their cities broad authority known as "home rule," but Nevada's charter cities could not really be described as home rule cities. Nevada's constitution and laws seem somewhat contradictory on this matter. Article 8, Section 8, of the state constitution reads:

> The legislature shall provide for the organization of cities and towns by general laws, and shall restrict their power of taxation, assessment, borrowing money, contracting debts and loaning their credit, except for procuring supplies of water; provided, however, that the legislature may, by general laws, in the manner and to the extent therein provided, permit and authorize the electors of any city or town to frame, adopt, and amend a charter for its own government, or to amend any existing charter of such city or town.

The portion of this article that begins with the words "provided, however" was added as a constitutional amendment in 1924. The legislature then enacted a law stating that an initiative petition signed by registered voters in the city equal in number to 15 percent or more of those who voted at the last general municipal election may propose an amendment that will be placed on the ballot at the next general municipal election.[12]

The authority to "frame, adopt and amend a charter for its own government" is very similar to the wording found in the home-rule articles of many state constitutions. In Nevada, the state appears to grant the authority and then take it away, for the legislature passed a law stating that the power of cities to adopt charters is "subject to the right of the legislature to create or alter the form of municipal organization by special act or charter."[13] Having constitutionally granted the cities a version of home rule, the legislature then reasserted its right to change the charters of the cities.

City Functions

Not surprisingly, the major city functions are similar to those provided by the counties and noted above. Reno expends a considerably larger percentage of its funds for public safety than does Las Vegas. The difference can be partially explained by the existence of the Las Vegas Metropolitan Police Department, which consolidated the former city police department and the county sheriff's office. The consolidation has led to a more efficient police operation with resulting financial savings. A consolidated communications center for fire services also operates in the area, with the center dispatching fire and emergency vehicles for the city of Las Vegas, Clark County, the city of North Las Vegas, and the unincorporated towns of Laughlin, Moapa Valley, and Indian Springs.

Sales and property taxes provided for 61 percent of the revenue for the general fund of Las Vegas and 60 percent of Reno's general fund budget for fiscal year 1991–92. Other sources included business and nonbusiness licenses, permits, and franchise fees; fines and forfeitures; and charges for services.

City Officials

The courts in most home-rule states have decided that cities have their greatest authority in the area of government structure. Cities in those states have greater flexibility in determining such matters as whether to have a city manager, whether members of the city council should be elected from districts or at large, whether the mayor should be directly elected or be chosen by the city council, and how large the council should be.

Most small cities in Nevada have a mayor-council form of government. In the general-charter cities, voters directly elect the mayor and city council, which consists of three to eight members, depending on the city's population. Cities with special charters may adapt the structure as they see fit, subject to approval by the voters or the legislature.

Most of the special-charter cities in Nevada, including the consolidated city-county of Carson City, have a council-manager form of government. The largest cities of Las Vegas and Reno have mayors who are directly elected by the people, whereas under some charters the mayor is elected for a term from and by the members of the city council. Reno tried the latter "weak mayor" approach in the 1960s in order to strengthen the position of the city manager in the administration of the city's business. However, the city returned to a directly elected mayor when the majority of the population favored a stronger mayor to counteract the increasing influence of developers. The elected mayor has more visibility than one selected by peers on the city council.

The advocates of the council-manager form argue that it combines the benefits of democracy and efficiency. The city council is elected directly by the people and sets policies, levies city taxes, and approves the annual budget. A professional manager, who is appointed by and serves at the pleasure of the council, appoints the heads of the city departments and has overall supervision of the city's administration. The city manager, who is more likely than the part-time council members to be current on how other cities throughout the nation are solving problems, also plays an important role in recommending policies for council approval.

In Nevada, city officials are elected on a nonpartisan basis. In addition to the council and mayor, the city attorney and municipal judges are generally elected in Nevada. Most special charters provide for the election of a city clerk, but the clerk is appointed in both Las Vegas and Reno.

SCHOOL DISTRICTS

Nevada was one of the nation's leaders in the consolidation of school districts. Each county has one school district; thus the Clark County School District, which enrolls about 60 percent of the state's elementary and secondary students, is one of the largest school districts in the country. Fewer than three hundred students were enrolled in each of the three smallest school districts in 1990. The voters in each county select the members of its school board in a nonpartisan election. The board in turn appoints a county superintendent of instruction, who supervises the schools in the county. Although the elected state board of education sets some policies that are binding on the county school boards, the latter have considerable latitude in determining school policy and curriculum.

SPECIAL DISTRICTS

In addition to the seventeen county school districts, the 1987 Census of Governments showed that Nevada had 146 other special districts. Some of these districts are countywide, while others are drawn to coincide with the area of the problem to be solved or the service to be rendered. The special districts include fire districts, sewer districts, flood-control districts, local improvement districts, library districts, and hospital districts. Airport authorities and housing authorities are also counted as special districts by the Bureau of the Census. One special district, the borders of which include a small portion of Nevada—the Tahoe Transportation District—is actually counted in the Census of Governments as a California special district.

REGIONAL ORGANIZATIONS

Many counties around the country have established regional organizations, in which the county and the incorporated cities are represented, to coordinate certain programs. Such an organization is often used as a conduit for distributing certain federal planning grant monies. One example is the Washoe Council of Governments (WCOG) established in Washoe County. The Regional Transportation Commission in Clark County serves some of the same purposes as WCOG; its membership is made up of the two county commissioners, two members of the Las Vegas City Council, and one city council member from each of the other four incorporated cities in the county.

The two largest counties have planning commissions to coordinate future land-use planning and to recommend approval or rejection of development projects in the areas. The Washoe County Planning Commission was established shortly after the end of World War II and has been much more active than its counterpart in Clark County, due to the Reno area's greater opposition to growth. However, overall coordination of planning in Washoe County has been complicated by the existence of separate planning commissions in the cities of Reno and Sparks.

Another type of regional organization is one that promotes tourism. The Las Vegas Convention Authority and the Reno-Sparks Convention and Visitors Authority are examples. These authorities are funded through the assessment of hotel and motel room taxes; their boards of directors are made up of representatives from the county commission and the incorporated cities and appointees from the public sector. For example, the Las Vegas Convention Authority Board is made up of two county commissioners, two members of the Las Vegas City Council, one member of the Henderson City Council, and one position that is rotated among the city councils of North Las Vegas, Boulder City, and Mesquite. The elected officials then appoint one person to represent the downtown Las Vegas hotels, one to represent the Strip hotels, one to represent the motels and small hotels, one to represent the Nevada Resort Association, and a person recommended by the Las Vegas Chamber of Commerce. Both the Reno and Las Vegas authorities support large convention centers and other tourist attractions, including concerts and sporting events.

CONSOLIDATION OF LOCAL GOVERNMENTS

There have been a number of government consolidations in Nevada. As noted above, school districts were consolidated from 167 to 17. In 1962 the legislature created health districts in Clark and Washoe Counties to consolidate the services formerly offered by city and county health departments. The aforementioned Carson City–Ormsby County consolidation took place in 1968. Five years later, the police departments of Clark County and Las Vegas were consolidated to form the Las Vegas Metropolitan Police Department, better known in the area as "Metro."[14]

Government consolidation is usually supported as a means to reduce overlapping jurisdiction, duplication of services, and general governmental inefficiency. It can be argued, however, that consolidation is not always desirable from the viewpoint of the individual citizen. A major advantage of local governments is that they are close to the people; this advantage may be diminished if local governments get too large or too distant from the citizen through consolidation. Some citizens in Clark County argue that its school district is "too big" and that the school system should be divided into two or more districts in order to bring the governance of the schools closer to the people.

Clark County uses a system of town boards in an attempt to address the issue of its size. The boards are used, especially in the rural areas, to give citizens an opportunity to express their views on local matters. The town boards are appointed by and are advisory to the board of county commissioners, with the latter body, of course, making the final decisions. The issue of when local governments should be consolidated or when they are already too large must be decided on a case-by-case basis.

CONTEMPORARY ISSUES OF LOCAL GOVERNMENTS

Clark and Washoe Counties, in which 83 percent of Nevadans resided in 1990, have the same problems that plague most urban areas in the nation: crime, gangs, traffic congestion, and pollution. These two counties have also experienced tremendous population growth in recent decades.

Citizens in the Reno area displayed concern about rapid growth much sooner than those in the Las Vegas area, where pro-growth sentiment dominated until recently. Barbara Bennett was elected mayor of Reno in the 1970s on a slow or limited growth platform. She was succeeded by Peter Sferrazza, who was elected to three four-year terms in the 1980s on a similar platform. In Clark County, the election for the county board of commissioners in 1990 was a watershed event with respect to the growth issue. A new commissioner was elected on a "managed growth" platform.

The attitude of the Clark County citizenry toward traffic congestion was also made clear at the 1990 election, when the voters overwhelmingly approved Question 10. This question proposed a "Fair Share Funding Program for the Master Transportation Plan" for Clark County, which would be funded by $100 million annually in new revenue. Most of the money comes from a five-cent increase in the gas tax and an increase in the county room tax. The plan was an "excellent example of intergovernmental and inter-departmental teamwork," as Clark County, its incorporated cities, and the Regional Transportation Commission worked together in the formulation.[15]

Conservation of water has become a pressing problem in Washoe County because of several consecutive drought years prior to 1994. With the huge increases in population, water conservation has also become a public concern in Clark County.

In the early 1990s ethics became an important issue in both Clark and Washoe Counties. In the Reno area, the question arose in connection with the charge that the membership of the Reno Planning Commission was heavily business-oriented. In the southern part of the state, Jan Laverty Jones was elected mayor of Las Vegas in 1991 on an ethical-reform platform that was a response to allegations of improprieties by city administrators in a land deal.[16]

Of the other counties, the city-county of Carson City, with a population that has more than quadrupled since 1960, has a traffic congestion problem downtown. A proposed bypass plan may alleviate the problem. Elko County has many of the problems connected with rapid growth because of the mining boom and because it was selected by a national magazine as one of the best retirement areas in the country.

CONCLUSION

Local governments in Nevada have some of the same problems as state government in trying to cope with a rapidly expanding population. Local governments have primary responsibility for the two areas of most concern to Nevadans in the mid-1990s—K–12 education and crime. The 1993 legislature treated the school districts comparatively well in the hold-the-line 1993–95 budget, and Governor Bob Miller gave the schools top priority in his 1995–97 budget proposal. The 1993 legislature's refusal to increase funding for social services, including AFDC, mental health, and general welfare, increased the burden of the counties. Increased welfare costs may lessen the funds available to the two metropolitan areas to fight gangs and crime.

Although the 1993 legislature swore off unfunded mandates, it did not give local governments more authority to raise revenues. The sharp increase in the amount of sales tax revenues, including the city-county relief tax, in 1993 and 1994 was encouraging and helped local governments meet their financial commitments. In the long run, however, the governor and the legislature should come up with a plan to give the local governments more flexibility. As it has turned out, the individualistic and conservative aspects of Nevada's political culture are hindering the ability of the urban local governments to cope with their pressing problems as they approach the twenty-first century.

CHAPTER THIRTEEN

Public Policy Issues: Education and Hospital Cost Containment

Harold Lasswell gave the title *Politics: Who Gets What, When, How* to his groundbreaking book in the 1930s. That title could be used to describe public policymaking in the 1990s. Governors, legislators, and interest groups have their program priorities, and often the content of the state budget is the best indication of whose priorities have prevailed in the political process, inasmuch as most public policies require funding to be effective.

In the federal system, the states often serve as laboratories by experimenting with various approaches to problems. The outcomes of those experiments can be important in the policymaking process. For example, the success of motor-voter registration in other states was key to its passage by Nevada's legislature in 1987 and then by Congress in 1993.

Long-range planning is an essential ingredient for effective policymaking in most areas, such as taxation. In 1990 the Corporation for Enterprise Development (CED) published a Development Report Card in which it graded each of the fifty states in four areas: economic performance, business vitality, development capacity, and state policy. Nevada was given an A for economic performance but a grade of F for state policy.[1] Colorado was one of four other states also given an F grade in the policy area. Cronin and Loevy explain Colorado's lack of long-range planning as follows: "Skeptical individuals are never sure that the planners' conception of a desirable future will be the same as theirs. And even if it is, they are concerned about the cost . . . and the possible loss of freedom that might come as part of the process."[2] This statement could also explain the lack of long-range planning in Nevada's highly individualistic political culture. As in Colorado, "the state budget document must serve in most cases as the state planning document."[3]

Most public policy decisions in Nevada are reactive in response to pressing problems or needs. The most important policy issues debated by the 1993 legislature were how to reform the State Industrial Insurance System (SIIS), which was headed toward insolvency, whether to make changes in the 1991 business tax, whether state support for social services should be increased, and whether funds should be added to the state Distributive School Account to compensate for the governor's cuts in 1991–93. Governor Miller was a key player in the decisions on all these issues, although he did not prevail in all cases. The important policy questions raised by Miller in his State of the State address to the 1995 legislature were prisons, crime prevention, class-size reduction in the lower elementary school grades, the use of the large general fund surplus for one-shot capital improvement projects, and a rainy-day fund.

Despite its general political conservatism, Nevada has been one of the leading states in structural school reform. In 1956 the voters approved a constitutional amendment to remove the state superintendent of public instruction as an elective official. Since that time the superintendent has been appointed by the elected State Board of Education; thus Nevada has been spared the unseemly battles between an elected state superintendent and the state board that have afflicted California at times. The state also consolidated its school districts into seventeen county districts in 1955 and was a national leader in providing basic support for each schoolchild in the state, including a wealth factor that helps poorer school districts.

The 1993–95 budget allocated over 55 percent of state general fund appropriations to K–12 and higher education, in addition to the funds allocated to school districts through local taxes and unrestricted federal grants. Thus, education funding continues to be the top priority among policy decisions facing the state every two years.

FUNDING OF EDUCATION

Historically, financing of education has been viewed as a shared obligation of the state and its local governments.[4] Indeed, the Nevada Constitution contains the following provision: "In addition to other means provided for the support and maintenance of said university and common schools, the Legislature shall provide for their support and maintenance by direct legislative appropriation from the General Fund."[5]

The Distributive School Account

An indication of the growth in population of the state—as well as the policy decisions of recent governors and legislators to provide more support for the public schools—is that the state's general fund transfers to the Distributive School Fund went from less than $12 million in the 1953–55 biennium to over a billion dollars in the 1993–95 biennium. Important players in the decision to expend more money for education were local units of the Parent-Teacher Association (PTA), which lobbied successfully for the passage of a general sales tax in 1955 and campaigned against the referendum to repeal the tax in 1956.[6]

General fund transfers to public schools were originally based on the school-age population in each district, according to the most recent federal decennial census.[7] The 1925 legislature changed the basis of apportionment of the monies to the number of students actually attending school in each district. Two studies of the financial and administrative problems of the schools after World War II recommended a consolidation of districts; in 1947, there were 143 one or two-teacher rural districts. The 1955 legislature passed the 2 percent sales tax, which made it possible for the state to increase its support of the public schools by 70 percent, and consolidated school districts so that there would be one school district in each of the seventeen counties.

The Peabody study that was presented to the 1955 legislature also recommended that the state "guarantee each local school system revenues at least equivalent to its basic school needs."[8] The legislature adopted the Peabody formula—which used the number of certified school employees, the number of students in average daily attendance, and bus transportation costs—for determining each district's basic school needs. The apportionment from the state general fund to each county's school district was then made on the basis of "the difference between the basic school need and the county contributions."[9] A portion (70 cents per $100 of assessed valuation) of the property tax constituted the county contributions.

The Peabody formula was used until 1967, when the Nevada Plan, which was devised by Lincoln Liston, the associate state superintendent of public instruction, and state senator Carl Dodge, was adopted by the legislature in connection with passage of the new school support tax. The Nevada Plan takes into account the differences among the counties in both population and wealth. In the smaller counties, the pupil-teacher ratio is of necessity smaller than it is in the larger counties, so the "basic per student support rate" guarantee is calculated by a formula that considers the demographics of each district. This rate also has "a moving base" in that it is reexamined and reset every two years. Transportation needs and the wealth of the county are factored in prior to the determination of the final guaranteed funding for the district that will come from the Distributive School Account (DSA).[10]

The Nevada Plan also includes locally generated revenues that are subtracted from the guaranteed support in order to determine how much money will be transferred from the state general fund to the DSA. Presently (1995), the locally generated revenues are the 2.25 percent school support tax and the 25-cent (per $100 assessed valuation) property tax that was earmarked for education by the 1983 legislature.

In addition to the general fund appropriation each biennium, the DSA receives other revenues that have been earmarked by the legislature. The largest additional source is the slot machine tax, followed by the 2.25 percent out-of-state sales tax, mineral leases, and the interest generated by the permanent school fund.

The county school district has other sources of revenue to supplement the funds from the above-named local taxes and the DSA. These sources include 50 cents on each $100 assessed valuation of the property tax, the motor vehicle privilege tax, and certain unrestricted federal revenues. Thus, the funding of public school education in Nevada is a complicated but workable process that depends on a variety of state and local taxes.

In the 1980s, the big push in education reform in Nevada was to reduce class sizes, especially in the early elementary grades. Nevada had consistently ranked among the states with the highest pupil-teacher ratio. The ratio for kindergarten through grade 3 was 28:1 in 1986, with some classes having as many as 40 students.[11] The State Board of Education in 1986 proposed that class size in K–3 grades be reduced to 22:1; the 1987 legislature responded by directing the school districts to prepare a plan to achieve that ratio by the year 2000.[12]

The year following the legislature's decision to work toward the 22:1 ratio for the lower elementary grades, a study was published by the U.S. Department of Education stating, "Unless the number of pupils per class is reduced substantially below 20—at least to 15 according to one celebrated research review—little improvement in student achievement may be expected."[13] Responding to this report and other expert testimony, an interim subcommittee set up by the 1987 legislature recommended to the 1989 legislature that a pupil-teacher ratio of 15:1 in the K–8 grades in language arts and mathematics be phased in over eleven years.[14] There was strong public support for class reduction. A poll conducted jointly by the survey research centers at the two state universities in November 1988 showed that 81 percent of the respondents favored a moderate tax increase to fund "smaller class sizes for public school children in elementary grades," with only 13 percent being opposed.

Governor Bob Miller asked the 1989 legislature to lower the pupil-teacher ratio to 19:1 over a period of eleven years, but only in the K–3 grades. Under the Miller plan, the reduction would have started with the first grade in the fall of 1990. However, the legislature found more money for the reduction by using some estate tax money; the 1989 legislature then funded a cut in the ratio to 15:1 for the first grade, beginning in the fall of 1990. The 1991 legislature continued to go beyond the governor's recommendation. The pupil-teacher ratio was reduced to 16:1 for the second grade in the fall of 1991 and for the third grade the following year. Although the budget shortfall in 1992 forced Governor Miller to request a postponement of the class-size reduction for the third grade, he restored the reduction in his 1995–97 budget request. However, the Republicans, led by Bill Raggio, forced the governor to accept a compromise of only one-third of the amount needed to fund the third-grade class-size reduction fully.

The legislature, prodded in many cases by the public and schoolteachers, has played the major role in the policymaking process that has resulted in the above structural and funding reforms for K–12 education. Although governors in the 1950s and 1960s, with the exception of Grant Sawyer, were reluctant to get out front on the tax issue in order to obtain more revenue for the public schools, the legislature enacted the sales and school support taxes in 1955 and 1967.[15] The NSEA, Governor Miller, and the legislature all played important roles in the enactment of the business tax, which made class-size reduction possible.

Higher Education

Similarly to public school financing, the cost of funding higher education in Nevada has escalated sharply in the last three and a half decades because of rising enrollments. As late as the early 1950s, there was only one institution of higher learning in the state—the University of Nevada in Reno. By 1980 there were two universities with extensive graduate programs and four community colleges in the University of Nevada System.

Although charged by the constitution with providing support for the university, the legislature appropriated only minimal funds for faculty salaries and library books during the first sixty years of the university's existence on the Reno campus.[16] With the small state population, the enrollment at the university was less than 1,500 students in the early 1950s. The enactment of the 2 percent sales tax in 1955 allowed the legislature to increase the appropriation for the university. The resultant increases in faculty salaries and the number of faculty positions then made it possible for the university to recruit promising young faculty from the nation's major graduate schools. The increased support came at a propitious time. Enrollments grew rapidly in the late 1950s and in the 1960s on the Reno campus and at Nevada Southern University, which had started offering classes in Las Vegas in 1954 and granted its first degrees in 1965.

In 1967 former governor Sawyer noted that no formula was used during his administration to allocate funds for the university in the executive budget. Basically, the university received what was left after allocating funds for other programs, including the support of the public schools, for which there was a formula.

Prior to the 1969 legislative session, a study committee appointed by Governor Paul Laxalt and a plan proposed by Chancellor Neil D. Humphrey of the University of Nevada System both recommended that a formula based on enrollment be adopted for funding higher education.[17] In 1967–68 the ratio of students (calculated on a full-time-equivalent basis) to faculty was 15:1 at the Reno campus and 19:1 at Nevada Southern University. (The name of the Las Vegas campus was changed in 1968 to the University of Nevada, Las Vegas.) The Board of Regents accepted the chancellor's plan to phase in a formula of 20:1 by 1980. Governor Laxalt and the 1969 legislature acquiesced to the regents' recommendation; however, Governor Mike O'Callaghan decided to move to the 20:1 formula in his first budget in 1971. This formula was changed to 22:1 in 1981. The community colleges are funded on the basis of a higher student-faculty ratio because they do not have the research mission of the two universities.

By the early 1990s, enrollment at UNLV was much higher than that at the Reno campus. UNLV's skyrocketing enrollment in the 1980s severely taxed its facilities. The existence of the Higher Education Construction Fund, which depended on the annual receipt of the first $5 million of the slot machine tax, from 1971 to 1983 was a boon for the use of bonds to construct new buildings, including the facilities needed at the four community colleges. With the governor's decision to divert the slot machine money to the general fund during the 1983 fiscal crisis, the legislature, which was very supportive of UNLV, was hard-pressed to find the money for the needed new buildings on the UNLV campus. The main problem was the state constitution's limitation on borrowing of 1 percent of the assessed valuation of the state.

Attempts by the legislature to gain voter approval of a constitutional amendment to increase the state debt limit had failed in 1960, 1968, and 1974. The 1987 and 1989 legislatures again proposed an increase to 2 percent in the debt limit. This time the legislature had an appealing argument for the voters—especially for the 60 percent who resided in Clark County—for more bonding capacity was needed to fund the UNLV facilities. A 62 percent "yes" vote in Clark County enabled the amendment to pass with a 54 percent majority statewide, even though a majority of the voters in thirteen of the seventeen counties voted "no."

Lacking the political clout of the schoolteachers, higher education was the biggest loser in the 1993–95 "hold-the-line" state budget after the 1992 recession. Despite rapidly rising enrollments, it received $10 million less than the 1991–93 budget passed by the legislature. The funding formula was set aside as higher education dropped from receiving 20.2 percent of the general fund budget in 1991–92 to 17.5 percent in 1994–95. However, the economic recovery allowed Governor Miller to return to the funding formula in his 1995–97 budget and to request that part of the general fund surplus be used for university equipment and capital construction needs.

Ever since the 1960s, the University of Nevada and the University of Nevada System (changed in 1991 to the University and Community College System of Nevada or UCCSN) have emphasized in their appropriations requests to the legislature the low state support for higher education compared to other states. In 1987–88 Nevada ranked thirty-ninth among the fifty states in legislative appropriations of tax revenue per full-time higher education student and forty-second in appropriations of tax funds per $1,000 of personal income for operating expenses of higher education.[18] In 1992–93 Nevada ranked fiftieth in the amount of grant money available for low-income students.

In the face of fast-rising enrollments, the two universities have tried to emphasize quality by increasing admission standards. The less expensive community colleges will still have an open admissions policy so that high school graduates denied admission to the universities will still be able to go to a community college. The quality of the programs offered at the two universities has also been aided by increased private donations. Former president Robert Maxson of UNLV and President Joseph N. Crowley of the University of Nevada, Reno, spearheaded funding drives that have resulted in large gifts earmarked for student scholarships and endowed faculty chairs.

OTHER HIGHER-EDUCATION ISSUES

The Board of Regents

Nevada has a more consolidated higher-education administration than most states. The Nevada Constitution stipulates that a Board of Regents shall "control and manage the affairs of the university and the funds of the same, under such regulations as may be provided by law."[19] Charles R. Donnelly, the first and only president of the Community College Division from 1970 to 1977, favored the establishment of a separate governing board for the community colleges; however, he not only lost his fight with the regents on the issue, but his position was abolished. The one Board of Regents continues to govern all public higher education in the state; hence, most disagreements among the various universities and colleges are generally fought out at that level rather than at the legislature.

In 1995 Nevada was one of only five states that have an elected university governing board. Because the regents are elected from districts, the board must be reapportioned after every decennial census. By 1981 five of the nine regents were elected by Clark County. In 1991 the board recommended that its membership be increased to eleven. The legislature agreed and created two new districts in the southern part of the state. One includes the northern parts of Clark County and all of Lincoln County. The other includes the western portion of Clark County and southern Nye County. Washoe County still elects two regents, and the remainder of the state elects two.

The WICHE Student Exchange Program

Since 1959 Nevada has been a member of the Western Interstate Commission for Higher Education (WICHE), which operates a student exchange program along with other cooperative programs in thirteen western states. Under WICHE, Nevada pays a fee to cooperating professional schools in other states in fields such as dentistry, law, library science, optometry, pharmacy, physical therapy, and veterinary medicine for a number of Nevada students, who are then treated as in-state students by the receiving schools. The legislature decides how many students will be supported in each field; and WICHE, which consists of three commissioners from each state, sets the support fees. The major advantage to the state is that it does not have to establish expensive professional schools or graduate programs in these fields.[20] Critics of the WICHE program have argued that need should be an important factor in the selection of student recipients.

CONTAINMENT OF HOSPITAL COSTS

The program to contain hospital costs has had mixed results in Nevada. In 1983 Governor Richard Bryan expressed concern about the rapidly rising

health-care costs in the state. In January 1984 he appointed to the Health
Care Cost Containment Committee a panel of individuals from various state
agencies who had expertise in the health field. The governor's proposals to
the 1985 legislature were based on the report from this committee and con-
sultation with others, including the State Health Coordinating Council.[21]
The main provision of the proposal was "a standby hospital rate-setting
commission which would become effective if the hospital industry did not
take immediate action to contain hospital costs paid by Nevadans."[22]

The hospital industry responded to the proposal by claiming that "Health
Maintenance Organizations, employer coalitions and other private sector
cost containment actions were now in place and proliferating, resulting in
lower costs for their members."[23] The hospital representatives urged the legislators to wait until they had data for 1984 and 1985 before acting on Bryan's
bill. The 1985 legislature decided to hold off action on the rate-setting commission; however, it enacted some other provisions in the governor's bill—
including the creation of a new Division of Health Resources and Cost Review. The law authorized the division to develop a system of collecting and
analyzing relevant information from health providers in the state.

The 1985 legislature also resorted to a familiar device when faced with a
controversial issue: the establishment of an interim committee chaired by
Senator Ray Rawson to study hospital costs and utilization and to report back
recommendations to the 1987 legislature. In the meantime, in June 1986
Governor Bryan gave a speech in which he cited a report of the American
Hospital Association on 1984 hospital cost information, which indicated the
following points about Nevada hospitals: first, Nevada's hospital occupancy
rate was only 58.6 percent of existing beds—a figure that placed the state
forty-eighth among the fifty states; second, Nevada's average daily charge of
$910 for every patient admitted to a hospital in 1984 was the highest in the
nation and compared unfavorably with a national average of $520 and with
the second highest daily charge of $801 in California; and third, the average
per day *profit* of $43 for each inpatient in Nevada hospitals was not only the
highest in the nation but was more than double the profit of Utah, the second
highest state.[24]

Bryan went on to say that "the question is no longer whether the state
needs to take direct action to control health care costs but rather which action
will be most effective." The governor also noted that after the hospital industry had helped kill his proposed rate-setting commission in 1985, "the in-
vestor-owned hospitals in the state increased their total charges by almost
$30 million ($28,900,000), and increased their profits over 1984 [which

were already the highest in the nation] by $14.1 million, in spite of declining utilization."[25] The public appeared to be solidly behind the governor on the issue. Survey research polls in both northern and southern Nevada in September 1986 showed that 89 percent of the respondents favored a statewide board to regulate hospital costs.[26]

Bryan's cost-containment proposal to the 1987 legislature included the rate-setting commission concept from his 1985 proposal and added an excessive-profit tax that could be used "as an alternative to, or in conjunction with" the commission. The Rawson interim committee noted that during the 1985–87 study period, several consumer groups, including the self-funded state insurance program, had negotiated substantial discounts with hospitals in the state by designating the hospitals as "preferred providers." The study showed that there had been a decrease in health-care costs for employers in Nevada between 1983 and 1986, while at the same time such costs had increased by 35.5 percent nationally.[27] The interim committee thus concentrated on the uninsured consumer and recommended that all uninsured Nevadans be offered "a preferred or discounted hospital rate."

As often happens, the bill that came out of the two health committees was a compromise between the proposals of the governor and the interim committee. The 1987 law mandated that some hospitals reduce their charges to a set level. Other hospitals were required to lower charges when the percentage of increases in income exceeded the percentage rise in operating costs. The law also included a provision to equalize the indigent patient load in counties with more than one hospital.[28]

Three years after its enactment, the plan had not solved the problem of high hospital costs. Nevada was still ranked close to the top in the nation in average daily hospital charges; and the average daily charge at both non-profit hospitals in Reno had risen to $1,800. Governor Bob Miller, who had worked closely with his predecessor on cost containment, met privately with hospital representatives to try to formulate a solution. Miller told them to come up with a satisfactory agreement, or he would ask the legislators to establish the rate-setting commission.

The day before the 1991 legislature convened, a major newspaper editorialized: "Lawmakers should give careful consideration to the idea of a state rate-setting agency for hospitals if the industry can't demonstrate an ability to get control of this problem."[29] In his State-of-the-State address, Miller revealed that he had negotiated a "pact" with the state's five largest hospitals—three in Las Vegas and two in Reno—to freeze their charges for a year and then to restrict increases in their charges in the future to the annual

increase in the Consumer Price Index. The agreement also provided a 30 percent rollback in prices charged the estimated 17 percent of the patients who
are uninsured. The governor's initiative was a surprise to most politicians,
and some consumer groups found the agreement hard to believe. One hospital spokesman commented afterwards that it was a pleasure to work with the
governor's office prior to a session rather than have a confrontation during
the legislative session.[30]

Governor Miller announced in early 1994 that the containment policy had
been successful. It was not clear, however, how much of the containment
was due to the program and how much was due to a decline in health-care
costs in general in response to the threat of congressional regulation.

OTHER CONTEMPORARY ISSUES

Crime, the environment, and welfare funding will continue to be other important policy issues in the state. The 1995 legislature enacted a tough truth-
in-sentencing measure drawn up by Senator Mark James and lowered the age
for trying juveniles as adults to sixteen as proposed by Governor Miller. Environmental issues have been explosive in the past, especially reclamation in
connection with mining activities in the rural counties. The legislature has
pushed the cities to adopt recycling and environmentally sensitive programs
for the disposition of garbage and trash.

As part of the agreement with the state's largest hospitals in 1991, Governor Miller promised to recommend increases in state funding for Medicaid.
He increased the funding originally without any additional state funds by the
use of a loophole in the federal law, but Congress has since closed the loophole.

CONCLUSION

Although Nevada has been weak in long-range planning, governors and legislators have worked with professionals to make Nevada one of the leaders in
education reform. The Peabody and Wyoming studies led to structural and
financing reforms in the 1950s and 1960s, and studies of the effect of smaller
class sizes were important in the 1989 and 1991 class-size-reduction programs.

The consistently strong popular support for increased funding for K–12
education, even if additional taxes are needed, has also played a major role
in the reforms. This support fits in with the individualistic political culture of
the state, for there is a strong belief that the polity must provide a good edu-

cation for its young people so that each individual will have the opportunity to maximize his or her potential.

It is difficult to determine the outcome of education policy in the short run, except for who won the battle of the budget. For example, it will be several years before comparative data will be available on the effect of class-size reduction in the lower grades in Nevada. It does appear that hospital cost-containment has succeeded, at least for a time.

Comments of legislators after the 1989 and 1991 sessions showed that there was a strong feeling that providing for some class-size reductions in the lower elementary grades had given them more satisfaction than anything else they had done during the sessions. However, despite a large budget surplus accumulated during the 1993–95 biennium, legislators at the 1995 session did not give class-size reduction the same top priority as did Governor Miller. The 1996 election will determine whether the governor's approach receives legislative support at the 1997 session.

CHAPTER FOURTEEN

Concluding Observations

The main theme of this study of Nevada politics and government has been that the highly individualistic political culture of Nevada has produced a conservative political philosophy in an open society. In addition, subthemes include the effects on the state's political system of the ever-increasing concentration of its population and the "love-hate" relationship with the federal government, which owns and manages 87 percent of the state's land. These concluding observations summarize the effects of these themes and comment on their importance—along with the potential impact of term limits—for the future of the state's politics.

THE HIGHLY INDIVIDUALISTIC ETHIC

Economic developments in the area that now constitutes Nevada reinforced and heightened the individualistic ethic that the early settlers brought with them. The ethic had its roots in the early state constitutions and the Declaration of Independence, both of which stressed individual rights. The discoveries of silver and gold in the 1850s attracted mainly transients concerned with striking it rich. A few of the new arrivals became settlers and brought with them experience in politics in the eastern part of the country or in California. They were needed because Nevada was granted statehood a mere thirteen years after the first permanent white settlement in the area.

Mining and cattle ranching reinforced the individualistic ethic. Along with the railroads, these industries were the important influences on the politics of the state during the first sixty-five years of its existence. The legalization of casino gaming in 1931 had a profound effect on the state's growth and development. Similar to mining, gambling tended to attract tourists and many transient workers looking for a way "to make a fast buck."

The general opposition of Nevadans to big labor, big business, and big government is also evidence of the highly individualistic political culture of the state. When the legislature refused to pass a "right-to-work" law in the 1950s, the populist initiative device was used to enact it. Opinion polls have consistently shown public support for taxation of corporations and the gaming industry. Even though the Nevada electorate's support of the *Roe v. Wade* decision's approach to abortion and its opposition to the Equal Rights Amendment might appear to be inconsistent, the two positions are similar in their opposition to a larger role for government. The results of the 1994 election, in which Republicans came within one assembly seat of controlling the organization of both houses of the legislature for the first time since 1931, seem to assure that the government's role in Nevada will not grow in the foreseeable future.

CONSERVATISM IN AN OPEN SOCIETY

Until recently when a large number of states turned to lotteries and casino gambling as a painless way to increase their revenues, Nevada was viewed by many outsiders as an "outlaw" state because of its strong economic dependence on gambling and accommodation of legal prostitution. Now Nevada's regulation of gambling is looked upon as a model by other states. Ironically, the wider acceptance of legal casino gambling in other states poses a threat to Nevada's economic future.

Nevada does have a more open society than other states. Yet its politics has generally been conservative. A definition of modern conservatism includes belief in the importance of family, an emphasis on property rights, a limited role for government, low taxation, and skepticism about innovation.

Although gambling and prostitution do not set well with some conservatives, especially religious conservatives, they are part of Nevada's tradition and do conform with the libertarian view of individual freedom of some conservatives. Economic factors were mainly responsible for the legalization of casino gaming.

Nevadans are mostly concerned with low taxes for residents. Polling has shown consistently that they favor increasing gaming taxes, inasmuch as tourists indirectly pay the lion's share of such taxes. The gaming taxes and sales tax revenue from tourists make it possible for the state to get by without an income tax, which is an important source of revenue for most states.

Although the gaming tax is the largest source of revenue for the state's general fund (39 percent in the governor's proposed 1995–97 budget), the sales tax is the largest source of revenue in the state when local government revenue is included. Only about 30 percent of the total sales tax revenues goes into the state general fund, with the rest going into school support and city-county relief funds. Overall, gaming taxes constitute only about 10 percent of the state and local government revenues.

Given the public sentiment in favor of higher gaming taxes, why is it that Nevada's tax rates on casino profits are much less than New Jersey's? For one thing, the survival of the economic health of the gaming industry is more important to Nevada than it is to New Jersey, which has a much more diversified economy. Thus, Nevada is more concerned about taxing gaming too much and driving an important segment of it out of business. What is perhaps more important, the gaming industry is by far the largest contributor to the campaigns of gubernatorial and legislative candidates. The industry also has the funds to hire top lobbyists to make its case at the legislature.

Some conservatives view those who favor higher funding for education as liberals because such funding often requires higher taxes and because the teachers' union has generally supported Democratic candidates. However, polling in the last decade has shown that a substantial majority of Nevadans—most of whom classify themselves as moderates or conservatives—favor funding for K–12 education even if it means having to pay a moderate tax increase. Most legislators in the 1987, 1989, and 1991 legislatures, whether Democrats or Republicans, were supportive of additional funding for class-size reduction. K–12 education was in great favor because of strong public and gubernatorial support. The election of many new conservative Republican members of the assembly and the defeat of a Clark County school bond issue in 1994 may presage a lessening of legislative support for education funding. However, Nevadans seem to favor education as a means of providing for equality of opportunity, a concept that is favored by present-day conservatives, moderates, and liberals alike.

The 1995 congressional movement for reform of the welfare system and putting able-bodied welfare recipients to work is in line with conservative politics and the individualistic culture in Nevada. Despite a large general fund surplus, Governor Bob Miller did not recommend an increase in individual AFDC payments in his 1995–97 budget proposal. In a state where the *liberal* label is unpopular with the great majority of the population, most politicians do not espouse more aid to poor families.

The moderate conservatism of the Nevada electorate has long influenced the behavior of politicians. Grant Sawyer has stated that he had to repress some of his liberal tendencies in the eight years he served as governor. Senator Alan Bible admitted that he tended to vote more with the "conservative coalition" and less with the presidents of his own party during the year when he was asking the Nevada voters to reelect him. James Santini was considered a liberal district judge prior to his election to Congress in 1974; yet by 1981 he was supporting much of President Reagan's conservative agenda. Richard Bryan was more liberal as a state legislator than he has been as governor or U.S. senator. Both Bryan and fellow Democrat Harry Reid voted over 40 percent of the time with the Senate's "conservative coalition" in 1994.

CONCENTRATION OF THE STATE'S POPULATION

The expansion of casino gambling in the Las Vegas area directly led to the rapid growth of the state's population in the last half of the twentieth century. Therefore, it was no surprise that the population became more and more concentrated in Clark County. Fortunately, the growth period has been prosperous for the state, with the exception of the recessions of 1981–82 and 1991–92. Therefore, the state and Clark County have generally been able to meet the increasing financial needs for more schools, highways and streets, and police protection.

Politically, the increasing concentration of the population in Clark County has not had as much effect as anticipated. In statewide elections, the large county has shown its muscle. Since 1970, three of the four governors and four of the five U.S. senators have hailed from Clark. Also, state senators from Clark County have served as majority leader of the upper house in eight of the twelve sessions since the 1971 reapportionment gave the county a majority of the seats in both legislative houses. However, members of the assembly from Clark County have occupied the Speaker's chair in only four of the twelve sessions in the lower house, despite their majority in the Democratic caucus that controlled the selection of the Speaker in eleven of the sessions. The speakership was held by rural county assembly members in seven of the sessions, including both co-Speakers in the 1995 session. The frequent turnover in assembly members from Clark County and the respect for the evenhanded leadership of Joe Dini, who served as Speaker or co-Speaker for six terms, account for the failure of Clark to hold the key position in the lower house since John Vergiels was Speaker in 1985. A Clark County assemblyman did chair the powerful Ways and Means Committee in seven of the twelve sessions, including the cochairmanship in 1995.

THE "LOVE-HATE" RELATIONSHIP WITH
THE FEDERAL GOVERNMENT

From its early years, when the state was a supporter of Lincoln and the Union party and a strong opponent of the demonetization of silver, Nevada has had a "love-hate" relationship with the federal government. Congress forced the state to include an ordinance in its constitution renouncing all rights to 87 percent of the land within its borders; this renunciation has irritated Nevadans, especially those residing in the rural areas of the state, ever since and this irritation was manifested in the ill-fated "Sagebrush Rebellion" of the late 1970s and early 1980s.

While ranchers and cattle raisers in the northern part of the state often battled with the federal Bureau of Land Management (BLM), workers involved in the construction of Hoover Dam, a major federal project, and federal employees at Nellis Air Force Base and the nuclear test site have benefited the southern part of the state economically. Even a fiscal conservative like Congressman Walter Baring, who generally decried federal grants to states as wasteful spending, was quick to claim credit for federal projects and monies for Nevada. Despite these federal monies, in 1993 Nevadans were paying much more in federal taxes than they were receiving back from the federal treasury. Only six states had a larger negative per capita balance of payments with the federal government than Nevada.[1]

Republican control of both houses of Congress in 1995 may herald a new relationship between the states and the federal government. The quick passage of restrictions on unfunded federal mandates should help the states financially. More opportunities for state responsibility and experimentation in social programs could turn out to be a mixed blessing, especially if Congress decides to reduce its financial contributions to such programs. However, both President Clinton and Republican congressional leaders appear to favor a more cooperative relationship with the states, which may in turn modify the "love-hate" relationship Nevadans have had with the federal government.

THE EFFECTS OF TERM LIMITS ON NEVADA POLITICS

At the same 1994 election in which Nevadans overwhelmingly approved a ballot initiative to amend the state constitution to limit the terms of legislators, judges, and other elected state and local officials, they elected eighteen new members to the forty-two-member assembly. In the 1995 legislature, twenty-seven members (64 percent) of the assembly were serving first or second terms and nine members (43 percent) of the senate were first termers. Thus, in the state legislative area, the present plan—with no term limits— appeared to be working in providing "new blood" to the political system. The amendment, which will go into effect if approved again in 1996, provides for a limit of twelve years in each house of the legislature. In the 1995 legislature, only three members of the assembly and six members of the senate would not have been able to run in 1994 if the amendment had been in effect.

What might be missing in future legislatures if the twelve-year limit goes into effect is the experience of certain key leaders. For example, if the limit had been in effect, the senate would have been deprived of Jim Gibson's valuable leadership from 1979 until his death in 1988. Also, such an amendment would have forced Joe Dini, the longest-serving and most respected Speaker in the state's history, to retire in 1978 after serving one term as the assembly's leader. Bill Raggio, who has been a strong Republican majority leader in the senate for four of the last five sessions, would never have served in that capacity if he had been forced to retire after three terms in 1982.

The resurgence of the GOP in 1994 assembly election races, especially in Clark County, allowed the party to share in the leadership of that body. However, two-thirds of the assembly Republicans were first termers, including ten of the eleven members from Clark County. At a time of strong public support for term limits, the 1995 legislature had an abundance of "new blood."

Even without term limits, Nevada's legislature has become more professionalized in recent years because of the amount of staff assistance now available to legislators through the Legislative Counsel Bureau. If term limits encourage even more turnover in the future, the professional staff and longtime lobbyists, who will have more institutional memory than the legislators, will become even more important. As former governor Sawyer has stated, "Generally speaking, people elected to the state legislature can be easily swayed in the wrong direction if they don't get strong leadership."[2]

Finally, with the stress in this study on the transiency of much of the population, perhaps more attention should have been given to those Nevadans who—because of the state's scenic beauty, climate, and friendliness—would not live anywhere else. It is a state in which the individual can still make a difference. Jim Gibson and Jim Joyce, two individuals who made a difference, were sorely missed after their untimely deaths in 1988 and 1993, respectively. Both had great integrity and were concerned with the best interests of the state as a whole. Again in Sawyer's words, "We are fortunate that there are a few strong, able, intelligent people who are willing to accept the rigors and dangers of public life in order to serve their state and nation."[3]

Suggestions for Further Reading

During the first century of Nevada statehood, systematic analysis of the state's political institutions and behavior was rare. In 1959 political scientist James S. Roberts founded the Bureau of Governmental Research at the University of Nevada. The Nevada Studies in History and Political Science series of the University of Nevada Press was established in 1961, and the Oral History Project, under the direction of Mary Ellen Glass, was initiated at the Getchell Library in the early 1960s. The ensuing publications of the Bureau of Governmental Research, the Senator Alan Bible Center for Applied Research, the Nevada Studies in History and Political Science, along with many of the oral histories, have provided valuable resources for understanding Nevada politics and government.

BIBLIOGRAPHIES AND LISTINGS

Many of the major sources for the study of Nevada politics and government can be found in this book's chapter notes. The bibliography with the most thorough compilation of books and pamphlets about Nevada (including its history, politics, geography, and economics) is *Nevada: An Annotated Bibliography,* assembled and published by Stanley W. Paher (Las Vegas: Nevada Publications, 1980). This bibliography contains over twenty-five hundred annotated listings. Paher did not include articles from periodicals or scholarly journals, except for what he termed "major articles" in the *Nevada Historical Society Quarterly.*

The best annotated bibliography of Nevada history is found in the "Sources" and "Addendum to Sources" sections at the end of Russell R. Elliott's *History of Nevada* (2d ed., rev.; Lincoln: University of Nebraska Press, 1987), pp.411–53.

LIBRARIES

The four main depositories in the state for documents and materials that can be useful in research in Nevada politics and government are the Nevada State Library and Archives in Carson City; the Special Collections Department of the Getchell Library at the University of Nevada, Reno; the Nevada Historical Society in Reno; and the Special Collections Department of the James R. Dickenson Library at UNLV. In addition, the papers of some prominent Nevada political figures are located in libraries outside the state.

All official letters and papers of state officials are by law housed in the State Archives in Carson City. However, the archives contain very few papers of governors prior to the administration of John Sparks, who served as the state's chief executive from 1903 until his death in 1908. The collections housed at the archives have been expanded in recent years.

The private papers of Governors Vail Pittman and Charles Russell, and the papers of U.S. senators Alan Bible and Paul Laxalt, two-term congressman George Bartlett, and four-term congressman James D. Santini are located in the Special Collections Department of the Getchell Library at the University of Nevada, Reno. The papers of other prominent politicos, such as Eva Adams, Norman Biltz, Pete Petersen, and Colonel Thomas Miller, are also located in Getchell's Special Collections.

The important collection of letters and papers of U.S. senator William M. Stewart is housed at the Nevada Historical Society in Reno. The papers of Senators Pat McCarran and Tasker Oddie, ten-term congressman Walter Baring, and single-term congressman David Towell are also located at the Historical Society.

The papers of U.S. senator Howard W. Cannon and Judge Foley's *Baneberry* case papers are housed in the Special Collections Department of the Dickenson Library at UNLV. The same department has one of the best collections in the nation on gaming.

HISTORIES

The best scholarly history of the state, including its political history, is the *History of Nevada* by Russell R. Elliott. A very readable history written for junior high school students is James W. Hulse's *The Nevada Adventure* (6th ed., Reno: University of Nevada Press, 1990).

The *Political History of Nevada* is updated periodically and published by the secretary of state. The names of each member of each house of the legislatures are listed, and the results of statewide elections from 1864 to the present are also included in the book, which was last issued in late 1990.

Perhaps the most thorough coverage of a substantial portion of the state's political history is Jerome E. Edwards's *Pat McCarran: Political Boss of Nevada* (Reno: University of Nevada Press, 1982). Edwards performed a masterful job of using oral histories and personal interviews to buttress his examination of the personal papers of many of the key players in the fascinating first half of the twentieth century in Nevada politics.

A decade later, Elizabeth Raymond covered much of the same period with her excellent biography, *George Wingfield: Owner and Operator of Nevada* (Reno: University of Nevada Press, 1992). Gary E. Elliott's *Senator Alan Bible and the Politics of the New West* (Reno: University of Nevada Press, 1994) is the best study of an important Nevada politician in the post-McCarran era and the contributions Bible made on the national level.

THE CONSTITUTION

The debates of the two state constitutional conventions are available in *Reports of the 1863 Constitutional Convention of the Territory of Nevada*, edited by William C. Miller and Eleanore Bushnell (Carson City: Legislative Counsel Bureau, 1972), and the *Official Report of the Debates and Proceedings of the Constitutional Convention of the State of Nevada, . . . July 4, 1864*, by Andrew J. Marsh, official reporter (San Francisco: F. Eastman, 1866).

In 1965 Eleanore Bushnell authored a study of the Nevada Constitution that was published primarily as a text to be used in university political science and history courses to satisfy the state's constitution requirement. The book went through six editions, the last two of which were updated with some additional material by Don W. Driggs. See Bushnell and Driggs, *The Nevada Constitution: Origin and Growth* (6th ed., Reno: University of Nevada Press, 1984). In 1993 Greenwood Press published Michael W. Bowers's *The Nevada State Constitution: A Reference Guide*.

STATE DOCUMENTS

The Legislative Branch

The *Nevada Revised Statutes,* which are updated after each legislative session, are available in all major libraries and many government offices throughout the state. The legislative proceedings of each regular and special session are published in the *Journal of the Senate* and the *Journal of the Assembly,* which are available at the university and community college libraries, as well as at the State Library and Archives and the Legislative Counsel Bureau.

Before each regular legislative session, the Legislative Counsel Bureau publishes a *Legislative Manual,* which is an important reference for legislators. The manual also contains much useful information for the student of the legislative process.

The Legislative Counsel Bureau (LCB) has published a large number of bulletins, reports and studies since 1948. Some of the reports and studies are available in the university libraries; however, the full complement of publications is housed in the library of the Research Division of the LCB in Carson City.

The Executive Branch

Gubernatorial messages to the legislature, including the biennial State of the State address, are published in the journals of the legislature. The reports of state officials, commissions, and boards are contained in the *Appendices to the Journals of the Senate and the Assembly* of each legislative session.

The secretary of state periodically publishes a booklet entitled *Election Laws* that contains the constitutional and statutory provisions related to campaign finance and elections, including bond elections and the amendment of city charters. In 1980 the secretary of state discontinued the publication of the official returns of the primary and general elections by precinct. Pamphlets of the election returns are available in the research libraries in the state for earlier periods.

The secretary of state's office also has the records of individuals or corporations that made contributions of over $500 to campaigns for state offices since the state's campaign finance reform act was passed in 1975. Such contributions for county and city offices are filed with the respective county or city clerks.

The Judicial Branch

The Nevada Supreme Court's decisions are published each year and are available in most law libraries throughout the state and in the research libraries mentioned above. A summary of the "Yearly Register" of cases filed, opinions written, cases disposed of, and cases pending at the end of the year is available from the clerk of the supreme court.

RESEARCH CENTERS

The Bureau of Governmental Research, first established by the University of Nevada's Department of History and Political Science in 1959, went through two name changes in the 1980s. The name of the bureau was changed to the Nevada Public Affairs Institute in 1982 and to the Senator Alan Bible Center for Applied Research in 1985. The name of the publications of these entities was changed over the years from *Governmental Research Newsletter* to *Nevada Public Affairs Report* to *Nevada Public Affairs Review*. The periodic publications have often dealt with one subject, such as "Higher Education in Nevada," "Health Policy in Nevada," "Betting on the Future: Gambling in Nevada and Elsewhere." In addition, a valuable resource for research on public policy is the biennial "Legislative Issues" publication distributed prior to the convening of each regular legislative session. The articles in this publication often give legislators and the public an opportunity to read pro and con arguments on an important public policy matter to be considered at the legislative session. Since 1983 the biennial "Legislative Issues" publication has also included the results of public opinion polling on selected legislative issues.

Since 1984 the University of Nevada Poll, a joint effort of the Senator Alan Bible Center for Applied Research at the University of Nevada, Reno, and the Center for Public Data Research and the Center for Survey Research at the University of Nevada, Las Vegas, has conducted polling on important issues facing the upcoming legislature. The two major newspapers in the state, the *Las Vegas Review-Journal* and the *Reno Gazette-Journal*, have jointly sponsored public opinion polls on the important political races in the state during election years.

The Bureau of Business and Economic Research at the University of Nevada, Reno, is a good source for information about the state's economy. The bureau publishes papers on business and economic subjects as well as the quarterly *Nevada Review of Business and Economics,* which carries information on such matters as unemployment and inflation in the state.

ELECTION ANALYSES

From 1948 through the 1970 elections, the *Western Political Quarterly,* a professional journal sponsored by the Western Political Science Association, devoted one of its issues every two years to articles about the elections in each of the thirteen western states. The Nevada articles contain analyses of the outcomes of the important state races in the twelve election years.

Analyses of later Nevada elections can be found in the following articles: Don W. Driggs, "The 1974 Election in Nevada," *Nevada Public Affairs Report* 14 (April 1976); Don W. Driggs, "The 1976 Election in Nevada," *Nevada Public Affairs Report* 15 (February 1977); Eleanore Bushnell and Don W. Driggs, "Nevada," in B. Oliver Walter, ed., *Politics in the West: The 1978 Elections* (Laramie WY: Institute for Policy Research, 1979), pp.90–102; and Eleanore Bushnell and Don W. Driggs, "Nevada: Business as Usual" (1980 election), *Social Science Journal* 18 (October 1981), pp.65–75.

DISSERTATIONS AND THESES

A small number of doctoral dissertations of graduates of the University of Nevada, Reno, Ph.D. program in political science are available in the Getchell Library. A larger number of master's theses from programs at both state universities are available at the respective campus libraries. The Special Collections Department of the Getchell Library on the Reno campus has copies of some dissertations and theses involving Nevada politics that were written at other universities around the country.

Notes

CHAPTER ONE

1 Eleanore Bushnell, ed., *Sagebrush and Neon: Studies in Nevada Politics*, rev. ed. (Reno: Bureau of Governmental Research, University of Nevada, Reno, 1976).

2 Russell R. Elliott, with William D. Rowley, *History of Nevada*, 2d ed., rev. (Lincoln: University of Nebraska Press, 1987), p.14.

3 See Russell R. Elliott, *Nevada's Twentieth Century Mining Boom* (Carson City: University of Nevada Press, 1965).

4 See Daniel J. Elazar, *American Federalism: A View from the States*, 2d ed. (New York: Crowell, 1972), pp.84–126.

5 Elazar, *American Federalism*, p.89.

6 See Jill M. Winter, Judy Calder, and Donald E. Carns, "Public Opinion on Selected Legislative Issues: November 1992," *Nevada Public Affairs Review* (hereafter noted as *NPAR*) 1993, Senator Alan Bible Center for Applied Research, University of Nevada, Reno, pp.4–10; Jill M. Winter and Donald E. Carns, "Public Opinion on Selected Issues: Fall 1990," *NPAR* 1991 pp.5–12; John S. DeWitt and Donald E. Carns, "Public Opinion in Nevada: Selected Issues, Fall 1988," *NPAR* 1989 no.1, pp.3–9; and James T. Richardson, John DeWitt, and Sandra Neese, "Public Opinions in Northern Nevada," *NPAR* 1987 no.1, pp.3–10.

7 DeWitt and Carns, "Public Opinion in Nevada," pp.3–6.

8 Elazar, *American Federalism*, pp.86–87.

9 Elazar, *American Federalism*, p.88.

10 Elazar, *American Federalism*, pp.88–89.

11 Winter, Calder, and Carns, "Public Opinion on Selected Legislative Issues," p.4.

12 See Marion Goldman, *Gold Diggers and Silver Miners* (Ann Arbor: University of Michigan Press, 1981).

13 *Cunningham v. Washoe County*, 66 Nev. 60 (1949). Also, see Ellen Pillard, "Rethinking Prostitution: A Case for Uniform Regulation," *NPAR* 1991 no.1, pp.45–49.

14 *Nevada Revised Statutes* (hereafter noted as *NRS*), 244.345.

15 *Nye County v. Plankinton*, 94 Nev. 739 (1978).

16 *NRS*, 1.030.

17 Pillard, "Rethinking Prostitution," p.46.

18 Pillard, "Rethinking Prostitution," p.46.

19 "Public Opinion in Nevada: The University of Nevada Poll," Senator Alan Bible Center for Applied Research, University of Nevada, Reno, February 1988, p.27.

20 Elmer R. Rusco, "A Demographic Description of Nevada," in "Ethnicity and Race in Nevada," *NPAR* 1987 no.2, p.8.

21 William Gillette, *The Right to Vote* (Baltimore: Johns Hopkins University Press, 1965), pp.31, 39–43.

22 *Journal of the Assembly*, 4th sess. (1869).

23 See Sue Faun Chung, "The Chinese Experience in Nevada: Success Despite Discrimination," *NPAR* 1987 no.2, pp.43–51.

24 See Roosevelt Fitzgerald, "The Demographic Impact of Basic Magnesium Corporation on Southern Nevada," *NPAR* 1987 no.2, pp.29–35.

25 See Joseph N. Crowley, "Race and Residence: The Politics of Open Housing in Nevada," in Bushnell, *Sagebrush and Neon*, p.60.

26 See Sammy Davis Jr., *Yes I Can* (New York: Farrar, Straus and Giroux, 1965), pp.88–91.

27 Elmer Rusco, "The Civil Rights Movement in Nevada," *NPAR* 1987 no.2, p.76.

28 Rusco, "Civil Rights Movement," p.76.

29 See Grant Sawyer, Gary E. Elliott, and R. T. King, *Hang Tough! Grant Sawyer: An Activist in the Governor's Mansion* (Reno: University of Nevada Oral History Program, 1993), pp.95–106.

30 See Crowley, "Race and Residence," pp.61–67.

31 Thomas C. Wright and Dina Titus, "Ethnicity and National Origin in the Las Vegas Metropolitan Area," *NPAR* 1987 no.2, p.70.

32 See Shayne Del Cohen, "The Reno-Sparks Indian Colony," *NPAR* 1987 no.2, pp.19–22.

33 Dina Titus, *Study of Gaming*, bulletin no.93–94 (Carson City: Legislative Counsel Bureau, December 1992), pp.24–25.

34 *Journal of the Assembly*, 58th sess. (1975).

35 *Journal of the Senate*, 58th sess. (1975).

36 See James T. Richardson and Sandie Wightman, "Religious Affiliation as a Pre-

dictor of Voting Behavior in Abortion Reform Legislation," *Journal for the Scientific Study of Religion* 11 (1972) pp.347–59.

37 *NRS*, 442.250.

38 Senate Joint Resolution 26, 58th sess. (1975).

39 *Webster v. Reproductive Health Services*, 489 U.S. 1063 (1989).

40 Nevada Constitution, art.19, sec.2.

41 Elmer Rusco, "Welfare in Nevada: The Great Anomaly," *NPAR* 1980 no.1, Bureau of Governmental Research, University of Nevada, Reno, pp.11–12.

42 Rusco, "Welfare in Nevada," p.16.

43 Rusco, "Welfare in Nevada," p.16.

44 Howard Hughes made his fortune as a builder of aircraft and the principal owner of an airline. As he aged, he became more eccentric. He purchased the Desert Inn and other property in the Las Vegas area in the 1960s and became a resident of Nevada when he moved to the penthouse of the Desert Inn.

45 See Peter Steinman and Richard Ganzel, "The Funding of Public Education in Nevada," *NPAR* 1979 no.2, pp.22–26.

CHAPTER TWO

1 A federal system is one in which governmental power is constitutionally divided and shared between a national government and regional units.

2 See Deil S. Wright, "A New Phase of IGR," in Richard H. Leach, ed., *Intergovernmental Relations in the 1980s* (New York: Marcel Dekker, 1993), pp.15–32.

3 U.S. Constitution, art.6, sec.2.

4 Nevada Constitution, art.1 sec.2.

5 Elliott, *History of Nevada*, p.290.

6 *Reno Gazette-Journal*, 2 November 1990, p.1.

7 See James W. Hulse, *The Nevada Adventure: A History*, 6th ed. (Reno: University of Nevada Press, 1990), pp.226–31.

8 For more commentary on the "Sagebrush Rebellion," see A. Constandina Titus, "The Sagebrush Rebellion: A Question of Constitutionality," in Titus, ed., *Battle Born: Federal-State Conflict in Nevada during the Twentieth Century* (Dubuque IA: Kendall/Hunt, 1989), pp.150–61.

9 Titus, "The Sagebrush Rebellion."

10 See Andrew C. Tuttle, "The Pervasive Military Presence in Nevada," in Titus, *Battle Born*, pp.139–49.

11 See Joseph C. Strolin, "Nuclear Waste Disposal: National Dilemma with Significant Implications for Nevada," *NPAR* 1987 no.1, pp.78–83.

12 James T. Richardson, John DeWitt, and Sandra Neese, "Public Opinion in

Northern Nevada," and Steven Parker, Donald Carns, and Frederick Preston, "Southern Nevada Opinion on Contemporary Legislative Issues: A Survey of the Las Vegas Metropolitan Population," *NPAR* 1987 no.1, pp.7, 11; DeWitt and Carns, "Public Opinion in Nevada: Selected Legislative Issues: 1989," edited by Jill Winter, *NPAR* 1989 no.1, p.7.

13 See John Kincaid, "From Cooperation to Coercion in American Federalism: Housing, Fragmentation, and Preemption, 1780–1992," *Journal of Law and Politics* 9 (winter 1993), pp.333–43.

14 See A. Constandina Titus, "The NIMBY Syndrome: Dealing with Nuclear Waste," in Titus, *Battle Born*, pp.162–80.

15 DeWitt and Carns, "Public Opinion in Nevada," p.7.

16 See Saundra K. Schneider, "Intergovernmental Influences on Medicaid Program Expenditures," *Public Administration Review* 48, no.4, (July–August 1988), pp.756–63.

17 For a thorough discussion of Tahoe area issues, see Douglas H. Strong, *Tahoe: An Environmental History* (Lincoln: University of Nebraska Press, 1984).

18 Courts sometimes appoint an expert or "master" to attempt to achieve a compromise among opposing parties in a complex case.

19 Gary E. Elliott, "Arizona v. California: Nevada's Intervenor Role in the Struggle for the Colorado River Water," in Titus, *Battle Born*, pp.97–106. For a general discussion of the Colorado River issue and the politics of water, see Marc Reisner, *Cadillac Desert: The American West and Its Disappearing Water* (New York: Viking Press, 1986).

CHAPTER THREE

1 See Norman F. Furniss, *The Mormon Conflict, 1850–1859* (New Haven: Yale University Press, 1960), pp.7–11.

2 Elliott, *History of Nevada*, p.54.

3 Elliott, *History of Nevada*, p.55.

4 "Utah Expedition," 35th Cong., 1st sess., 1857, H. Exec. Doc. 71, pp.212–14.

5 See Furniss, *Mormon Conflict*, p.56, and Philip S. Klein, *President James Buchanan* (University Park: Pennsylvania State University Press, 1960), p.316.

6 Mathias F. Cowley, *Wilford Woodruff* (Salt Lake City: Deseret Press, 1909), p.387.

7 Effie Mona Mack, *Nevada: A History of the State from the Earliest Times through the Civil War* (Glendale CA: Arthur H. Clark, 1936), pp.169–70.

8 Frankie Sue Del Papa, *Political History of Nevada*, 9th ed. (Carson City: State Printing Office, 1990), p.54.

9 Elliott, *History of Nevada*, p.61.

10 *Congressional Globe*, 36th Cong., 1st sess., 1860, p.2068.

11 *Congressional Globe*, 36th Cong., 2d sess., 1861, p.1334.

12 Mack, *Nevada*, p.221.

13 Mack, *Nevada*, p.221.

14 Mack, *Nevada*, p.222.

15 T. B. H. Stenhouse, *The Rocky Mountain Saints* (London: Ward Rock, and Tyler, 1874), p.410.

16 For an excellent biography of Stewart, see Russell R. Elliott, *Servant of Power* (Reno: University of Nevada Press, 1983).

17 George R. Brown, ed., *Reminiscences of Senator William M. Stewart of Nevada* (New York: Neal, 1908), p.141.

18 Myron Angel, ed., *History of Nevada* (Oakland CA: Thompson and West, 1881), p.81.

19 *Congressional Globe*, 37th Cong., 3rd sess., 1863, p.1549.

20 Del Papa, *Political History of Nevada*, p.83.

21 See William C. Miller and Eleanore Bushnell, eds., *Reports of the 1863 Constitutional Convention of the Territory of Nevada* (Carson City: Legislative Counsel Bureau, 1972).

22 Miller and Bushnell, *1863 Constitutional Convention*, p.395. Also, see David A. Johnson, "A Case of Mistaken Identity: William M. Stewart and the Rejection of Nevada's First Constitution," *Nevada Historical Society Quarterly* 22 (fall 1979), pp.186–98.

23 Elliott, *Servant of Power*, p.26.

24 Johnson, "Mistaken Identity," p.191.

25 *Virginia Daily Union*, 3 January 1864, p.2.

26 Angel, *History of Nevada*, p.85.

27 *Congressional Globe*, 38th Cong., 3d sess., 1864, p.521.

28 See Andrew J. Marsh (official reporter), *Nevada Constitutional Debates and Proceedings* (San Francisco: Frank Eastman, 1866), pp. x–xii for the provisions of the enabling act.

29 Marsh, *Nevada Constitutional Debates*, p.14.

30 David A. Johnson, "Industry and the Individual on the Far Western Frontier: A Case Study of Politics and Social Change in Early Nevada," *Pacific Historical Review* 51 (August 1982), p.247.

31 Angel, *History of Nevada*, pp.85–86.

32 Mack, *Nevada*, p.264.

33 Effie Mona Mack, "James Warren Nye," *Nevada Historical Society Quarterly* 4 no.3/4 (July–December 1961), p.33.

34 Elliott, *History of Nevada*, pp.108–9.

35 Elliott, *Servant of Power*, pp.64–67.

36 Elliott, *History of Nevada*, pp.162–63.

37 Elliott, *Servant of Power*, pp.80–82.

38 Elliott, *History of Nevada*, p.164.

39 Elliott, *Servant of Power*, p.91.

40 The "Black" nickname derived from the term *Black Republican*, which was applied by southern Democrats to those Republicans who were avid in their support
of the newly freed slaves after the Civil War. See Mary Ellen Glass, *Silver and
Politics in Nevada, 1892–1902* (Reno: University of Nevada Press, 1969), p.48.

41 Elliott, *History of Nevada*, p.156.

42 *Appendix to Journals of Senate and Assembly, 1883,* vol. I (Carson City, NV
1883), p.12.

43 Elliott, *History of Nevada*, pp.157–58.

44 Elliott, *History of Nevada*, p.161.

45 Sam P. Davis, *The History of Nevada*, vol. I (Reno: Elms, 1913), p.441.

46 *Nevada State Journal* (Reno), 21 March 1891, p.2.

47 Glass, *Silver and Politics*, p.41.

48 *Morning Appeal* (Carson City), 21 January 1893, p.1.

49 See Elliott, *Servant of Power*, pp.182–83, 307.

50 See *Morning Appeal*, 6 January 1897, p.3, and 19 January 1897, p.3.

51 Elliott, *History of Nevada*, p.90.

52 See Elliott, *History of Nevada*, pp.195–215.

53 Elliott, *History of Nevada*, p.235.

54 Elliott, *History of Nevada*, p.243.

55 *Nevada State Journal*, 30 March 1904, p.2.

56 Glass, *Silver and Politics*, p.85.

CHAPTER FOUR

1 Elliott, *History of Nevada*, pp.211–24.

2 See Loren B. Chan, *Sagebrush Statesman: Tasker L. Oddie* (Reno: University of
Nevada Press, 1973).

3 See Hulse, *The Nevada Adventure*, pp.177–85.

4 For an excellent biography, see C. Elizabeth Raymond, *George Wingfield:
Owner and Operator of Nevada* (Reno: University of Nevada Press, 1992). Also,
see Barbara Cavanaugh Thornton, "George Wingfield in Nevada from 1896 to
1932" (master's thesis, University of Nevada, Reno, 1967).

5 See Jerome E. Edwards, *Pat McCarran: Political Boss of Nevada* (Reno: University of Nevada Press, 1982), p.7.

6 Raymond, *George Wingfield*, p.1.

7 Elliott, *History of Nevada*, pp.236–37.

8 See Anne Bell Howard, *The Long Campaign: A Biography of Anne Martin* (Reno: University of Nevada Press, 1985).

9 See Christopher G. Driggs, "Governor Emmet D. Boyle of Nevada: A Man of His Times" (master's thesis, University of Texas at Austin, 1987), p.32. (Copy of thesis is available at Getchell Library, University of Nevada, Reno.)

10 *Reno Evening Gazette*, 7 May 1921.

11 See Elliott, *History of Nevada*, p.268.

12 Elliott, *History of Nevada*, p.268.

13 Raymond, *George Wingfield*, pp.174–75.

14 Raymond, *George Wingfield*, p.154.

15 See Fred Balzar Papers, Nevada State Archives, Carson City.

16 See Elliott, *History of Nevada*, p.245.

17 Raymond, *George Wingfield*, p.195.

18 See Raymond, *George Wingfield*, pp.193–99, for national response to legislation.

19 See Raymond, *George Wingfield*, pp.159, 185.

20 See Raymond, *George Wingfield*, pp.6, 41, 254–56, 310. Also, see Elliott, *History of Nevada*, pp.270–71.

21 Raymond, *George Wingfield*, p.186.

22 Raymond, *George Wingfield*, p.182.

23 See Edwards, *Pat McCarran*, pp.19–22, 25.

24 Edwards, *Pat McCarran*, pp.43–44.

25 Edwards, *Pat McCarran*, p.47.

26 Edwards, *Pat McCarran*, p.57.

27 Pete Petersen, "Reminiscences of My Work in Nevada Labor, Politics, Post Office and Gaming Control" (Oral History, University of Nevada, Reno Library, 1970), pp.54–55.

28 See Edwards, *Pat McCarran*, pp.155–57, 163.

29 Edwards, *Pat McCarran*, p.147.

30 See Edwards, *Pat McCarran*, pp.110–13, 134–36, 170–80.

31 Gary E. Elliott, *Senator Alan Bible and the Politics of the New West* (Reno: University of Nevada Press, 1994), p.77.

32 See Elliott, *Senator Alan Bible*, pp.107, 135–36, 194.

33 See Eleanore Bushnell and Don W. Driggs, *The Nevada Constitution: Origin and Growth*, 6th ed. (Reno: University of Nevada Press, 1984), pp.100–101.

34 See Don W. Driggs, "The 1974 Election in Nevada," *NPAR* April 1976.

35 Driggs, "1974 Election in Nevada."

36 *Reno Gazette-Journal*, 5 November 1982, p.2C.

37 *Reno Gazette-Journal*, 24 October 1982, p.1A.

38 Jim Joyce, conversation with D. Driggs, Carson City, 17 January 1983.

39 *Reno Gazette-Journal*, 5 November 1982, p.2C.

40 *San Francisco Examiner*, 21 September 1986, p.A4.

41 See Myram Borders, "Nevada's Leading Democrats Work to Unite Party," *Reno Gazette-Journal*, 4 May 1986, p.10D.

42 *Reno Gazette-Journal*, 10 April 1987, p.1A.

43 *Reno Gazette-Journal*, 18 December 1987, p.2C.

44 *Reno Gazette-Journal*, 1 July 1988, p.1C.

45 Norman Biltz, "Memoirs of the Duke of Nevada" (Oral History, University of Nevada, Reno Library, 1967), p.149.

46 Charles H. Russell, "Reminiscences of a Nevada Congressman, Governor, and Legislator" (Oral History, University of Nevada, Reno Library, 1987), p.127.

47 See Edwards, *Pat McCarran*, pp.186–88.

48 Russell, "Reminiscences," pp.229–30.

49 Many of the "McCarran boys" became political leaders in the state. See Sawyer, Elliott, and King, *Grant Sawyer*, pp.34–35.

50 Sawyer, Elliott, and King, *Grant Sawyer*, pp.53–55.

51 See Don W. Driggs, "The 1958 Election in Nevada," *Western Political Quarterly*, March 1959.

52 See Edwards, *Pat McCarran*, pp.101–2.

53 Edwards, *Pat McCarran*, p.67.

54 Edwards, *Pat McCarran*, p.67.

55 Edwards, *Pat McCarran*, p.104.

56 Edwards, *Pat McCarran*, pp.200–201.

57 *Las Vegas Sun*, 30 August 1952. Greenspun had high praise for Bible when he died in 1988. See *Las Vegas Sun*, 14 September 1988.

CHAPTER FIVE

1 Daniel J. Elazar, "The Principles and Traditions Underlying American State Constitutions," *Publius: The Journal of Federalism* 12 (winter 1982), p.21.

2 *Book of the States, 1992–93* (Lexington KY: Council of State Governments, 1990), p.20.

3 *Gitlow v. New York*, 268 U.S. 652 (1925).

4 Alpheus Thomas Mason and Gordon E. Baker, *Free Government in the Making: Readings in American Political Thought* (New York: Oxford University Press, 1985), p.125.

5 Joseph R. Grodin, Calvin R. Massey, and Richard Cunningham, *The California*

State Constitution: A Reference Guide (Westport CT: Greenwood Press, 1993), p.7.

6 *Schenck v. United States*, 249 U.S. 47 (1919).

7 John Kincaid, "The New Judicial Federalism," *The Journal of State Governments* 61 (September/October 1988), p.163.

8 Kincaid, "New Judicial Federalism," p.164.

9 See Howard, *The Long Campaign*.

10 *State ex rel. Herr v. Laxalt* 84 Nev. 382, 441 P.2d 687 (1968).

11 Elazar, "American State Constitutions," p.17.

CHAPTER SIX

1 *Nevada State Journal*, 25 February 1915, p.3.

2 *Colegrove v. Green*, 328 U.S. 549 (1946).

3 *Reynolds v. Sims*, 377 U.S. 533 (1964).

4 *Baker v. Carr*, 369 U.S. 186 (1962).

5 See *Dungan v. Sawyer*, 253 F.Supp. 358 (1966).

6 See Bushnell and Driggs, *The Nevada Constitution*, pp. 100–101.

7 Sawyer, Elliott, and King, *Grant Sawyer*, p.72.

8 In contrast with the U.S. vice president, who seldom presides over the Senate unless there is the prospect of a tie vote, Nevada's lieutenant governor presides over the upper house most of the time during a legislative session.

9 See Bushnell, *The Nevada Constitution*, pp.88–94.

10 *Dunphy v. Sheehan*, 92 Nev. 259.549 P.2d 332 (1976).

11 *NRS*, 281.481, sec.11.

12 *NRS*, 281.455, sec.5.

13 *Legislative Manual, 61st Session of the Nevada Legislature* (Carson City: Legislative Counsel Bureau, 1981), pp.144–46.

14 *NRS*, 218.695.

15 For additional tasks performed by the Research Division, see *Legislative Manual*, pp.148–49.

16 *NRS*, 218.740.

17 Citizens Conference on State Legislatures, *The Sometimes Governments: A Critical Study of the 50 American Legislatures* (New York: Bantam Books, 1971), p.253.

18 See Citizens Conference, *The Sometimes Governments*, pp.44–47, for the criteria and subcriteria of each area.

19 Citizens Conference, *The Sometimes Governments*, p.254.

20 Citizens Conference, *The Sometimes Governments*, pp.253–54.

CHAPTER SEVEN

1 Nevada Constitution, art. 5, sec. 3.

2 *Sawyer v. District Court*, 82 Nev. 56 (1966). See Bushnell and Driggs, *The Nevada Constitution*, pp. 111–12.

3 Bushnell and Driggs, *The Nevada Constitution*, p. 112.

4 *Nevada State Journal*, 5 June 1985, p. 1C. Also, see Bushnell and Driggs, *The Nevada Constitution*, p. 112.

5 *Reno Gazette-Journal*, 5 June 1985, p. 1C.

6 See Clinton Rossiter, *The American Presidency*, 2d ed. (New York: Harcourt, Brace, and World, 1966).

7 Nevada Constitution, art. 5, sec. 14.

8 See Don W. Driggs, "The List-Bryan Transition in Nevada, 1982–1983," in Thad Beyle, ed., *Gubernatorial Transitions: The 1982 Election* (Durham NC: Duke University Press, 1985), pp. 279–300.

9 Marlene Lockard, Bryan's transition director, interview with D. Driggs, Carson City, 4 March 1983; and Andrew Grose, Bryan's chief of staff, interview with D. Driggs, Carson City, 1 April 1983.

10 Driggs, "The List-Bryan Transition," p. 291.

11 Nevada Constitution, art. 5, sec. 10.

12 Nevada Constitution, art. 4, sec. 17.

13 Nevada Constitution, art. 5, sec. 9.

14 See John F. Galliher and John Ray Cross, *Morals Legislation without Morality: The Case of Nevada* (New Brunswick NJ: Rutgers University Press, 1983) for a more extensive history of gambling and its regulation in Nevada.

15 Galliher and Cross, *Morals Legislation without Morality*, p. 56.

16 Jack Stevenson, "He Fathered Nevada Gaming Growth," *Nevada State Journal*, 29 August 1976, p. 1.

17 James W. Hulse, *Forty Years in the Wilderness: Impressions of Nevada, 1940–1980* (Reno: University of Nevada Press, 1986), p. 68.

18 See Jerome H. Skolnick, *House of Cards* (Boston: Little, Brown, 1978), p. 117.

19 See Mary Ellen Glass, *Nevada's Turbulent Fifties: Decade of Political Turmoil and Economic Change* (Reno: University of Nevada Press), pp. 28–33.

20 Glass, *Nevada's Turbulent Fifties*, pp. 34–37. Also, see Hulse, *Forty Years in the Wilderness*, pp. 70–75.

21 Edward A. Olsen, "The Black Book Episode—An Exercise in Muscle," in Bushnell, *Sagebrush and Neon*, pp. 1–2.

22 Olsen, "The Black Book Episode," p. 2.

23 See Olsen, "The Black Book Episode," pp. 5–21.

24 *Marshall v. Sawyer*, Civil no.360, D. Nev. (25 September 1964).

25 *Marshall v. Sawyer*, 365 F. 2d 105 (1966).

26 *Reno Gazette-Journal*, 23 April 1984, p.4A.

27 *Reno Gazette-Journal*, 18 March 1985, p.3B.

28 Sawyer, Elliott, and King, *Grant Sawyer*, p.74.

29 *Nevada Weekly*, 22–28 June 1994, p.6.

30 *Reno Gazette-Journal*, 8 January 1995, p.4C.

CHAPTER EIGHT

1 *NRS*, 284.

2 *Book of the States, 1990–91* (Lexington KY: Council of State Governments, 1990), p.362.

3 *Book of the States, 1990–91*, p.349.

4 *Las Vegas Review-Journal*, 12 May 1991, p.4A.

5 *Las Vegas Review-Journal*, 12 May 1991, p.4A.

6 George J. Gordon, *Public Administration in America*, 3d ed. (New York: St. Martin's Press, 1986), pp.358–60.

7 *NRS*, 286.

8 Deil S. Wright, *Understanding Intergovernmental Relations*, 2d ed. (Monterey CA: Brooks/Cole, 1982), p.63; Terry Sanford, *Storm over the States* (New York: McGraw Hill, 1967, p.80.

9 *Las Vegas Review-Journal*, 19 May 1991, p.2C.

CHAPTER NINE

1 For comments on the Gunderson-Manoukian feud and an explanation of Chief Justice Mowbray's problems, see Michael W. Bowers, "Personality and Judicial Politics in Nevada," *State Constitutional Commentaries and Notes* 2, no.4 (summer 1991), pp.7–10.

2 See Julius Goebel Jr. and T. Raymond Naughton, "Judges and the Law: The Role of the Courts," in Marvin Meyers and J. R. Pole, eds., *The Meanings of American Interpretations of American History,* vol.1, *Colonial Origins to the Civil War* (Glenview IL: Scott, Foresman, 1971), pp.115–28.

3 Robert L. Clinton, *Marbury v. Madison and Judicial Review* (Lawrence: University Press of Kansas, 1989), p.18.

4 See Charles G. Haines, *The American Doctrine of Judicial Review* (New York: Russell and Russell, 1959), pp.88–121.

5 1 Cranch 137.

6 *Book of the States, 1992–93* (Lexington KY: Council of State Governments, 1992), pp.229–30.

7 Alexis de Tocqueville, *Democracy in America* (reprint, London: Oxford University Press, 1953), p.205.

8 Tocqueville, *Democracy in America*, p.205.

9 *Statutes of 1915 Legislature*, chapter 285, p.507.

10 Bushnell and Driggs, *The Nevada Constitution*, p.135.

11 See Michael Bowers, "The Impact of Judicial Selection Methods in Nevada: Some Empirical Observations," NPAR 1990 no.2, pp.3–8.

12 Nevada Constitution, art.7, sec.2.

13 Nevada Constitution, art.7, sec.3.

14 See Gordon Morris Bakken, "Judicial Removal in Nevada," *The Rocky Mountain Social Science Journal* 8 (April 1971), pp.109–18.

15 *State v. McClinton,* 5 Nevada 329 (1869).

16 Nevada Constitution, art.6, sec.2.

17 Marsh, *Nevada Constitutional Debates*, p.642.

18 Nevada Constitution, art.6, sec.3.

19 384 U.S. 436 (1966).

20 *Tarkanian v. National Collegiate Athletic Association*, 103 Nev. 741 P.2d 1345 (1987).

21 John Kincaid, "The State and Federal Bills of Rights: Partners and Rivals in Liberty," *Intergovernmental Perspective* 17, no.4 (fall 1991), p.31.

22 *Stumpf v. Lau*, 108 Nev. 826, 839 P.2d 120 (1992).

23 Nevada Constitution, art.6, sec.6.

24 See Dina Titus, "Toward a Consolidated Approach to Legally-Related Domestic Problems: Nevada Creates a Family Court," NPAR 1990 no.2, pp.18–22.

CHAPTER TEN

1 See Don W. Driggs, "Nevada: Powerful Lobbyists and Conservative Politics," in Ronald J. Hrebenar and Clive S. Thomas, eds., *Interest Group Politics in the American West* (Salt Lake City: University of Utah Press, 1987), p.85. Some of the analysis of interest groups in this chapter was published in the Hrebenar and Thomas book.

2 NRS, 293.1715.

3 V. O. Key, *Politics, Parties, and Pressure Groups*, 4th ed. (New York: Thomas Y. Crowell, 1958), p.411.

4 Pat McCarran letter to Pete Petersen, 19 January 1950, Petersen Papers, Getchell

Library, University of Nevada, Reno, as quoted in Jerome E. Edwards, *Pat McCarran: Political Boss of Nevada* (Reno: University of Nevada Press, 1982), p.138.

5 *NRS*, 293.128-163.

6 *Reno Gazette-Journal*, 8 February 1995, p.1A.

7 Nevada Constitution, art.2, sec.1; *Dunn v. Blumstein*, 405 U.S. 330 (1972).

8 424 U.S. 1 (1976).

9 Individuals are limited to contributing no more than $10,000 to a candidate for statewide office and $2,000 for a local government candidate. Groups may give up to $20,000 for a statewide candidate and $10,000 for a local candidate.

10 Norman Biltz, "Memoirs of the Duke of Nevada," pp.211–12.

11 Freeman Lincoln, "Norman Biltz, Duke of Nevada," *Fortune* 50 (September 1954), p.146.

12 Biltz, "Memoirs of the Duke of Nevada," pp.104–5.

13 See Driggs, "Nevada," p.87.

14 See Faun Mortara, "Lobbying in Nevada," in Bushnell, *Sagebrush and Neon*, pp.41–57.

15 *NRS*, 218.926.

16 *Reno Gazette-Journal*, 11 February 1995, p.5A.

17 *Reno Gazette-Journal*, 30 January 1984, p.2C.

18 Driggs, "Nevada," p.88.

19 James T. Richardson, conversation with Don W. Driggs, Reno, June 1993.

CHAPTER ELEVEN

1 David R. Berman, *State and Local Government*, 6th ed. (Dubuque IA: William C. Brown, 1990), pp.257–60.

2 *Book of the States, 1990–91*, pp.282–86.

3 John S. DeWitt and Donald E. Carns, "Public Opinion in Nevada: Selected Legislative Issues, Fall 1988," *NPAR* 1989 no.1, p.4.

4 *Journal of the Assembly*, 44th sess. (1949), p.540. See Don W. Driggs, "Taxation and the Financing of Education in Nevada," in Bushnell, *Sagebrush and Neon*, pp.83–90.

5 See Driggs, "Taxation and Financing," pp.90–95.

6 Mary Gojack, "Remove the Tax on Food," *NPAR* 1979 no.2, pp.19–21.

7 Glen W. Atkinson and James Newman, "Nevada's Fiscal System in Flux: Jeopardizing Economic Stability and Diversification," *NPAR* 1985 no.2, p.21.

8 The Urban Institute and Price Waterhouse, "Fiscal Affairs of State and Local

Governments in Nevada: Executive Summary," *NPAR* 1989 no.1, p.72.

9 Urban Institute and Price Waterhouse, "Fiscal Affairs," p.73.

10 Stuart E. Curtis, "The Growth in Gaming," *NPAR* 1979 no.2, p.13.

11 Curtis, "The Growth in Gaming," p.13.

12 Curtis, "The Growth in Gaming," p.13.

13 See Nevada Constitution, art.10, sec.2.

14 See Bushnell and Driggs, *The Nevada Constitution*, pp.147–48.

15 Urban Institute and Price Waterhouse, "Fiscal Affairs," p.75.

16 See Lou Cannon, "The Gold Rush out of California: Business Is Finding Better Prospects in Other States," *Washington Post National Weekly Edition*, 9–15 September 1991, p.20.

17 *Reno Gazette-Journal*, 2 July 1993, p.6A.

18 Urban Institute and Price Waterhouse, "Fiscal Affairs," p.75.

19 See *State Fiscal Capacity and Effort:* 1988 (Washington DC: U.S. Advisory Commission on Intergovernmental Relations, 1990), pp.132–33.

20 *NRS*, 353.210.

CHAPTER TWELVE

1 Nevada Constitution, art.4, sec.25.

2 Nevada Constitution, art.4, sec.20.

3 J. F. Dillon, *Commentaries on the Law of Municipal Corporation*, 5th ed., vol.1 (Boston: Little, Brown, 1911), p.448.

4 11 Nev. 223 (1876).

5 James Bryce, *The American Commonwealth* (London: Macmillan, 1889).

6 Lincoln Steffens, *The Shame of the Cities* (New York: McClure, Phillips, 1904).

7 Henry C. Gilbertson, *The County* (New York: National Short Ballot Association, 1917).

8 Glen Atkinson and Ted Oleson, "Nevada Local Governments: Coping with Diversity under Centralization," *NPAR* 1993, p.34.

9 See Bjorn P. Selinder, "Unfunded Mandates: An Unfair Solution to Government Budgetary Woes," *NPAR* 1993, pp.40–43.

10 Titus, *Battle Born*, p.169.

11 For an excellent article on the Bullfrog County controversy, see A. Constandina Titus, "Bullfrog County: A Nevada Response to Federal Nuclear Waste Disposal Policy," *Publius: The Journal of Federalism* 20, no.1 (winter 1990), pp.123–35.

12 *NRS*, 268.010.

13 *NRS*, 266.010.

14 Albert C. Johns, *Nevada Politics*, 3d ed. (Dubuque IA: Kendall/Hunt, 1973), pp.103–6.

15 *Clark County Performance Report, 1990* (Las Vegas, 1990), p.6.

16 *Las Vegas Review-Journal*, 3 November 1991, p.3F.

CHAPTER THIRTEEN

1 See David R. Morgan, Robert E. England, and George G. Humphreys, *Oklahoma Politics and Policies: Governing the Sooner State* (Lincoln: University of Nebraska Press, 1991), pp.172–73.

2 Thomas E. Cronin and Robert D. Loevy, *Colorado Politics and Government: Governing the Centennial State* (Lincoln: University of Nebraska Press, 1993), p.286.

3 Legislative Council, Interim Committee on Organization of State Government, December 1973, quoted in Cronin and Loevy, *Colorado Politics and Government*, p.286.

4 Nevada School Finance Survey Group, *Financial and Administrative Problems of Nevada Schools, and Suggested Solutions*, bulletin no.5, (Carson City: Legislative Counsel Bureau, 1948), p.9. Some material in this section on the funding of education was used in Driggs, "Taxation and Financing," pp.83–90.

5 Nevada Constitution, art.11, sec.6.

6 See Glass, *Nevada's Turbulent Fifties*, pp.58–60.

7 Nevada School Finance Survey Group, *Problems of Nevada Schools*, p.9.

8 Division of Surveys and Field Surveys, George Peabody College for Teachers, December 1954, p.27.

9 See Driggs, "Taxation and Financing," p.86.

10 See "The Nevada Plan," Nevada Department of Education handout, 1992.

11 Eugene T. Paslov, "The Politics of Educational Excellence: The Dilemma," *NPAR* 1987 no.1, p.70; *Reno Gazette-Journal*, 21 June 1989.

12 Donald O. Williams, "Nevada Public Schools: Legislative Concerns and Proposals," *NPAR* 1989 no.1, pp.36–37.

13 T. M. Tomlinson, *Class Size and Public Policy: Politics and Panaceas* (Washington DC: U.S. Department of Education, 1988) p.1, as quoted in Williams, "Nevada Public Schools," p.37.

14 Williams, "Nevada Public Schools," p.38.

15 Driggs, "Taxation and Financing," pp.81–98.

16 Hulse, *The Nevada Adventure*, p.264.

17 See James T. Richardson and K. Donald Jessup, "The History of Formula-Based Budgeting for Nevada Universities," *NPAR* 1981 no.1, pp.64–68.

18 Warren H. Fox and Kimberly Harris, "Nevada's National Rank in Higher Education: State Revenues and Tax Capacity," *NPAR* 1991 no.1, p.62.

19 Nevada Constitution, art. 11, sec. 7.

20 Don W. Driggs, "WICHE and Professional Education in Nevada," *NPAR* 1981 no. 1, pp. 51–57.

21 Governor Richard H. Bryan, "Health Care Containment," *NPAR* 1987 no. 1, p. 19. Also, see *NPAR* 1985 no. 2, pp. 39–42.

22 Bryan, "Health Care Containment," p. 20.

23 Bryan, "Health Care Containment," p. 20.

24 Bryan, "Health Care Containment," pp. 19–20.

25 Bryan, "Health Care Containment," p. 23.

26 James T. Richardson, John DeWitt, and Sandra Neese, "Public Opinion in Northern Nevada," *NPAR* 1987 no. 1, p. 8; Steven Parker, Donald Carns, and Frederick Preston, "Southern Nevada Opinion on Contemporary Legislative Issues," *NPAR* 1987 no. 1, p. 13.

27 Senator Raymond D. Rawson and Natalie Birk-Jenson, "Controlling the Cost of Nevada's Health Care," *NPAR* 1987 no. 1, p. 28.

28 See Raymond D. Rawson and H. Pepper Sturn, "Cost and Access Issues for Nevada's Health Care," *NPAR* 1989 no. 1, p. 30.

29 *Reno Gazette-Journal*, 20 January 1991.

30 *Reno Gazette-Journal*, 24 January 1991.

CHAPTER FOURTEEN

1 Office of Senator Daniel Moynihan, as cited in *Time* 145, no. 22 (29 May 1995), p. 12.

2 Sawyer, Elliott, and King, *Grant Sawyer*, p. 74.

3 Sawyer, Elliott, and King, *Grant Sawyer*, p. 228.

Index

In the Politics and Governments of the American States series

Alabama Government and Politics
By James D. Thomas and William H. Stewart

Alaska Politics and Government
By Gerald A. McBeath and Thomas A. Morehouse

Arkansas Politics and Government: Do the People Rule?
By Diane D. Blair

Colorado Politics and Government: Governing the Centennial State
By Thomas E. Cronin and Robert D. Loevy

Illinois Politics and Government: The Expanding Metropolitan Frontier
By Samuel K. Gove and James D. Nowlan

Kentucky Politics and Government: Do We Stand United?
By Penny M. Miller

Maine Politics and Government
By Kenneth T. Palmer, G. Thomas Taylor, and Marcus A. LiBrizzi

Michigan Politics and Government: Facing Change in a Complex State
By William P. Browne and Kenneth VerBurg

Mississippi Government and Politics: Modernizers versus Traditionalists
By Dale Krane and Stephen D. Shaffer

Nebraska Government and Politics
Edited by Robert D. Miewald

Nevada Politics and Government: Conservatism in an Open Society
By Don W. Driggs and Leonard E. Goodall

New Jersey Politics and Government: Suburban Politics Comes of Age
By Barbara G. Salmore and Stephen A. Salmore

North Carolina Government and Politics
By Jack D. Fleer

Oklahoma Politics and Policies: Governing the Sooner State
By David R. Morgan, Robert E. England, and George G. Humphreys

South Carolina Politics and Government
By Cole Blease Graham Jr. and William V. Moore